SHAPING IDENTITY IN MEDIEVAL FRENCH LITERATURE

UNIVERSITY PRESS OF FLORIDA

Florida A&M University, Tallahassee
Florida Atlantic University, Boca Raton
Florida Gulf Coast University, Ft. Myers
Florida International University, Miami
Florida State University, Tallahassee
New College of Florida, Sarasota
University of Central Florida, Orlando
University of Florida, Gainesville
University of North Florida, Jacksonville
University of South Florida, Tampa
University of West Florida, Pensacola

SHAPING IDENTITY IN MEDIEVAL FRENCH LITERATURE

THE OTHER WITHIN

EDITED BY

Adrian P. Tudor and Kristin L. Burr

University Press of Florida
Gainesville · Tallahassee · Tampa · Boca Raton
Pensacola · Orlando · Miami · Jacksonville · Ft. Myers · Sarasota

Copyright 2019 by Adrian P. Tudor and Kristin L. Burr
All rights reserved
Published in the United States of America

This book may be available in an electronic edition.

24 23 22 21 20 19   6 5 4 3 2 1

Library of Congress Cataloging-in-Publication Data
Names: Tudor, Adrian, editor. | Burr, Kristin L., editor.
Title: Shaping identity in medieval French literature : the other within / edited by Adrian P. Tudor and Kristin L. Burr.
Description: Gainesville : University Press of Florida, 2019. | Includes bibliographical references and index.
Identifiers: LCCN 2018060739 | ISBN 9780813056432 (cloth : alk. paper)
Subjects: LCSH: French literature—To 1500—History and criticism. | Identity (Psychology) in literature. | Literature and society—France.
Classification: LCC PQ155.I35 S53 2019 | DDC 840.9/001—dc23
LC record available at https://lccn.loc.gov/2018060739

The University Press of Florida is the scholarly publishing agency for the State University System of Florida, comprising Florida A&M University, Florida Atlantic University, Florida Gulf Coast University, Florida International University, Florida State University, New College of Florida, University of Central Florida, University of Florida, University of North Florida, University of South Florida, and University of West Florida.

University Press of Florida
2046 NE Waldo Road
Suite 2100
Gainesville, FL 32609
http://upress.ufl.edu

CONTENTS

Acknowledgments vii

Introduction: Shaping Identity in Medieval French Literature 1
Adrian P. Tudor and Kristin L. Burr

1. The Medieval *Moi Multiple*: Names, Surnames, and Personifications 15
Douglas Kelly

2. "Je vueil ung livre commencier": The Othernesses of Othon de Grandson's "Je" 30
Jane H. M. Taylor

3. *Huon de Bordeaux*: The Cultural Dream as Palimpsest 42
William Burgwinkle

4. Ringing True: Shifting Identity in *Le Roman de la Violette* 53
Kristin L. Burr

5. Inside Out and Outside In: (Re-)Reading the Other in the Guillaume Cycle 67
Sara I. James

6. *Ami et Amile* and Jean-Luc Nancy: Friendship versus Community? 79
Jane Gilbert

7. The Devil Inside: Merlin and the Dark Side of Romance 92
Francis Gingras

8. Melly and Merlin: Locating Little Voices in Paris BnF fr. 24432 107
James R. Simpson

9. Sex, the Church, and the Medieval Reader: Shaping Salvation in the *Vie des Pères*   121
   Adrian P. Tudor

10. Roland's Confession and the Rhetorical Construction of the Other Within   137
    Mary Jane Schenck

   Notes   151
   List of Contributors   189
   Index   193

ACKNOWLEDGMENTS

This book evolved over a long period of time for unexpected personal reasons. The editors would very much like to express their gratitude to contributors who have been so patient and loyal to the project. Sincere thanks from us both.

We would like to thank the team at University Press of Florida, in particular Stephanye Hunter and Linda Bathgate, for guiding us through the publication process. We would also like to acknowledge the contribution of two anonymous readers, whose careful reading and thoughtful suggestions have led to a variety of positive modifications. This is a better book for their reports. The book has also profited from the sharp expertise of our copy editor Ann Marlowe.

Finally, we would like to thank our families. The book is dedicated to them, for it would not have seen the light of day without their patience and support.

Introduction

Shaping Identity in Medieval French Literature

ADRIAN P. TUDOR AND KRISTIN L. BURR

Identity matters. As is evident in contemporary political discourse, both the groups that have traditionally been marginalized and those who have long held positions of authority realize that the stakes are high in the quest for acknowledgment, for respect, for visibility, for a voice that is heard and listened to. Defined by those with the power to decide which groups "count"—those who "belong"—and which groups do not, the identity of individuals might determine where they live, what they do, or who and how they can love. Today, we recognize that the complex interplay of gender, race, class, religion, sexuality, and cultural norms—among other factors—make us who we are. We are able to occupy multiple positions at once, with certain aspects of our identity privileged depending on the setting; we may also find ourselves acting in the role of subject, of object, or of both simultaneously. At times, we choose the ways in which others identify us; in other moments, we may have identities imposed upon us. We might describe the ability to define ourselves—and to shift that definition over time—as the "shaping of identity," the theme at the heart of this book. To be sure, terms used to identify oneself and characteristics deemed acceptable by general society have changed since the Middle Ages. Nevertheless, as contributors to the present book show, a wide variety of medieval French texts point to the process and consequences of forming and re-forming identity, at the same time highlighting how identity may be imposed and self-imposed by authors, characters, and audiences.

More precisely, the collection taken as a whole focuses on the concept of the Other Within. Chrétien de Troyes's *Le Conte du Graal* offers the perfect example of this phenomenon. The tale opens with the hero hunting alone in the forest, entirely absorbed in his own pursuits, his own world, and his own thoughts. Perceval's aloneness and self-absorption are quite transparent as the text charts the hero's passage toward an integration into society from which he emerges both accepted and yet even more "different." Such distance, deliberately erected, presents the reconstructed self as the Other Within. This term, which we may consider a marker of social and cultural change, offers the chance to explore the relationship between an individual and a group: one may simultaneously exist within and outside of society, finding oneself a member of a community without being entirely defined by it.

This ambiguous space results in large part from the mutability of identity. One is able to be variously Other or not Other or Other Within—or indeed Others Within or even Other Without—throughout a text because identity is not stable. The concept of the Other Within, and more broadly the process of shaping identity, thus provides a framework that invites the study of identity in all its facets. These include imposition of character type, a sense of not belonging, split identity, religious anxieties, a desire to copy a role model, and the embracing of a community or group by an individual. Characters assume or discard identities, and authors do likewise; attitudes toward textuality and individuality evolve markedly, the purpose for writing develops, and audiences change. Within this burgeoning cultural world, identities are imposed in many ways, revealing what Jane H. M. Taylor speaks of in her contribution to this volume as a "variousness of the self" in the later Middle Ages, a most useful way of summing up a fluidity of identity and distance. Case studies across traditions and periods add up to more than the sum of their parts. They allow the present book to explore the complex interactions between and among individuals and groups—at the same time revealing the richness of medieval French literature.

This inclusivity and variety is not to ignore the importance of context. Modern notions of identity reflect the historical and cultural circumstances of the twentieth and twenty-first centuries rather than those of the medieval period. One of the clearest ways to understand how identity was perceived in the Middle Ages, at least by intellectuals, might be to consider medieval mappae mundi, of which the greatest extant example has been housed at Hereford Cathedral possibly since its fabrication. Marginal commentaries and most other textual aspects of the Hereford Mappa Mundi are in French, the native language of those who commissioned and used it. At the center of the world map is Jerusalem. Biblical places and events are depicted, as are a wide variety of peoples, creatures, and mythical beasts. Heaven and hell and other legendary places are here. This is not to say the map is not geographical: it accurately depicts land masses and seas, towns and mountains, and could probably have served as a map to help the user find the way from one town to another. But that was not its primary function. This Anglo-Norman artefact—part literary, part religious, part scientific, part mythical—is an encyclopedic visual depiction of the sum of all knowledge. It illustrates how the approach to the world in the Middle Ages is drastically different from ours. Medieval people were perfectly capable of using the same document in many ways, including to situate themselves in God's plan. Educated people in the Middle Ages seeking to establish their identity in the world or in a particular situation might refer to a mappa mundi and be satisfied by what they saw or read.

Evidence such as this suggests that "medieval identity" as a concept per se does not pose a problem. Moreover, a frequently assumed broad uniformity of medieval Western European culture—witness pan-European architectural movements, oral and written narrative traditions, and especially the overarching Christian presence—may further the impression of an overarching notion of identity in the Middle Ages.[1] Indeed, at first glance, it may seem possible to establish a set definition of identity in medieval texts, at least within a specific corpus of texts. A study limited solely to *La Chanson de Roland* or a saint's life, for instance, might lead to fairly firm conclusions: namely, a distinct feudal and religious identity for the first, and an accepted place in God's plan for the second. Likewise, an initial reading of the works of Villon or Rutebeuf alone might suggest that each poet has an understanding of his place in society and of how his works fit in, allowing a relatively stable idea of medieval French literary identity to emerge within this context.

Even texts that seem to imply the potential for shifts in identity may in fact reveal that such changes are merely superficial. It is important to distinguish between identity and function, a difference illustrated well by the fabliau tradition. Characters continually pretend to be something or someone they are not—sometimes a priest, sometimes a corpse, sometimes a member of the opposite sex—but pretense does not necessarily suggest a change in identity. Transitory identity switching seems to be a vital tool in the fabliau trickster's tool kit, yet most fabliau characters do have a fixed identity: they may pretend to be a husband or a dead person or a ghostly voice or a wise woman, but at the end of the tale such characters appear to return to who they were when first encountered by the audience: in short, they remain fools, cuckolds, or tricksters. Similarly, characters in romance may cross-dress without necessarily altering their identity. When the eponymous hero of Robert de Blois's *Floris et Lyriopé* dons female garb, his goal is purely masculine: he wishes to be near and seduce Lyriopé. Other characters, too, switch function but maintain their identity. Reynard the fox is a slippery and malleable character who will do and say almost anything to convince his foes of his sincerity. The wily fox's function arguably differs depending on whether he is the star of an oral tale, the trickster of stories written down on the manuscript page, or carved on the misericords under the backsides of monks, but assuming an identity of his choice in a given narrative episode does not result in a transformed identity overall.

The same may be said of characters who first appear to shift identities. Ganelon is a case in point. Known as a spy who switches function at will, on the surface he is the ultimate Other Within, a knight with excellent credentials—very much an insider—who turns against Roland on the basis of a perceived sleight. Here is the enemy within, one of "us" who plots with the Saracens to satisfy his personal (if not actual) need for revenge. It might be argued that Ganelon's greatest crime is not his treachery but rather his association with the pagan Blancandrin. However, is this type of treachery truly an example of the variousness of identity, of confused, imposed, or self-imposed identity? Ganelon is evil throughout *La Chanson de Roland*, a twisted knight who is well respected but rejects such respect for personal vengeance. His is not the most complicated of identities. The same holds true for Méléagant in Chrétien de Troyes's *Le Chevalier de la charrete*: he is a malicious villain regardless of his words and actions. More complex is Kay, and yet even this knight—at times virtuous, at times less so—does not really struggle with identity complications within a single narrative: it is more from author to author, narrative to narrative, and text to text, that his identity changes. These are interesting characters, certainly, but in essence just "baddies" (or for Kay, at times, "goodies").

Yet the line between function and identity may also be blurred: the notions converge at times, and both can be either temporary or permanent. Just how are we to understand the confessions—most notably in *Le Plaid*—that punctuate the *Roman de Renart*? Are these (albeit temporary) sincere expressions of remorse, indicating a shift in Reynard's personality?

If so—and it is not to be dismissed out of hand as a possibility—then the fox is, perhaps under pressure, undergoing a shift in his very identity. Moreover, despite the usual stability of identity in the fabliaux, if the characters' situation changes in the course of the tale—something is gained or lost, someone duped, wealth vanished—then a part of who they are will have altered at the end: a wife put in her place, a source of food made available, a new social position adopted. Successful fabliau characters (and indeed the losers, too) are somehow "changed" when the page is turned. Identity is absolutely connected to power in the fabliaux: The peasant and his wife in *Les quatre souhaits Saint Martin* are given the power to change their lot and therefore themselves, but eventually, through their own stupidity and lascivious nature, they do not grab the opportunity to better their situation. In *Frère Denise*, who is to know what goes through the cross-dressing fabliau character's mind? And *Du vilain asnier* is very much a story about identity ("am I more at home with perfume or shit?"), as is its contemporary pious pendant *Merlin Mellot*, the longest tale of the *Vie des Pères*, discussed in James R. Simpson's chapter in this book. Although counterintuitive, it might be argued that, thanks to their ability to change their identity through successful ruse, fabliaux "winners" are more in control of their identity than many characters in most other traditions, with the possible exception of hagiography.

All of the previous examples also testify to identity's inherent instability: the basis upon which an individual becomes part of a group can change over time, as can the desire to be a member of a particular community. Moreover, identity can be created and re-created, adopted, conferred, refused, imposed, and self-imposed. These identity shifts reveal and result from diverse motivations. Some characters' transformations—whether imposed or self-imposed—are straightforward and relatively easy to justify: witness a knight reassessing his priorities in a chanson de geste, the fairy queen imposing a new identity on Lanval in Marie de France's lai, or the recipients of a miracle turning their back on sin. The reasons behind such shifts are varied, but the result is much the same. Individuals may choose to create an alternative identity for a limited period of time—exemplified by the number of knights who appear incognito for particular reasons before their "true" identity is revealed—or seek to discover their lineage because of an initial lack of specific identity; characters originally qualified by monikers such as the Fair Unknown are cases in point. At times, political or social constraints lead to the imposition of an identity, as when Silence's parents decide to raise their daughter as a boy in Heldris de Cornuälle's *Le Roman de Silence*, whereas at other times characters have identities forced on them out of spite or for reasons of revenge. The heroines of wager romances serve as perfect illustrations of the latter; the tales' villains seek to preserve their own interests or enhance their social status and landholding by offering fraudulent proof of the heroine's infidelity. In some instances, imposed and self-imposed identities converge, as characters adopt a persona that was first placed on them by another. Gauvain's supposed death in *L'Âtre périlleux* erases his identity temporarily, and the paragon of chivalry becomes "Cil sans non" [the Nameless One], taking on the identity determined for him by the men who claim to have killed him. This identity—or rather, lack of identity—marks Gauvain until he can once more claim his name, after re-creating himself and reestablishing his place in society.

Whereas radical transformations of identity are infrequent, more modest shifts are continual. We repeatedly change ourselves in small ways through reactions and responses to others. With expectations that vary depending on the circumstances, characters may privilege one identity in one setting and then another in a different situation. Although love and chivalry are closely intertwined, for instance, the skills that make a knight formidable on the battlefield are not necessarily the same ones that will make him a success when he is alone with his lady. Others' reactions may also reveal a gap between expectations and reality. In thirteenth-century romances including *Hunbaut, Le Chevalier aux deux épées*, and *La Première Continuation de Perceval*, Gauvain finds himself in difficulty when a lady who has fallen in love with the celebrated knight sight unseen fails to recognize him in person and in fact refuses her affections to the man before her because she is saving her heart for Gauvain. In these cases, the lady's response leads Gauvain to alter his own behavior. Internal standards, too, guide shifts. In Marie de France's *Bisclavret*, the noble-turned-werewolf's moral character leads him to behave courteously with the king, yet attack the two people who have forced him to remain transformed as a beast. Similarly, when the eponymous hero of Raoul de Houdenc's *Meraugis de Portlesguez* has lost his lady—who erroneously believes the knight to be dead—he finds himself in the odd position of becoming the ally of the man holding his beloved captive when he is brought to the man's castle to recuperate from severe wounds. This turn of events means that the hero pits himself against his friends from the Arthurian court, who have come at the lady's request to besiege the castle and free her, raising the question of how to recognize a "bad guy."

At times, identity may change constantly in a literary work if an especially gifted composer seeks a degree of instability, or if a character is particularly ambiguous. In other cases, shifts are extratextual and call attention to the role that the audience plays. At times, it is a question of modern perception and a desire to classify tales and their composers: just why was a text labeled a fabliau in the nineteenth century, a pious tale in the twentieth century, and now a *dit* in the twenty-first? Is Gautier de Coinci an entertainer, a preacher, a musician, or a poet? Readers and listeners play a role in the process of shaping identity in each text, as well, through their interpretation of how they are meant to understand a character. Poets generally create a text within a tradition, but once their works are in circulation, they have little, if any, power over how their creation will be read, received, and interpreted. Their characters are left to the mercy of an audience, whether medieval or modern. Furthermore, works may implicitly or explicitly invite interpretation and discussion by their audience, allowing for members of the public themselves to impose identity upon key and minor characters. The Arthurian corpus is perhaps the most obvious example: the notion of the "once and future king" leaves an understanding of Arthur's identity to the reader or listener, and plenty of space for continuations and new texts to be authored.

Whether intra-, inter-, or extratextual, shifts in identity do not exist in a vacuum; all reveal the stakes for both the individual and the group. Linked intimately to the term "identity" and the construct of an Other are concepts such as community, inclusion and exclusion, society, and kinship, each of which is itself complex and multiple. Cultural politics, religious and regional stereotypes, social status, age, gender, occupation, time period, and (in the case of composers) reason for writing—idiolect and sociolect—all help to establish norms that influence whether an individual belongs, wishes to belong, or is excluded from a particular community, with "community" understood in the broadest possible sense. While notions of identity—particularly national identity—most easily correspond to the framework of the modern world, they played a key role in the Middle Ages as well. The question of national identity is difficult for medieval scholars, attached as it is to territory, lordship, and kinship. A sense of shared identity was an essential but complex necessity for lords to manage their lands effectively. Political circumstances would require rulers to shape multiple identities, depending on the situation; for those beneath them such a discussion of changing political identity might be a great deal less important. There are some interesting examples of the need to "claim" national, local, and other political identities in French, from the histories of Wace and Geoffrey Gaimar's *Estoire des Engleis* to the entire Arthurian corpus. Seen through the lens of twenty-first-century notions of nation-building, historiography appears an imposition of identity; in the Middle Ages, the reality for most would likely have been a blissful ignorance of such arguments and discussions.

Modern scholars have understandably been intrigued by the interest in exploring identity shifts, identity switching, and the imposition of a new identity in literary works of the Middle Ages. Over the years, a good deal of critical attention has been devoted to examining how individuals belong, consider their own status, have new functions imposed upon them, or are considered by others—in short, how they have a fixed identity or an identity in flux. Nevertheless, until now there has been no direct attempt to bring together the whole medieval period, a broad range of traditions, and the construction of identity, notably by looking at ways of shaping identity and the questions of the Other Within. This is not to say that some rich works do not feed into and off of the issues raised in this volume. Studies such as Donald Maddox's *Fictions of Identity in Medieval France* and *Medieval Identity Machines* by Jeffrey J. Cohen focus specifically on how identities are constructed. Maddox, for example, insists that narrative poets' audiences were "receptive to much more than an eventful tale: on occasion one has the sense that between the specular enlightenment of characters and the audiences that enjoyed such arresting moments there might also have existed a virtually specular relationship."[2] This sort of relationship is precisely the type of bond worthy of examination by modern scholars, a mutual understanding of identity at a particular moment in time.

The concept of the Other, too—whether defined by gender, sexuality, religion, or another attribute—often intersects with an investigation of identity. The two merge in works including Kirsten A. Fudeman's *Vernacular Voices: Language and Identity in Medieval French Jewish Communities*; Sylvia Huot's *Madness in Medieval French Literature: Identities Found and Lost*; Sharon Kinoshita's *Medieval Boundaries: Rethinking Difference in Old French Literature*; *Gender and Difference in the Middle Ages*, edited by Sharon Farmer and Carol Braun Pasternack; and recent studies on the medieval Mediterranean, such as Megan Moore's *Exchanges in Exoticism: Cross-Cultural Marriage and the Making of the Mediterranean in Old French Romance*. Questions of identity and the Other may also be explored in terms of the author, as in *The Medieval Author in Medieval French Literature*, edited by Virginie Greene, or of the relationship between humans and beasts, the case in Jill Mann's *From Aesop to Reynard: Beast Literature in Medieval England*, or of marginalized groups, seen in Jean-Marie Fritz's *Le Discours du fou au Moyen Âge, XIIe–XIIIe siècles*.[3] There is a rich modern interest in examining issues concerning all aspects of identity, if not always overtly interconnected. This book makes full use of such work while setting itself apart through its direct and sustained focus on shaping identity in all of its forms while exploring the Other Within.

As our discussion makes apparent, the question of identity in the Middle Ages is not quite so straightforward as it may first seem. In fact, it proves to be particularly complex. There is no single "medieval French" treatment of how identity is considered, no unified understanding of emerging authorial distinctiveness, no specific perception of "text," no consistent view of how characters should be drawn or indeed read. Stories evolve, attitudes toward authorship develop, and wider philosophical ideas concerning the individual mature. These issues thus remain in constant flux.

Even as these changes occur, inclusion and exclusion serve as powerful tools in encouraging—whether overtly or tacitly—members of a group to conform to societal expectations, thereby shaping identity in notable ways. Yet it is also possible to take one's place in a group while remaining foreign to it, as we saw was the case with Perceval in Chrétien de Troyes's *Le Conte du Graal*. The ability to exist simultaneously inside and outside of a community serves as the focal point for this volume, which illustrates the breadth of perspectives from which one may view how identity is shaped and the possibility of the Other Within. With an opportunity to consider identity in all its guises, from the very notion of identity to how identity both of and within texts may shift, contributors take diverse approaches to these topics. They examine the themes through a wide range of lenses—from marginal characters to gender to origins to questions of voice and naming—in works that span genres and date from the twelfth century to the late Middle Ages. While romance and epic figure prominently, essays also treat saints' lives, lyric, and historiography. Together the studies offer, in the most positive of senses, a kaleidoscopic snapshot of the Other

Within in medieval French literature. They invite readers to consider how multiplicities of understanding may exist and interact, leading to new insights regarding identity shifts.

Douglas Kelly explores the relationship between personification and the *moi multiple*, highlighting the ways in which forms of personification can express multiple attributes of characters. Kelly looks closely at several narratives from the late twelfth and early thirteenth centuries—Chrétien de Troyes's *Conte du Graal*, Guillaume de Lorris's *Roman de la Rose*, and Huon de Méry's *Tournoiement Antéchrist*—before a more general analysis of late medieval works by authors such as Froissart, Machaut, Christine de Pizan, Thomas de Salluste, Evrart de Conty, and Villon. By studying the importance of the name (or names) of a personification, the links between names and surnames, and changes in context with the passing of different ages of life, Kelly reveals that personification is especially rich for evoking the *moi multiple* of characters. The importance of personifications extends far beyond an individual work, Kelly argues, for they can have an impact on how audiences understand and construct their own inner selves.

The dream accounts in Othon de Grandson's *Livre Messire Ode* are at the center of Jane H. M. Taylor's essay, which also evokes the *moi multiple* of Kelly's study. Reading Othon's dream garden in dialogue with Guillaume de Lorris's *Roman de la Rose*, Taylor evokes contrasts between the works to argue that the inhabitants of Othon's garden serve a very different purpose than Guillaume's allegories. With Othon's dreaming "I" indistinguishable from his writing "I," his encounters in the dream garden offer him the chance to interact with his own potential selves: instead of fragmented qualities of the dreamer, as is the case in the *Rose*, here the characters in the garden represent projections of who the dreamer could be. Taylor contends that, thanks to the *Rose*'s influence, Othon's choice to humanize the garden's inhabitants renders them strange to the audience. With Othon's series of potential selves, the work is an act of self-scrutiny as the poet tries to experience his self as Othered.

A different type of dream world appears in William Burgwinkle's essay. Burgwinkle studies the ways in which *Huon de Bordeaux*—itself a hybrid text that mixes elements of chansons de geste and romance—blurs boundaries and raises questions about geographical, cultural, philosophical, and religious difference. Analyzing Huon's interactions with Auberon and the world that he inhabits, Burgwinkle demonstrates that cultures may take on the customs of others and thus become Other themselves. He argues convincingly that *Huon* is a tale that, in Roger Kennedy's terms, "dreams history" by imagining Carolingian revenge and the return of Islamic lands to Christians. In the end, however, the West's victories are hollow. The text presents itself as a middle ground that mediates difference, yet the extremes that it depicts are less distinct than they appear.

The next two essays consider questions of gender. Kristin L. Burr examines the ways in which the hero and heroine make themselves Other Within the courtly system in Gerbert de Montreuil's *Le Roman de la Violette*. Initially forced into the role of outsider as they face reversals in fortune, both characters then consciously adopt the role, resisting attempts to categorize them easily. They transform their identities through stories that others impose upon them and the tales that they tell about themselves, inviting the audience to question assumptions concerning chivalry, love, the qualities of a courtly lady, and gender stereotypes. Focusing on episodes that center on a ring given to the heroine by the hero, Burr points to the gap between words and acts and argues for nuancing the understanding of activity and passivity in the tale. She demonstrates that the object plays a key role in establishing identity and reintegrating the couple fully into the courtly world.

Like Burr, Sara I. James examines questions of gender in her essay as she analyzes the complicated range of ways in which Rainouart and Orable/Guibourc evoke the Other in the chansons de geste of the *Cycle de Guillaume*. She notes that ambiguity surrounds the characters' Otherness, as they are noble Saracens who convert to Christianity, thus positioning themselves simultaneously inside and outside of certain groups. Their constant shifts from outsider to insider and back again raise questions about how we are to understand an epic "center," particularly when Rainouart and Guibourc are portrayed more favorably than Louis and Blanchefleur, the Frankish king and queen. James concludes that in these rich, complex texts, the Other is never inherently lesser, even while being appropriated, assimilated, or feared.

The fluid boundaries between "insider" and "outsider" appear in Jane Gilbert's contribution as well. Noting that many important characters in chansons de geste are internal "outsiders" even as the genre displays a strong collectivist element, Gilbert turns to Jean-Luc Nancy's work to study both how it enhances our understanding of the heroes in *Ami et*

Amile and the ways in which chanson de geste adds a new layer to Nancy's analysis of community. Gilbert demonstrates that reading *Ami et Amile* through the lens of Nancy's concepts of "l'être-en-commun" and "la communauté"—rendered here as "communialty"—reveals the tensions rather than the harmony in the relationship between the titular characters. In the tale, the acts of each man, which could highlight sameness, instead testify to singularity and its associated ethical obligations. In the end, reading Nancy's work and chanson de geste together teases out their nuances, allowing a deeper appreciation for both.

Merlin plays a key role in the next two essays. The question of origins is at the heart of Francis Gingras's study. Gingras argues that the founding of the Arthurian world rests on otherness thanks to the role of Merlin, a character simultaneously good and bad. Examining works spanning the centuries from Geoffrey of Monmouth and Wace to the late thirteenth-century *Claris et Laris*, Gingras traces the tale of Merlin's origins along with the story of Arthur's conception. Whether the texts treat the material directly or through allusions, they all elicit questions concerning the relationship between history and fable, truth and lies. While early works privilege the historical aspects, Robert de Boron blurs the boundary between fiction and history, and *Claris et Laris* abandons claims to historical truth and chooses to underscore fiction instead. Ultimately, Gingras concludes, the genre of romance resides on the permeable boundary between history and fiction.

James R. Simpson looks closely at questions of voice in his contribution. Studying BnF fr. 24432 and focusing particularly on Jehan de Saint-Quentin's *Merlin Mellot*, Simpson uncovers the uncertain space where marginalized individuals belong—or half-belong—to a community. He demonstrates that voice is a living presence in *Merlin Mellot*, highlighting as well the influence of epic on this version of the tale. With an emphasis on collections of small objects and the role of exchange, Simpson uncovers the tensions created between faith communities by differing material and spiritual values. Voice is suggestive or directive, whispering or booming, and central to the narratives examined here to a startling degree. In the end, the "little voices" in the manuscript speak to the construction of identities.

Analyzing the interaction between sex, the Church, and the medieval reader allows Adrian P. Tudor to highlight the conflicts and sense of "marginality" that underpin the message of conversion in the *Vie des Pères*, a work central in Simpson's study as well. Tudor demonstrates that sex is a motif rather than a lesson in itself: characters from many backgrounds can shape their own identity or have their identity shaped by another party, overcoming the pitfalls of carnal sin in the process. The characters' eventual conversion comes less often through divine intervention than through human agency: their spiritual transformation—to be imitated by the medieval reader when positive—arises generally from compassion rather than compunction. Instead of simply illustrating the dichotomy between good and evil, the authors of this "collective text" provide examples for those in the "real world." The spiritual journeys undertaken by characters in the *Vie des Pères* frequently feature sexual sin. The objective of these tales is to edify and entertain, but not to titillate. By creating a world where, under the right circumstances, sex and salvation can coexist, the *Vie des Pères* invites the audience to reassess their own conduct, potentially identifying a "penitent within."

Mary Jane Schenck, too, considers the bonds between a text and its public. Pointing to the ways in which religious difference can encourage the audience to identify with characters, Schenck focuses on Roland's confession scenes in the Oxford *Roland*, the Châteauroux version of the epic, and the vernacular translation of the *Pseudo-Turpin* chronicle. Schenck views the scenes through a rhetorical lens to examine the ways in which each uses ethos, pathos, and logos to create a relationship between interiority and the audience. In each version, the confession is designed for a different effect and group of observers or hearers. In the Oxford *Roland*, Roland creates a self of memories and evokes audience empathy as he offers a lesson on how to die as a warrior. Shifts in the Châteauroux version direct the message to the common man who must think about heaven and hell as much as to a warrior audience. The *Pseudo-Turpin* reveals an emphasis on salvation theology and a confession of faith in the presence of a witness to position Roland in a place of common humanity, as a soul in need of a proper death.

By focusing on the Other Within and crossing traditional boundaries of genre and time period, this book underscores both the richness of medieval French literature and its engagement with questions that are simultaneously more and less modern than they may initially appear. Characters, authors, or audiences can remain outsiders throughout a work or eventually take their place once more as fully within the social order: such an easily shared and shareable characteristic offers scholars a fruitful point of departure and allows for easy dialogue with students of all areas of medieval French literature. Every study in this book invites us to consider the role that distance and difference play, and encourages readers to consider the ways in which we, too, may be an Other Within.

1

The Medieval *Moi Multiple*

Names, Surnames, and Personifications

DOUGLAS KELLY

"Paris se trouve filtré, intériorisé par l'esprit du poète, qui, en retour, peut se projeter sur Paris (enfer et paradis), extériorisant son moi multiple" [Paris is filtered, interiorized by the poet's mind, which, in turn, can project itself on Paris (Hell and Heaven), exteriorizing his *moi multiple*].[1] Villon's projection of his *moi multiple* onto a Parisian landscape illustrates a common medieval way of depicting the self. That is, his interior self emerges as a projection that identifies his place in his urban environment. This environment is then interiorized, where it becomes a part of his interior self. Personification is one device used for such projection. In what follows, I examine several instances of personification, ranging from *abstracta agentia* through personification proper to allegory.[2]

Personification as the term is used here includes the full range of rarely precise devices to represent a fictional or pseudo-autobiographical character's inner self. Three topics are prominent in this scheme: the name or names of the given personification, the linking of complementary and contrasting names and surnames, and changes in context as the ages of life pass by and the inner self evolves. I focus on personifications prominent in late twelfth-century and early thirteenth-century narratives: Chrétien de Troyes's *Conte du Graal*, Guillaume de Lorris's *Roman de la Rose*, and Huon de Méry's *Tournoiement Antéchrist*, with some attention to Raoul de Houdenc's *Roman des Eles* and *Songe d'enfer*. I conclude with a summary review of analogous phenomena in later medieval literature.

Personifications have names. The name, including the surname, is a topos that can reveal something about the character or actions of the person or the personification. "Por neant n'ai ge pas cest non" (v. 962)

[It's not for nothing that I have this name], as Chrétien puts it in *Cligés* for Soredamors, whose name means "gilded over with love."[3] A personification may represent a virtue or a vice or, in narrative, now the one, now the other. This is frequently the case with Amour. Referring to personified names, Raoul de Houdenc emphasizes the importance of the name's meaning in both poems. For example, the chevalier should understand the meaning of the name he goes by and how he should properly represent it: "Por ce fust droiz sanz contredit / Qu'il fussent tel com lor nons dit"[4] (vv. 27–28) [That's why it would be absolutely right for them to conform to their name's meaning]. Raoul goes on to explain that "Chevalerie" is the fountainhead of "cortoisie" (vv. 12–13) and that it is the "propres nons de gentillece" (v. 39) [proper name for nobility]. Taken together, these names anticipate how the narrator will depict *chevalerie* in descriptions and narrative: "Li nons m'en aprent la matire" (v. 464) [the name teaches me its subject matter].

With Raoul's words in mind, we may turn to Chrétien's *Conte du Graal.* Perceval's adventures confirm his mother's counsel: "Par le sornon connoist on l'ome"[5] (v. 562) [one knows the man by his surname]. This young man discovers his given name after his Grail Castle fiasco. Before that, Beau Fils (v. 373), as his mother calls him, knows only what she taught him, and then only to the extent and in the ways his isolated experience in the "gaste forest soutaine" (v. 75) [solitary waste forest] permits. He does not even know what a knight is (vv. 176–78), a name he gradually comes to understand as the romance progresses. He must, like Villon, understand and then interiorize that word and, finally, let it show in his actions in the outside world.

To the knights he encounters in the forest while hunting, Beau Fils "ne set pas totes les lois" for "Galois sont tot par nature / Plus fol que bestes en pasture; / Cist est ausi comme une beste" (vv. 236, 243–45) [is ignorant of all the rules of conduct . . . Welshmen are naturally more foolish than beasts in pasture; this one too is like a beast]. Both astonishing successes and bumbling failures result from his "bestiality." The young man emerges from his Grail Castle adventure to acquire his given name and other identifying surnames: "Perchevax li chaitis! / Ha! Perchevax maleürous, / Comme iés or mal aventurous" (vv. 3582–84) [Perceval the wretch! Ah, unhappy Perceval! How unfortunate you are now]. Some thousand lines further on, the Hideous Damsel exclaims: "tu, li maleüreus" (v. 4665) [you unhappy man], again recalling his silence at the Grail Castle, a silence that his mother's Beau Fils thought conformed to Gornemant de Goort's counsel. In fact Gornemant warns against "Trop parlans" [talking too much]; he does not tell Beau Fils to be mute (vv. 1648–56).

We learn further on that the young man went wrong from the beginning when he failed to come to his mother's aid after she collapsed as he departed (vv. 622–28, 6394–402). He failed to understand, or recall, that ladies in distress should be helped. "Qui as dames honor ne porte, / La soe honor doit estre morte" (vv. 539–40) [whoever does not honor ladies, his honor is necessarily dead]. The loss of honor in this case is a sin. Only his mother's prayers saved him from a worse fate (vv. 6403–8). That sin, more than his misunderstanding of Gornemant's admonition, caused his failure to ask the Grail questions. It also explains his surnames. His last counselor, the hermit uncle, is categorical: "Pechiez la langue te trencha" (v. 6409) [Sin cut off your tongue]. Perceval is a sinner. According to this passage, Sin made him mute.

His sin, then, is a personification lurking in the young man from the moment that he abandons his mother. The hermit's words bring it out into the open. Sin initiates a narrative trajectory during which Perceval gradually interiorizes and comes to understand himself as knight and his place in the world. How could he know what sin is if he does not even know what a church is (v. 573) and, after more than five years in quest of the Grail Castle in order to right the wrong, he had not once entered a church (vv. 6220–23)? Isolated with his mother in the forest, he was totally ignorant of life outside the "lawless" world he knew, including the *us*, or customs, that govern the knight's life as well as the *lois*, or commandments, of the Christian religion. The prime fault comes out as Sin personified. As a personification, it is there for all readers to learn why Perceval failed to speak at the Grail Castle.

Sinners are not hopeless. Perceval can atone for his sin, as he can for his other faults in the different milieus whose *lois* he must learn to obey. He can do so, as Gornemant points out, with "cuer et paine et us" (v. 1467) [heart, pain, and practice]. Perceval is a fast learner, thanks to other personifications,

Car il li venoit de nature,
Et quant nature li aprent[6]

> Et li cuers del tot i entent,
> Ne li puet estre rien grevaine
> La ou nature et cuers se paine. (vv. 1480–84)

[for it came to him naturally. And, when Nature instructs him and he strives wholeheartedly to heed these lessons, nothing can be arduous for him when Nature and Heart strive together.]

Perceval merely needs the right kind of education. His efforts and encounters provide that education.

The Smiling Damsel at Arthur's court foresees Perceval's destiny to become the best knight in the world, a unique excellence that promises him a new surname. He will become a *seigneur*—"Celui qui de chevalerie / Avra toute la seignorie" (vv. 1061–62; cf. vv. 1039–44) [He who will be lord over all knighthood]—not so much over an *honor* as fiefdom[7] but, in the personification mode, lord over knighthood and chivalry. The damsel makes this prediction despite the fact that Perceval is still, obviously, a fool and that "Molt grief chose est de fol aprendre" (v. 1173) [to teach a fool is a grievous task], as Yvonet learns when he tries to teach Perceval how to put on the armor of the Red Knight. Yet fools do learn (vv. 1012–16), especially when Nature bestows on one of them the potential to become the best knight in the world. So, although uncouth, Perceval kills the Red Knight, showing that another, knightly Perceval is beginning to emerge.

I have dwelt on Perceval because his experiences rely on the stylistic feature that looms large in subsequent medieval writing: personifications, including their names and surnames, that depict the *moi multiple* of the medieval person. Chrétien's depiction of Perceval, *jeune héros en construction*[8] [young hero in the making], illustrates this. It is evident as well in a romance written some fifty years after the *Conte du Graal*. Guillaume de Lorris's *Roman de la Rose* relates the adventures of a young man impelled by Nature and Cuer but ignorant of the *us* and *lois* of the world he enters. He too sets out, entirely absorbed in his own pursuits, his own world, and his own thoughts. His grail is a rose. His attributes, multiple, diverse, and mutable, become personifications that act with him.

As Guillaume leaves his chamber, Terre, a personification, appears. She suggests he visit a beautifully adorned world far different from the wild, unpopulated forest of Perceval's childhood. Eschewing the demeaning toil of the personified defects in the wall of Deduit's garden, Guillaume discovers the marvelous charm of a highly stylized, courtly *locus amoenus*. Oiseuse opens the way into this world. This feminine personification, like Guillaume, "Mout avoit bon tens et bon mai, / qu'el n'avoit sousi ne esmai / de nule rien fors seulement / de soi atorner noblement" (vv. 569–72)[9] [had her good time in the merry month of May, for she had no care or anxiety at all except solely how to attire herself nobly]. Entering the enclosed space inhabited by a *compaignie* "bele . . . / et cortoise et bien enseignie" (vv. 627–28) [beautiful . . . and courteous and well versed in etiquette], that is, by those who know the *us* and *lois* of this marvelous realm, Guillaume encounters personifications that define his new personality. He, like all of them, is "liez et bauz et joienz" (v. 632) [happy, lively, and joyous]. That is, he interiorizes the qualities that constellate about him. He too enjoys good looks (Beauté), nobility (Richesse),[10] generosity (Largesse), free birth (Franchise),[11] courtliness (Courtoisie), leisure (Oiseuse), and youth (Jeunesse).[12] He joins these personifications in a carol.

When the carol ends, the personifications retire in the shade to make love ("donoier,"[13] vv. 1289–92). Guillaume is not yet Amant, but only a courteous young aristocrat, "[j]olis, gais et pleins de leesce" (v. 103) [joyful, gay, and full of gladness]. He therefore leaves the personifications to themselves as he meanders through the garden. Guillaume, like Perceval when he meets the knights, seems to sense that there is more to life than he has experienced heretofore. Restless, but not yet in love, he wanders about, the god of love stalking him with Doux Regard, who is well equipped with the god's bow and arrows. At Narcissus's fountain the god of love's *coup de flèche* changes everything. Guillaume's *gradus amoris* begins, and he acquires the new surname Amant.

The process begins when he sees the rosebuds, and especially the rose that becomes the poem's central image.[14] Doux Regard fixes Guillaume's gaze with the arrows of extramission[15] on five human attributes ascribed to the rosebud: Beauté, Simplece (this word signifies a lack of duplicity; it is the opposite of disingenuous),[16] Courtoisie,[17] Compaignie, and Beau Semblant (not Faux Semblant), an attribute that can refer to attractive features and affable conduct, or *bel acueil*. In this first encounter, therefore, Amant as Guillaume meets Bel Acueil who offers him a gift: "une vert fueille / vers le bouton . . . / por ce que pres ot esté nee" (vv. 2860–62) [a green leaf not far from the rosebud because it was born near to it]. All these features betoken Rose as both name and surname, like Soredamors in *Cligés* and Blancheflor in *Perceval*. The rose complex in the *Roman de la Rose* represents a person, obviously a young woman who is attractive, well brought up, affable, *honnête*. I shall henceforth refer to her by her surname, Rose, as I do to Guillaume as Amant—"Par le sornon connoist on" not only "l'ome" but also "la dame et la pucelle."

Rose's attributes depict her own *moi multiple* but include no vices. Just as in the *Roman des Eles* "li nons de chevalerie / Est contrepois de lecherie" (vv. 453–54) [the name knighthood is the antonym of debauchery], so the name Love in the *Rose* should also exclude debauchery. Groups of personifications and their corresponding attributes are virtual *conjointures* of complementary virtues or vices. Such groupings should avoid improper *disjointures* that link virtues and vices like *courtoisie* and pride.[18]

> Qu'entre cortoisie et orgueil
> Ne porroient conjoindre ensamble.
> —Por qoi?—Por ce que il me samble
> Qu'en toz poins naist de cortoisie
> Honor, et d'orgueil vilonie. (*Eles*, vv. 298–302)

> [For courtesy and pride could not be conjoined. Why? Because it seems to me that in every respect honor is born of courtesy, and villainy is born of pride.]

Of course, *contraires choses* (*Rose*, vv. 21543–52) may be revealing, as when lovers are called lovers but, by their actions, they reveal their depravity. Amant lurches in that direction too as the romance moves into Jean de Meun's environment.

However, this movement actually begins in Guillaume's narrative when Amant asks for Rose's rose. The sight of Rose produces his *rage* (v. 1581), or the mad desire to pluck this rose and then go on to pluck the other beautiful roses, suggesting debauchery. His indiscriminate desire, though, is quickly fixed on the single rose his eyes first fall upon. The confrontation does remain erotic. Hope, *doux penser*, *doux parler*, and *doux regard* constitute the next stages in a *gradus amoris* reflecting the personifications' *donoier* after the carol in the Garden of Deduit. But now the fresh springtime setting in the garden becomes the stormy summer of Amant's frustrated passion.

This happens as Amant confronts other personifications that emerge from the rose complex in response to his actions that, like Perceval's, reveal Amant's ignorance of the *us* and *lois* of *fin'amor*. When Bel Acueil offers Rose's leaf, Amant rebuffs it and asks point-blank for the rosebud. Bel Acueil's response is immediate, sharp, and transforming: he vanishes and four other personifications rise up from Rose's own *moi multiple* to thwart Amant's desire: Peur, Honte, Malebouche, and Dangier. Of these four guardians of the rosebud, Honte is the most worthy (v. 2821). As Reason's daughter, she is conceived and therefore comes forth when Reason sees blameworthy acts. More specifically in the context of Amant's brash request, God has brought Honte to life when "Chasteez, qui dame doit estre / et des roses et des boutons, / ert asaillie de glotons / si qu'ele avoit mestier d'aïe" (vv. 2830–33) [Chastity, who should be lady over roses and rosebuds, was attacked by sexual gluttons so that she needed assistance]. When Rose rejects Amant's request, he assaults her chastity and produces her shame. "Gloton" becomes Amant's implicit surname in this configuration. He has much to learn about the *us* and *lois* of love if he wants to lose this new surname and regain Rose's *bel acueil*.

Rose is, of course, not a visible woman in time and space like Soredamors or Blancheflor in Chrétien's romances. Amant is still dreaming. But Guillaume as Amant is no Gauvain or even Perceval. Like Rose, he is a complex of attributes. The pair's contrasting actions and reactions (*rage* and *shame*) conform to the give and take of the commonplace *gradus amoris*, itself applicable to a wide range of specific amorous scripts. There is more than one way to tell a love story, depending on the kind of love described and the changes that lovers may experience. These distinctions determine the choice, meaning, and semantic scope of personifications as they emerge in the narrative. Audiences can perceive the commonplaces all the while reflecting on how they may reveal unexpected or original meanings by the way the narrative evolves. The *Roman de la Rose* illustrates this, both in Guillaume de Lorris's part and, even more so, when Jean de Meun's continuation is appended to it and Amant becomes a full-fledged *gloton* and, indeed, a vulgar womanizer (vv. 21363–404).

Before Amant reveals his self as a sexual *gloton* (vv. 21509–31), Rose's own character is beginning to emerge and evolve.

Bel Acueil se poine de faire
quen qu'il sot qui me doie plaire.

> Sovent me semont d'aprochier
> vers le bouton et d'atouchier
> au rousier qui estoit chargié. (vv. 2853–57)

[Bel Acueil strives to please me in every way he knows how. He often invites me to draw near to the rosebud, to touch the heavy laden rosebush.]

But this will not suffice. Amant wants the rose, right now! Of course, the dream encounter may stand for numerous such encounters, making Amant's demand less precipitous than the literal dream depicts it. Rose's reaction is not only to Amant's accelerated *gradus amoris* but also to his threat to her chastity and therefore to her honor. "Me volez vos honir?" (v. 2894) [Do you want to dishonor me?], exclaims Bel Acueil; "Vilains estes du demender!" (v. 2899) [your request is villainous]. Rose's wish to preserve her chastity is obvious when Bel Acueil voices his refusal to grant the rose to Amant: "nou voudroie avoir deserté / dou rosier qui l'a aporté / por nul home vivant, tant l'ains" (vv. 2901–3) [I would not have taken it from the rosebush that produced it for any living man; I love it so much]. Then Bel Acueil disappears.

Dangier "li vilains" (v. 2904) [the villein] takes Bel Acueil's place and Amant takes to his heels. The change in Rose's personifications from the affable Bel Acueil to the villein Dangier is her response to the kind of love Amant proposes. *Dangier* in Old French is usually a noble prerogative implying dominion and domination.[19] Had Amant's relation with Rose remained "courteous," we might have seen Dangier depicted as "lordship" over her suitor, a commonplace of medieval love poetry in which a noble lover humbly serves his lady. But Rose's Dangier is a "peïsant" (v. 3653), much as Amant has become a villein. Dangier's ugly appearance and the club he is armed with attest to his villeiny as well as to his villainy. He represents an imposition that is no longer courteous or forthcoming like Bel Acueil. His is a villeinous response to a villainous request.[20] Rose's reaction is an emotionally violent response to male aggression. No wonder Jealousy comes forth, not as fear of infidelity with multiple lovers, but of his inconstancy that may lead to her public shame.[21] Rose senses the *gloton* assailing her chastity in order to pluck her rose. He wants to fornicate before they have even kissed.

The *gradus amoris* in Guillaume's *Rose* (as far as it goes) shows that with the passage of time people change. Huon de Méry's *Tournoiement*

Antéchrist illustrates such mutability in its broad, ongoing psychomachia of vices and virtues. This work is nearly contemporary with Guillaume de Lorris's *Rose*, but it draws material from Chrétien de Troyes and, more important here, from Raoul de Houdenc.[22] The *Tournoiement* confronts its first-person narrator with choices: to love or not to love and what his choices will reveal about his place in the broad moral context of virtues versus vices and in the special moral conflict of love versus fornication. The choice is no longer merely between being a good and a bad lover, as in the *Roman de la Rose*, but between being virtuous and being a sinner, as in the *Conte du Graal*. Both backsliding and redemption are possible as the narrator moves between Heaven and Hell, much as Dufournet shows Villon doing in his Parisian topography composed of the churches, taverns, and brothels his poetry depicts.

The *Tournoiement* also illustrates the transition from adventure romance like the *Conte du Graal* to personification romance like the *Roman de la Rose*. At the Perilous Fountain in Chrétien's *Yvain*, Calogrenant and Yvain confront Esclados le Roux after unleashing a violent storm by pouring water from the fountain onto a stone beside it. In the *Tournoiement* the narrator pours twice as much water on the stone, thereby unleashing a storm so violent that Heaven opens briefly, perhaps anticipating the moral context of the ensuing tournament between Antichrist and Christ's armies.[23] But here the narrator confronts not Esclados but Bras-de-Fer. This Moor who serves the Antichrist[24] leads the narrator to a banquet in Hell.[25]

In the *Tournoiement* Huon de Méry looks to Raoul de Houdenc's *Roman des Eles* and *Songe d'enfer* for models of personification. Personifications emerge not only at a banquet and during a brief quest but also, more extensively, in the tournament referred to in the poem's title. This tournament is a psychomachia that pits personified Virtues as God's knights against personified Vices under the Antichrist.[26] The combatants are therefore *contraires choses*—for example, Virginité opposes Fornicacion (vv. 2505–35). The Virtues win, but the Vices, although subdued, escape to do battle again on another day (vv. 3402–63).[27] Through all this, the narrator plays the largely passive role of observer and reporter, following Bras-de-Fer to the infernal feast at which he opts to neither eat nor drink (vv. 449–71). Later, during the Virtues' victory banquet, he does drink, this time the wine of honor (vv. 3256–65), not the wine of shame that was served in Hell.

The *Tournoiement* begins with the narrator returning as a knight from battles in Brittany. It ends when he withdraws into the religious life at Saint-Germain-des-Prés (vv. 3515–25). In the psychomachia framework, he passes from Desespoir, the Montjoie d'enfer, to Esperance, the Montjoie de paradis (vv. 1224–39). This transformation, a *gradus redemptionis*, relates his emergence through personification metamorphoses in the context of sin and human instability.

Love enters the fray at the *Tournoiement*'s midpoint or, more accurately, in its middle section (vv. 1713–1822).[28] Love is an unstable emotion. The word can, as in the *Rose*, refer to a broad range of diverse, mutable emotions, from lust to platonic love; it may even refer to fornication and virginity as well as to friendship, familial affection, and love for God. As the specific emotion emerges as a personification, it colors the description of Amour and suggests how, as a personification, it may be defined and understood in a specific narrative context. Therefore, in the *Tournoiement*, the narrator initially locates Amour on Christ's side, but with a caveat: love is unstable. It can easily slide from virtue into vice and back again.

> Pour ce, se j'ai amour descrit
> Ci entre la gent Jhesu Crit,
> N'est il mie toz jours des suens,
> Fors tant com il est fins et buens,
> Si comme en maint païs avient:
> Ce que l'en doit, ce qu'il convient,
> Doit l'en amer courtoisement.
> Qui aime bien et lëaument,
> Il est de la gent courtoisie,
> Ou se ce non, il n'en est mie. (vv. 1813–22)[29]

[For this reason, if I have depicted Love in Jesus Christ's army, he is not always on His side but only when he is subtle and good, as happens in many a land. One ought to love courteously what it is proper and suitable to love. Whoever loves well and faithfully is on Courtoisie's side; if not, then that person is not on that side at all.]

Accordingly, the good Amour is in the company of appropriate personifications such as Courtoisie, Prouesse, Sapience, Providence, and Charité. He (Amour is a male personification in the *Tournoiement*) fears betrayal:

"De traïson la poitevine / Se doute molt" (vv. 1730–31) [he is very suspicious of betrayal like that attributed to people from Poitou].[30] Betrayal can kill Love. This is Rose's fear when Amant asks for the rose and Bel Acueuil withdraws while Jealousy walls up the rosebushes.

The Round Table knights are an equally unstable part of Christ's host in the *Tournoiement*.[31] Borrowed from Chrétien's Arthurian world, they include Kay, who evinces his usual slander, felony, and villainous backbiting. Perceval, still wearing the Red Knight's armor (vv. 2004–7), so lustily produces storms in Brocéliande that they kill more than a hundred of Arthur's knights (vv. 2026–30). Meraugis de Portlesguez and Gorvain Cadrus survive from Raoul's romance *Meraugis de Portlesguez*, still at odds on the quality of ideal love: should it derive from beauty alone or from courtesy (vv. 1994–99)? These aberrations and variations[32] among exemplary figures reflect the mutability and range of meanings and characteristics of love in medieval narratives. With all this diversity, the question arises: how will the *Tournoiement*'s narrator love? He finds himself involved in a choice between two personifications, Virginité and Fornicacion, and, therefore, between Heaven and Hell.

Virginité successfully jousts with Fornicacion and Avoltire, who, unhorsed, fall into malodorous muck. But Venus, Fornicacion's mother, and Amour, her renamed son Cupido, remount Fornicacion, then join her in renewed attack, this time against Virginité's companion, Chasteté. We are back in the *Rose* context; Amour is again a striking illustration of the adaptation of a given personification to the instability evident in its semantic range in diverse moral and social contexts. Venus lets fly an arrow at Virginité. It misses because the virtue takes refuge in an abbey while the arrow flies on to strike the narrator (vv. 2596–99). With that he succumbs to desire and becomes personally involved in the tournament on Antichrist's side. The crossover signals a change in the narrator that betrays Christ's army, a betrayal that he earlier avoided at the Antichrist's banquet. His is a willing crossover and betrayal because his heart agrees to the change (vv. 2655–56).

Wounded by Venus's arrow, the narrator dismounts and falls to the ground,[33] as Bras-de-Fer and Esperance comfort him. The manuscripts offer two different, albeit problematical, readings for Esperance here, readings reflected in the divergent editions of the *Tournoiement*. In Wimmer's base manuscripts, "Esperance me tint le chief / Deseperée entre ses meins" (vv. 2618–19) [In despair Hope held my head in her hands]. Stéphanie Orgeur prefers a reading based on Wimmer's variant manuscripts: "Esperance me tint le chief / Desesperé entre mes meins" (vv. 2618–19) [Hope held my despairing head in my hands], in which the adjective *desesperé* modifies the narrator's head, or *chief*, not Esperance as in Wimmer's version. The sense of both readings is not fundamentally contradictory. In Orgeur's version Esperance overcomes the narrator such that he falls into a faint and despair. Wimmer's reading, a *lectio difficilior*, recalls the commonplace oxymoron that Jean de Meun's Reason calls "esperance desesperee" (*Rose*, v. 4268). This is the irrational hope of love poetry, not the hope for heavenly paradise implied heretofore in the *Tournoiement*. This sense is evident when Amour gives the lover a potion from Esperance as comfort: "Amours m'aporta d'Esperance / Une merveilleuse poison, / C'avoit confite en sa meson / Delectacïon l'espiciere" (vv. 2660–63) [Love brought me from Esperance a marvelous potion that the druggist Delectacion had concocted in her home]. Together with Tentacion, Amour gives the potion to the narrator, who gulps it down. Despair follows. Esperance intervenes once again to comfort him by inscribing the name Diane on his forehead (vv. 2706–7).[34] Eventually the Virtues capture and imprison the Antichrist. After backsliding, the narrator now feels compunction, confesses, and finds his way toward redemption at Saint-Germain-des-Prés. Esperance as Virtue triumphs over Esperance that serves an erotic Amour.

After the thirteenth century there is a general shift away from personification in favor of exemplification.[35] Nevertheless personification does not disappear entirely, especially in Froissart's *dits*. Two personifications offer subtle adaptations of commonplace notions in his *Joli Buisson de jonece*.[36] One would expect moral admonitions from Philosophie analogous to Philosophy's *chastoiements* in Boethius's *Consolation of Philosophy*, whereas Jonece might be expected to promote the *carpe diem* morality commonplace among youth and exemplified by Jeunesse in the *Rose*'s Garden of Deduit. These lessons are forthcoming, but in an unconventional and therefore striking restatement of these commonplaces. Philosophie teaches *carpe diem*, apparently ignoring the ages of life commonplace. Jonece, though, is well aware of the ages of life of which she is a part, a script the narrator learns in Jean Froissart's *Espinette amoureuse* when he is still a young man,[37] but which he then ignores in the later *Joli Buisson*. Once again we find the scope of the word personified, however specialized or generalized it may be, that is a fundamental consideration in understanding personifications in context[38] and in constructing and showing forth a *moi multiple* as it changes over time.

The multiple contexts within which personifications emerge are possible because of the semantic range of the word personified and the ways in which that range can be exploited in literal and allegorical narratives. A number of fourteenth- and fifteenth-century *dits* illustrate this adaptability. Machaut frequently uses personifications such as Esperance and Boneurté to state his moral views on love and other topics.[39] Philosophie in Christine de Pizan's *Advision Cristine* is also renamed Théologie, Sapience, and Sérénité in order to suggest different aspects of Christine's Philosophie. They are defining surnames.[40]

In Froissart's *Prison amoureuse* the prison functions as Amour's commonplace prison, from which Rose, a male lover, seeks release while he languishes there. But it also designates the prison where Wenceslas de Brabant, Froissart's patron, found himself after his defeat in the battle of Bastweiler.[41] Medieval love poems and *dits* may rely on philosophical, religious, and other broad moral contexts as well as on political and social contexts that the intricacies of love illustrate literally.[42] In Froissart's *dit* the personifications the Wenceslas figure encounters act in these different contexts. There are parallels to the narrator's crossover in the *Tournoiement*. For example, prior to the battle the Wenceslas figure rejects Avis. Therefore, the personification passes over to his enemy and becomes the decisive factor in the outcome of the battle; Avis[43] thus functions much as Reason does in many allegories, whether in a love context or in other contexts. When Avis returns to Wenceslas, the prisoner is released and resumes a reasonable political and amorous life.

Thomas de Saluste's *Chevalier errant* uses a three-stage *cursus aetatum* script to plot the "errant" knight's trajectory from love in youth, through fortune in midlife, to Connaissance in later life.[44] The realm of love and fortune shows this when the knight's beloved disappears and, later, when the hapless knight's encounters are as unfortunate as Perceval's in quest of the Grail Castle. Much as the *Tournoiement* narrator initiates a religious life, the Chevalier errant approaches Connaissance.[45] Evrart de Conty's *Echecs amoureux* and its moralization, the *Echecs moralisés*, relate a similar choice that appears to go wrong when the lover rejects Diana in favor of Venus and the Garden of Deduit.[46]

In the fifteenth century, too, personifications evoke the ages-of-life topos, whether it be long or short. Among the latter, Villon suggests acquisition of self-knowledge in his Parisian environment.

> Or est vray qu'aprés plains et pleurs
> Et angoisseux gemissemens,
> Aprés tristresses et douleurs,
> Labeurs et griefz cheminemens,
> Travail mes lubres sentemens,
> Esguisez comme une pelocte,
> M'ouvrist plus que tous les commens
> D'Averroÿs sur Arristote. (vv. 89–96)[47]

[It's true that after complaints and tears and anguished groans, after sad experiences and pain, suffering and grievous roaming about, Hard Life revealed to my mutable senses, as sharp as a ball,[48] more than all of Averroes's commentaries on Aristotle.]

Villon acknowledges this knowledge acquired by experience as he ages (*Testament*, vv. 429–36).

In another life patterned by the ages in human life and in a poem Villon may have heard at Blois, Charles d'Orléans too claims that "Folie et Sens me gouvernent tous deux" (Ballade 94, v. 4)[49] [both Folly and Intelligence govern me]. As companions throughout Charles's life, these two personifications find their place in his *cursus aetatum*: they provide *connaissance*, for "Plus ne puis fournir, / Se Sens ne m'aprent / Remede" (Rondel 137, vv. 10–12) [I can't achieve more if Intelligence doesn't teach me a remedy].[50]

"Si la critique moderne est d'accord pour ne plus voir dans la poésie lyrique courtoise une *Erlebnisdichtung* à la manière des romantiques, elle devrait cependant reconnaître que cette poésie, insérée dans des textes narratifs,[51] doit être considérée comme un modèle possible de l'actualisation d'un *Erlebnis*, qu'elle acquiert le statut d'un *Erlebnismuster*" [Although modern scholarship no longer views courtly lyric poetry as relating experience (*Erlebnisdichtung*) like that in Romantic literature, it should acknowledge that medieval poetry, when inserted as a potential model for experience (*Erlebnis*), can become the means to comprehend and explain such experience (*Erlebnismuster*)].[52] In this way they inform narratives and, potentially, the ways medieval audiences patterned their own experience and lives—including, among other devices, what personifications can reveal. For example, "Larges ne set contremander / La larguece qu'il a ou cors / Que la pointe n'en pere fors" (*Eles*, vv. 74–76) [the generous person cannot hide the largess inside him so that the tip doesn't show through]. The same holds for vices: "li relens de la paresce / Qu'il a ou cuer covient qu'il isse" (vv. 102–3) [the stench of idleness in his heart must come out]. When personifications appeared, audiences would heed the personified words' semantic range, mark attributes and surnames attributed to the person or the personification that might reveal its subtleties in diverse contexts, and pay attention to the settings and topoi in which the personifications act. In doing so they would ascribe to their own lives significance and meaning perceived in personifications, their attributes, and their actions. For this to happen, the author must name them appropriately, then personify them so that audiences can observe how they function or literally act, both generally and for particular individuals. In the *moi multiple*, virtues or vices conjoin with those of their own kind or their contraries, displaying their moral or social self.[53] As the *moi multiple* passes through life, it ages naturally. Deployed and set out in this way, personifications can reveal how individuals may understand, evaluate, and construct an inner self; then they let the self appear in descriptions of personifications and in the environment they inhabit, much as Villon projects himself into the Parisian landscape that he then interiorizes as a feature of his own self.

2

"Je vueil ung livre commencier"

The Othernesses of Othon de Grandson's "Je"

JANE H. M. TAYLOR

"Graunson, flour of hem that make in France":[1] Othon de Grandson's reputation has fallen away sadly since Chaucer saluted him as the flower of fourteenth-century French poets. He is better known today, perhaps, for his dashing, debonair death in a duel in 1397; his works were for many years available only in the edition published by Arthur Piaget in 1941, although this has now been superseded by Joan Grenier-Winther's of 2010.[2] This neglect is undeserved: Othon is a more than competent poet, highly regarded by his contemporaries, and author of a considerable body of work which is more complex and demanding than one might imagine. In this essay I intend to concentrate on the longest and most elaborate of his poems, the so-called *Livre Messire Ode*.[3] I want particularly to explore an incidental feature, but one that is central to late-medieval "autobiography":[4] an account of a dream which may at first sight seem merely perfunctory, a secondhand echo of the *Roman de la Rose*, but which, I hope to suggest, is actually an unexpected take on that hackneyed motif, and deployed as part of a battery of means to distance, to "alienate," and so to define, the *je*.[5]

First, however, the *Livre Messire Ode*.[6] This poem, some 2,500 lines long, is what Laurence de Looze has called a pseudo-autobiography:[7] that is, it purports to be the record of Othon's pursuit of a pitiless *maistresse*. Like so many late-medieval pseudo-autobiographies—Machaut's *Voir Dit*, Froissart's *Espinette amoureuse*, Villon's *Testament*—it is also a vehicle, or frame, for ballades, rondeaux, epistles, *complaintes* which he composes for and about his lady,[8] and which he hopes will win her heart. Briefly, the poem opens with Othon proposing to write "ung livre" where "seront tous mes faiz escripz" (1, 4) [a book where all my deeds will be recorded].⁹ The poet is sleepless on his bed, besieged by conflicting abstractions: Desir, Souvenir, Espoir, Reffuz, and Dangier. He composes a ballade—a cri de coeur: he is "raemply de dueil et de plains doloreux" (104) [filled with grief and sad laments]—and then falls into a despairing sleep. As he sleeps, he dreams that he finds himself in a beautiful garden, where he meets a number of characters to whom I shall return in detail. As these meetings progress, Othon composes a suite of verses and fixed-form poems: a letter (*Lectres*) for his lady (452–519), a *Chanson* begging for her mercy (583–603), a *Lay de plour* (702–833), and then a sequence of ballades, the tone of all of which is despairing. As the poem continues, we find, successively and among other things, a debate between Othon's body and his heart, yet more ballades and *complaintes*, expressions of such despair that he is tempted by suicide. There follows a brief awakening, then the poet founders into what seems to be a second dream,¹⁰ this time called a "pasmerie" (1987) [swoon],¹¹ until he wakes up again and pictures himself composing a long sequence of fixed-form verses. The *Livre* finishes with these, and on an ambiguous note since it may well be unfinished.¹² Othon, he says, vows himself henceforth to his lady's service: "Puisqu'Amours, a qui suis obeissant, / Veult que du tout a amer m'appareille, / J'aymeray tant que ce sera merveille / Et serviray" (2494–97) [Since Love, whom I must obey, wishes me to devote myself to love, I shall love to a marvellous degree, and serve].

Of Othon's two dreams, my focus will be primarily on the first (193–1726), which is far more complex and developed than the second,¹³ and is where the intertextual echoes of the *Roman de la Rose* are, of course, inescapable.¹⁴ Inescapable, immediately, in the dream setting: a *locus amoenus*, a garden that is "bel et plaisant et gracieux" (197) [fair and pleasing and elegant], carpeted with flowers, alive with birdsong. The narrating "I" is, however, unmoved by the beauty of the garden: he slips into yet another *complainte* ("A vous me plains de [la] tresgrant ardour / Du mal d'amer," 218–19) [I complain to you about the burning pain of love"] and—this is the first point to which I want to draw attention—scrupulously writes it down in his *livre*, "affin que mieulx m'en sovenist" (216) [so that I can remember it better]. Now, it is worth comparing this exordium with that of the *Roman de la Rose*. It too opens with the act of poetic composition: an "I" in the present is composing a poem that will recount the actions of an "I" in the past who has dreamt an "I" moving through a dream garden. Guillaume de Lorris's *Rose* therefore gives the reader an "I" with a triple identity: as writer, as dreamer, and as dreamt.[15] What is different in Othon's dream, and startlingly so in view of the inescapable intertextual dialogue with the *Rose*, is the fact that Othon makes his dreaming "I" indistinguishable from his writing "I." Gone, it seems, are the multiplied perspectives that, in the *Rose*, derive from changes in selfhood and changes in temporal viewpoint. Othon's dreamer is simply his writing self, pointlessly transposed, one might think, into the conventional late-medieval dream landscape where it will simply continue to write and to "register" his writings in a *livre* identical to that in which he records his waking self.[16] I have just—provocatively—used the word "pointlessly," and it is indeed tempting to dismiss Othon's reduction of "selves" as a diminishment; I return to this question later. But first, I want to turn to another contrast with the *Rose*: the ways in which the poet-lover "peoples" his dream. Briefly, the dream provides for a number of encounters:

1. First, coming toward him through the woods, the poet sees an elegant young man singing his happiness in love: "De mener joye n'est lassez" (403) [he never tires of showing joy], celebrating the fact that he has "ce que desiroie" (335) [what I desired], that he feels "nulle tristesse" (365) [no sadness].
2. Second, he sees "ung jeune joliz escuier" (617) [an elegant young squire], "plain de lermes, le chief enclin" (615) [full of tears, his head bowed], who is lamenting the "douleur mainte" (621) [many a grief] that love is causing him. But just as Othon is about to commiserate with a fellow sufferer, a *damoiselle* emerges from the wood: the squire's lady has had pity and has sent the *damoiselle* to invite him to join her.
3. The poet then dreams (1024–50) that he, Othon, offers his *maistresse* his heart—but, heartlessly, she accepts only "une partie" (1037) [a part].
4. Othon meets a young man, "dedans le vergier embuschié" (1141) [hiding in the orchard] and who also seems "durement . . . courchié" (1142) [very distressed]. They exchange stories: Othon's grief for his unrequited love, the young man's dismay because he has lost, successively, a magnificent "esprevier" (1250) [sparrowhawk], a "faulcon pelcrin" (1280) [a peregrine falcon], and a "tiercellet"

(1299) [tercelet, or male falcon]. Othon is unimpressed, not to say scornful: "suis de vous fort esbahiz / Dont vous prenez telle doulour . . . Pour ung oysel" (1367–70) [I am astonished that you feel such grief . . . for a bird]. The young man comes to recognize Othon's greater claim to sympathy (1484–1519).

5. Finally, Othon is witness to a *complainte*, a debate between his Corps and his Cueur (his Body and his Heart); his Body complains that his Heart is damaging, even killing him; his Heart responds that the Body has only to endure, and to accept its martyrdom in the cause of love (1702–26).

Now, of course, anyone who knows Guillaume de Lorris's *Rose* will be very struck by the fact that all the inhabitants of Othon's dream garden are incontrovertibly human (or, in the case of Heart and Body, human-derived): gone are the allegorical figures and the gods, Nature, Deduit, Amour, Bel Accueil, Malebouche, Venus. Despite the dream motif, in other words, despite the similarities of setting, this is an euhemerized world, quite different from that of the *Rose*. As a corollary, therefore, Othon's *Livre* ceases to be an exemplary discussion where the "I" remains receptive and virtually silent as speakers promulgate and discuss opposing and mutually contradictory views of love and compete for the "I"'s allegiance.[17] Rather, the protagonists of the *Livre* are themselves representative, of fortunate love, despairing love, sentimental regret. What I want to suggest is that they become projections of the poet, multiple selves, rather than forces that act upon him.[18]

No one will be surprised that I should describe the last of these encounters, between the poet-as-spectator, his Corps, and his Cueur, as a dialogue between projected selves. We cannot but be reminded of a better-known equivalent instance, rather more sophisticated, of the same phenomenon, Villon's so-called "Debat du cuer et du corps," which is, say Rychner and Henry, "un dialogue dramatique engageant la destinée et le salut d'un être physiquement et moralement à bout" [a dramatic dialogue involving the fate and the salvation of a being physically and morally exhausted].[19] Othon's dialogue has his Corps—resolutely terre-à-terre—complain bitterly of a grief he/it will not be long able to endure, and his Cueur, with a neat oxymoron, urging him/it to celebrate the pleasure of pain: "Je me merveille / Que tu ne prens a ta paine plaisir, / Quant tu scez bien que c'est la non pareille / D'onneur, de biens quë on pourroit choisir" (1558–61) [I am surprised that you don't take pleasure in your pain, when you realize that it is the greatest honor, the greatest good that you can choose]. In the end, Othon's Corps and his Cueur agree to embrace love's martyrdom: "son plaisir estoit / D'estre vray martir par amours" (1697–98) [his pleasure was to become a true martyr to love]. In a sense, then, the fragmented, alienated self (Heart, Body) is reintegrated—and merged, one might say—with the observing and narrating self, the *je*, whose "wholeness" they invoke, explicitly, in a *chançon* addressed to "their" lady couched in a first person plural that includes the observer: "Mectez *nous* en droit souvenir / Du parfont de vostre pensee. / *Nostre* princesse desiree, / Faictes *nous* devers vous venir" (1711–14) [Remember *us*, in the very depths of your mind, *our* most desired princess, and let *us* come before you].

The *je* here, in other words, fulfills precisely the function of the *je* of the *dit* as Jacqueline Cerquiglini defines it: the clerkly persona, the *je*, plays off different perspectives against each other, in an example of what she calls "méta-écriture," the conjoining of different sorts of discourse to form a unitary projected self.[20]

What will have seemed less obvious, however, is to describe the other encounters of Othon's dream as encounters with projections of his "self"—and yet what we are presented with, I believe, is a series of complex and imaginative self-projections (I am tempted to use the word "avatars"), whose identity with the narrating *je* is suggested by a variety of means: lexical, metaphorical, dialectic. Take, for instance, the poet's first encounter, with the elegant and carefree squire. The latter is not only happy in love, he refuses to contemplate the possibility of unhappiness. He is cheerfully indifferent to, resistant to, the claims of the stock figures of the courtly love repertoire: "Se plaigne qui veult et se clame / De *Dangier*, *Reffuz* et Destresse. / Je ne les loe ne les blasme, / Car point ilz ne me font de presse" (382–85; my italics) [Let anyone who wishes to complain of or protest about *Danger*, *Refusal*, Distress, I neither praise nor blame them, for they do nothing to bother me].

Stock figures, true, but what is significant is the lexical echo here that invites what we might call a *lecture en filigrane*, or reading through a prism. When we first meet the *je* of Othon's *Livre*, we remember, he is, says the poet, consumed with regret. Having chosen a *maistresse* for her youth, her beauty, her *doulceur* (kindness), her *chiere lie* (merry face), he has revealed his love, alas unwisely. The lady is pitiless:

Maiz Reffuz, le tresenvieulx,
Est contre moy de sa puissance.
. . . .
Emprés elle huche Dangier,
Et Reffuz est d'autre cousté.
En ce point suis je gouverné. (22–30)

[But Refusal, full of envy, brings all his forces against me. . . . And then she [my lady] enlists Danger to one side, Refusal to the other: that is how I am brought under control.]

The cheerful young squire, then, is the obverse of, the counterpoint to, Othon's *je*: where the latter is persecuted, driven to near despair, by Dangier and Reffuz, the young lover discounts those very entities, dismisses them with a cheerful carelessness. Diegetically speaking, that is to say, the elegant young man's is an "alien" voice penetrating the central communicative fiction of Othon's *livre*; his throwaway presence introduces an ironic insouciance which is an alternative to Othon's unremitting—perhaps even, we might think, chosen—*destresse*.

But the elegant young man is not the only alternative, "alien" self staged in Othon's *livre*, and with whom Othon and his *je* invite a cross-reading. Take, this time, the second of the dream episodes, in the course of which, we remember, the despairing squire is revived when his *dame* sends a *damoiselle* to summon him: "Ma dame m'envoye / Vous dire que soyez en joye. / Or sus, avecques moy venez / Et plus ne vous desconfortez" (638–41) [My lady sends me to you to say that you should be happy. Now get up and come with me, and do not despair any longer]. Rather later in the *Livre*, we find what is in fact a replica of this scene, when a grieving Othon is sent a messenger not by his lady but by Douleur—and the messenger's words pick up the same lexical cross-referencing, and indeed play with phonetic cross-referencing (m'envoye/joye/moy), which we have already seen with the elegant young squire:

Ung messagier qui vint vers moy,
Disant: "Douleur m'envoye a toy
Et te mande qu'il vient logier
Dedans ton cueur sans atargier
Et avec luy Reffuz sera,
Ne Dangier pas ne lessera" (917–22)

[A messenger came toward me, saying, "Grief has sent me to you to say that he is about to come and take up residence in your heart; with him will be Refusal, and Danger will follow close behind."]

By an interesting chiasmatic effect, Othon builds a contrasting potential self: a young man consumed as he, Othon, is by tearful love, but comforted in the avatar's case by a "demoiselle . . . jolie et belle" (636–37) [a damsel . . . gay and fair], whereas Othon is driven to renewed despair by a heartless messenger sent by Douleur to bring him Reffuz and Dangier.

I turn now to the fourth encounter, with the young man who has lost his *esprevier*.[21] What is interesting here is the ironic, even faintly comic, counterpoint that Othon creates between the young man's "courtship" of his hawk and Othon's own pursuit of his *dame*.[22] The young man is consumed by "parfait desir" (1233) [perfect desire] for the beautiful creature. His only wish is to please it: "Et ne faisoie qu'estudier / Comment peusse cest esprevier / Acoincter" (1225–27) [I did nothing but consider how I might get close to the hawk]; "je miz tout mon pensement / A lui, sans penser autre rien, / Pour l'amour de son beau maintien" (1234–36) [I concentrated entirely on the bird, thinking of nothing else, so much did I love its fair appearance]. Never, says the young man, had there been "oysel / Si gent, si plaisant, ne si bel" (1257–58) [a bird so elegant, so attractive, so beautiful], and now that the bird is lost, he longs only for death: "pour ce rien je ne vouldroie, / Fors que la mort" (1330–31) [for that reason I would wish for nothing except death]. The manifest absurdity of this hyperbolic devotion is ironically reminiscent of the *je*'s own hyperbole: his lady too has reduced him to near death: "a la belle plaist moy faire finir" (994) [it pleases the lady to have me die]. He is reduced, like the absurd young man with the hawk, to despair and accidie: "Je suis pensifz et mellencolieux, / De la servir je suis tresenvieux, / Et si crains fort prés d'elle remanoir" (1017–19) [I remain sad and melancholy; I have no wish other than to serve her, but I am very afraid of spending time in her company]. The young man mourning his *esprevier* is a fantasy "other," an alien entity—but also a projected self, a metaphoric equivalent of the narrating *je* of Othon's *Livre*. The reader familiar with the discourses of the lyric may well have taken the hyperboles of the *je* for granted, since they are those also of the medieval courtly love-lyric; cross-reading them against the hyperboles of the young man who has lost his *esprevier* makes them, however, inescapably unstable:

it makes the speaking *je* of the *Livre* profoundly unreliable and faintly comic.

What, then, is the virtue of these fragmentations of the lover-self? Why the elaborate dream mise-en-scène, the proliferation of selves? On one level, as I have suggested, Othon is tributary to the *Roman de la Rose*, in the wake of which "autobiographical" *dits* framed by dream-visions proliferate: the *cadre* of the poem, the beautiful garden, and the multiple encounters are strongly reminiscent of what was, in the later Middle Ages, as Pierre-Yves Badel has shown, a standard reference point.[23] Badel has also drawn attention, however, to a particular aspect of the dream-vision that will be useful for our purposes: what he calls "les frontières du songe" [the frontiers of the dream], the introductory and concluding sections of dream-vision poetry which, he suggests, are valuable in explaining the role that the notion of "dream" is to play in the poem.[24] In Badel's terms, the prologue to Othon's dream is what he calls an introductory motif—that is, one where the dream "rattache le songe aux pensées diurnes du rêveur" [links the dream to the waking thoughts of the dreamer].[25] The writing *je* is, he says, keeping a promise to his *dame*: a promise to write her a *livre*: "Je vueil ung livre commencier / Et a ma dame l'envoyer, / Ainsi que je lui ay promis / Ou seront tous mes faiz escripz" (1–4) [I want to begin a book in which I shall write all my deeds, and send it to my lady as I have promised her].

Now, there is of course no reason to take this seriously—the "autobiography" here may or may not have any connection to reality—but it is the case that Othon's prologue is unusually developed.[26] Amours, he says, has instructed him to choose a *maistresse*;[27] alas, when he tells her of his love, he is rejected. That said, he is determined to remain true to her, hoping that in time "sa voulenté retournera" (46) [she will change her mind]. Awaiting that happy moment, however, is reducing him to suicidal despair: "ma mort vueil et pour mort me tien" (62) [I long for death, and consider myself dead]. He flings himself on his bed where, unable to sleep, he composes a ballade (103–44) on the refrain "J'ay le rebours de ce que je desire" [I have the opposite of what I long for] and inscribes it in his *livre*. He addresses an ardent prayer to Amours and to his lady: he will be her *serf* (185) [servant]. At this point, already in a state of *resverie* (76) [daydreaming], he falls asleep and enters the dream state in which he will continue to compose and, crucially, to write: the *Livre* consists largely of fixed-form lyrics, and since the vision appears to be unfinished, it is difficult to know how Othon might have intended it to conclude.[28] The prologue, however, performs two maneuvers that suggest, interestingly, how the dream is to be understood. First, *resverie* suggests that the state of the dreamer is somewhat ambiguous:[29] Corbellari has pointed to Othon's "rôle quelque peu démystificateur"[30] [somewhat puzzle-solving role] via which he makes the frontiers between dream and "reality" surprisingly porous. Take, for instance, the letter that, the narrating *je* tells us, he composes within the dream to send, beyond the dream, to his lady: "Lors pensay que jë escriproye / Et mes lectres lui envoyroie" (450–51) [Then I decided to write to her, and to send her my letter]. Having written it, signed and sealed it, he sends it by "Ung mien tresloyal serviteur / Que j'aymoie de tout mon cueur, / Qui autrefoiz avoit esté / Vers celle ou est ma voulenté" (526–29) [A very loyal servant of mine, of whom I was very fond, and whom I had on other occasions sent to the lady to whom I am devoted]. The messenger, and the letter, can move effortlessly in and out of the dream state that Othon has made the frame for his *Livre*, and in which, in principle, he is still immured, since there has been no awakening.

The major virtue of the interpenetration of dream and reality stems from the way in which it allows entirely human, rather than allegorical, characters to circulate—and from the way therefore in which Othon invites his readers into a dialectical cross-reading with the *Roman de la Rose*. I have argued elsewhere for the importance of this reading process in the later Middle Ages, and have suggested that it involves not some mechanical redeployment of commonplace but rather a dynamic recuperation and resolution of opposing texts.[31] In the present instance, an intertextual reading of this sort suggests a refusal of allegory, and this creates an interesting, and revelatory, paradox. Allegory, it is now conventional to say, creates what Gay Clifford calls "strangeness and intensity . . . to communicate certain generalized formulations about the nature of human experience and the organization of the world";[32] it is endowed, to use medieval terminology, with a *senefiance* (meaning) that derives precisely from its strangeness, from the creating, as it were, of alien selves. One might suppose, therefore, that to humanize dream encounters would render them banal, and meaningless. But that is to reckon without the dialogue with the *Roman de la Rose*. Precisely because the *Rose* is ubiquitous, precisely because Othon has refused to allegorize the "experiences" that he recounts, his other "selves" are rendered strange, or alien. Guillaume de Lorris had, says David Hult, dissected "his being into several *personae*"[33]—that is, different selves all subsumed under the pronoun *je*—and had further fragmented his self, and the self of the *Rose*, into a string of their respective qualities. Othon's procedures are very different, and because of their difference from the ubiquitous personifications of the *Rose*, his fragmentation of his self creates a series of potential and "other," or alien, selves. The cheerful young squire, for instance, is Othon's self had he disregarded (sensibly, perhaps?) Reffuz and Dangier; the disconsolate lover saved from despair by a messenger is Othon's self had he been rescued by a similarly generous impulse on the part of his inflexible lady. Othon is able to see the absurdity of the squire being inconsolable at the loss of a mere bird; is that not Othon's self, had he been able to stand back and recognize the absurdity of his own unmitigated, unrelieved despair?

What is instituted via these carefully insistent alien selves is, I suggest, a process whereby the informed reader recognizes the ways in which the "I" and his dreamed alternative selves intersect with, and relativize, each other. Othon's exploration of the self, when read dialectically, is more than a mechanical redeployment of commonplace; rather it is a dynamic move that allows the poet to dramatize an ironic distance. Let me turn now to the third of the five "encounters" I mentioned above, and which I have so far left to one side. Othon dreams, as I said, that he has offered his heart to "celle / Qui est du monde la plus belle" (1026–27) [her who is the fairest in the world]; the lady's response uses that by-now familiar lexicon that invites cross-reading, but with an oxymoron that might perhaps have suggested a glimmer of hope: "Lors me faisoit ung doulx dangier / Et ung si gracieux reffuz / [Qu'estoye] du tout esperduz"[34] (1033–34) [Then she made me so gentle a rebuttal and so gracious a refusal that I was completely nonplussed]. She will not, she says, accept his heart, although "une partie / De vostre cueur bien garderay, / Et l'autre si vous renderay" (1037–39) [I will keep a part of your heart, and return the remainder to you].

Othon refuses to take back any part of his heart and is left devastated by her refusal. The narrative octosyllables shade, unprecedentedly, into an urgent present tense—"Helas! quel est son pensement? / Est il piteux de mon martire? / Je ne sçay que penser ne dire" (1051–53) [Alas! What are her thoughts? Are they sympathetic to my martyrdom? I do not know what to think or to say]—and then into an absurd endeavor. Othon (the dreamer? the dreamt?) issues a challenge in a prose missive, *Lectres closes* (1090–1122), to the *sire de Cornoiaille*: they are to fight a duel in which Othon, now deprived of his heart and consequently of "ma vertu et ma force" (P1109) [my courage and my strength], will be easily defeated, and killed; in the unlikely event that, by his lady's grace, Othon prevails, his vanquished opponent is simply to forfeit "ung dyament pour envoyer a celle qui desconfit vous auroit" (P1119–20) [a diamond to send to her who will have undone you]. What this palpably absurd little interlude provides is, as it were, a dis-integrated self; the lady refuses his heart and returns it to his own keeping, but this, paradoxically, shows that she wishes his death: "Or est ainsi qu'il ne luy plaist mon cueur tenir pour serviteur. Et a ce puis apparcevoir qu'elle veult abreger ma mort" (P1100–1102) [Now I can see that she does not wish to keep my heart for her servant, and from that I can guess that she wants to hasten my death]. Othon pictures himself as fragmented and unlocatable: his heart can survive only if it is alienated, detached from his self, entrusted to the safekeeping of his lady. This is, in other words, a dramatic representation of a complex and paradoxical self; Othon's self is diverse, his heart cast aside, and fatally alienated since it is no longer his, yet it has been refused refuge by his lady. The heart, here, is not the personified Cueur of the debate between heart and body in the fifth and final encounter of Othon's dream. Rather, it is a mere object, an objective correlative, as it were, of Othon's better self, the self that inspires and energizes. As a mere object, the heart is already, in a sense, an alien object; vested in the alien object, however, is Othon's despair.

I do not pretend that Othon makes his fragmented selves entirely coherent, or fully realized: on the contrary, he often fails to exploit all the potential of his play with personae. But what is interesting, in the *Livre Messire Ode*, is his attempt to experience his self as "othered." What the poet provides—and what is most visible when the *Livre* is read in dialogue with the *Rose*—is an inventory of "other," alien selves which are nevertheless sufficiently realized to redefine the speaking, narrative self. The *dit*, of course, is conventionally always a vehicle for self-scrutiny. Othon's writing self, here, uses multiple, competing (alien) selves to perform an act of self-scrutiny that, while sometimes absurd, permits a new complexity. Othon visibly draws inspiration from Guillaume de Machaut with his *Voir Dit*, and from Froissart with, for instance, his *Prison amoureuse*. Like them, he uses verse and prose, lyric set pieces and showcase prosodies;[35] like them he plays with dream, fiction, and reality.[36] This indeterminacy, Othon's multiplication of alien selves, is, he recognizes, a way to encompass his single, waking self: when, after the end of this first dream and following the debate between Cueur and Corps, he wakes up completely, it is as a first-person-plural *nous* which embraces the *je*, the Cueur and the Corps: "Quant nostre debat fut finé / Et en ce livre enregistré" (1727–28) [When our debate had ended and been noted down in this book]. But that self is, now and following the despair of the dream, annihilated: "Elle m'a tout. Je n'ay rien mien. / Et si ne me veult tenir sien" (1865–66) [She has taken all of me, I have nothing of mine left, and yet she does not want to make me hers]. In one sense, then, the alien selves that the poet has imagined are reunited, reintegrated, into a single *I,* into something, perhaps, equivalent to the royal "we."

It has, I think, been only too easy to dismiss Othon de Grandson as a facile imitator of the *Roman de la Rose* and of Guillaume de Machaut: just another dreamer with a portfolio of lyrics to set in a narrative frame. But a closer reading of his *Livre* should invite us to a reappraisal of his ambivalences. Like so many late-medieval writers, and especially in the wake of the *Rose,* Othon pays due lip-service to the traditional forms and the traditional discourses—but also like so many late-medieval writers, he is not content simply to parrot the *Rose.* Rather, he engages in a dialogue with the paradigms set by Guillaume de Lorris and Jean de Meun to produce an exploration of self via the invention of alternative, and othered, selves: an exploration in which those diverse, alien selves represent, perhaps, a recognition of the variousness of the self.[37]

3

Huon de Bordeaux

The Cultural Dream as Palimpsest

WILLIAM BURGWINKLE

This essay addresses the fragile bases upon which medieval stories about identity were sometimes constructed and those identities' subsequent miscomprehension. The case in point is the early thirteenth-century hybrid text *Huon de Bordeaux*, a tale of travel to the Middle East and of rightful feudal vengeance.[1] Its conflation of the personal and the collective, and of one identity with another, involves a feudal tale of revenge and another of cultural conquest, in which a Western, Christian hero is both vanquisher and vanquished, knightly and benighted, unwitting double to his foe. A reading of *Huon* would suggest that although literary texts inevitably bear witness to their historical times—this is, after all, a tale of travel to the Middle East, an encounter with local religious groups and ethnicities, and a testimony to Christian ingenuity—that testimony is often enigmatic, highly reflective, and clearly biased in favor of a particular version of truth. *Huon de Bordeaux*, for example, can be read in multiple ways: as an allegorical interpretation of the crusading imperative that developed under the French king (Saint) Louis IX, as a chanson de geste about rebel barons, and as an adventure about the exotic East. Moreover, Huon's absorption of his otherworldly host and that host's culture, plus his host's concurrent absorption of him, make for a psychologically compelling tale. This is cross-cultural interaction that poses serious questions about how cultures take on others' customs, convince themselves that they are right in doing so, and become "other" themselves as they begin to believe in their own recuperative fictions.

Huon de Bordeaux was composed around 1225, at the beginning of the reign of Louis IX (1214–1270), just as the teenaged king was formulating his dream of recapturing Jerusalem, some forty years after its loss. Dreams of conquest, or rather reconquest, are never far from the surface of *Huon de Bordeaux*, yet they are never mentioned explicitly. While most epics of the period purveyed fantasy reconstructions of historical material involving genealogical, religious, and regional conflicts, *Huon de Bordeaux* favors a mixed or hybrid approach to both its material and its form. It falls vaguely into the category of "rebel barons" epic, those texts in which the ideal figures of Christian kingship, Charlemagne and his sons, are shown as slow-witted, shortsighted, and tyrannical—always looking to solve a problem with a quick fix. Most important, however, in distinguishing *Huon de Bordeaux* from its chanson de geste brothers is its inclusion of that typical romance feature, the *merveilleux*, or supernatural, as its backdrop. The *merveilleux* is given body most strikingly in the person of Auberon, the most famous sprite of medieval and modern literature, the King of Shadows and Fairies, best known today from William Shakespeare's play *A Midsummer Night's Dream*, where he appears as Oberon, King of the Fairies. Though the origins of this figure go back to Merovingian mythology, and a similar figure appears as well in the early thirteenth-century *Nibelungenlied* as Alberich the sorcerer, the author of *Huon de Bordeaux* ignores this literary genealogy and portrays Auberon as a vaguely unhappy and certainly misunderstood outcast, jealously guarding his forest outside Jerusalem, waiting for something, or someone, to save him.

Huon thus calls into question geographical, cultural, philosophical, and religious difference and blurs distinctions between truth and fiction, East and West, Christianity and Islam, the human and the divine. Again and again we are asked to believe that this particular story of travel and adventure is capable of mediating these differences by establishing *itself* as a middle ground, a discourse that brings together cultural and religious extremes and supplements the radical deficiencies of Christian empire and kingship, even when, as we shall see, this often amounts to nothing more than pseudo-distinctions between self and other.[2]

Before any further discussion, a summary of the plot is required:

The story opens in the ninth century. Huon is the son of Seguin, the deceased Duke of Bordeaux, and he and his brother have been accused by an ambitious lord at Charlemagne's court, Amaury, of having refused to pay homage to their emperor, Charlemagne. The two young brothers (referred to as "effans," children, throughout the text) travel to Paris with the intention of clearing their names but are intercepted on the way by a hostile militia as they pass through a forest outside Paris. Charlemagne's corrupt son and heir, Charlot, has been provoked by the disloyal Amaury to attack the Bordeaux brothers, convinced that they have come to disrupt his authority. A battle ensues, during which Huon's brother, Gérard, is severely wounded. Huon, enraged by this injustice, kills the disguised Charlot in retribution.

The boys finally reach the imperial court, full of tales of their ambush, and are welcomed, but then Amaury arrives to announce that Huon has murdered Charlemagne's only son, and the emperor gives vent to his grief and rage. First, he orders that Huon be tied to horses and dragged through the streets until dead. When Huon protests that he was attacked illegally, that he never knew who was leading the attackers, and that he acted in self-defense, the most senior and respected of the knights, Naymes, threatens Charlemagne with the desertion of his *own* knights and the ruination of the emperor's reputation if he does not follow legal custom. A single combat is arranged between Amaury and Huon in which Huon is victorious; yet Charlemagne still banishes him, giving him the following conditions for reentry into Christian lands: he must (a) travel to Babylon and kill the first man he meets at the emir's table, (b) kiss the emir's daughter three times in front of the assembled nobility, (c) ask for tribute from the emir in the name of Charlemagne, and then (d) request the emir's white mustache and his four molars and take them by force if the request is denied. Needless to say, he will not be allowed home without the proof.

Huon is up for the challenge. He goes first to the pope for the remission of his sins, then travels to Brindisi, where he meets up with Garin de Saint-Omer, a merchant friend of his deceased father, who transports him to Saint Jean d'Acre. He prays at the Sepulchre in Jerusalem, then moves on to the land of Femmenie, the Coumans, and La Foy before arriving at a forest controlled by the fairy Auberon, who can unleash the power of nature against those who do not play his game.

Huon is at first warned not to acknowledge Auberon or even to speak to him. If he should do so, he is told, the fairy will gain full control of him and he will never again be free. Huon tries to follow this advice, but as Auberon gets ever more angry at being ignored, Huon gives in, seduced by Auberon's beauty and profession of Christian faith. Auberon then tests Huon: only the purest of heart can drink from a certain magic wine cup that the fairy carries with him. When Huon drinks his fill with no problem, Auberon embraces him and tells him the story of his life. Son of Julius Caesar and Morgan la Fée, he was cursed with his tiny size (he stands just three feet tall) by a jealous fairy at his birth; in compensation for that evil curse, the other fairies present offered him magical powers. Auberon now becomes Huon's closest ally, helping him cross the Red Sea, gaining him entry into the emir's palace, and ensuring his successful completion of Charlemagne's tasks. Interestingly, it is only the sexual side of conquest that proves a stumbling block. Auberon has forbidden Huon any sexual relations before marriage, but when Huon escapes with the daughter of the emir, who is now desperately in love with him, he succumbs to his sexual desire on an isolated island. Auberon immediately withdraws his support in anger, and the couple are attacked by pirates. Huon is left naked and without provisions, while his Saracen love is kidnapped.

There ensues a war between Muslim forces—those of the emir Galafre and his rival Yvorin. With Auberon's help, Huon eventually saves the day and is reunited with his love, who converts to Christianity in Rome. He then returns to Bordeaux and is going to take control when he is betrayed by Gérard, the very brother whose life he once saved. Huon is about to be put to death by Charlemagne for having failed his tasks (Gérard has stolen his proof of completion) when Auberon, who has now somehow forgiven Huon's earlier youthful hubris, saves him for the last time. In a final appearance, the fairy subdues the anger of Charlemagne and ensures justice through a humiliating show of magical power, proving once and for all the superiority of his powers over those of the emperor.

As is evident from this summary, there are so many odd and interesting facets to the story that I will have to limit myself to a discussion of those that relate most directly to the fantasy narrative that dominates.[3] The author moves quite swiftly to these episodes once we leave Paris, suggesting that this is where his real interests lie, and the text takes on a distinctly dreamlike tone: nothing, including genre, is as expected. First the men travel through the infertile lands of Femmenie, a land in which the sun does not shine and women are barren.[4] They then pass through the land of the Coumans, in which they meet hairy savages with burning red eyes who have no shelter, no clothing, and ears the size of elephants.[5] From there they move to the Land of Faith, where nature is backwards, men can take provisions at will, and faith and loyalty reign supreme.[6] At this point they meet a hermit, Gériaume, who has been living in the woods for thirty years after having completed a penitential pilgrimage to the Sepulchre in Jerusalem (also referred to as Outremer), and it is he who gives the warning about Auberon's forest as they approach it.[7] This is an enchanted space, he warns Huon, ruled by the irascible but incredibly beautiful fairy himself. From this moment on, we must read doubly: the forest is evil *and* it is Huon's salvation; it is an enchanted space but also the only Christian space that Huon encounters in the Middle East.

Huon's entry into this forest is also his entry into fantasy, into a space that acts as the filter through which all subsequent experience will be read. Once Huon has entered this space, its spell can never be cast off: it sets the parameters for how to visualize, how to desire, how to establish right from wrong. Imagine, if you will, *The Wizard of Oz*, for a contemporary parallel. Young Dorothy must also travel through an enchanted forest on her way to the Land of Oz to meet the Wizard and find the solution to her problems; and once she has accomplished this, nothing will ever again look the same. Once Huon has passed through Auberon's Christian woods, he has become subject to Auberon's will. Auberon will set for him rules of behavior, sexual ethics, and a code of morality. Only near the end of the text is it revealed that after having completed all of Charlemagne's tasks and returned to his rightful seat of power in Bordeaux, Huon will rule for only three years in Bordeaux before being called back to the forest to take up Auberon's position. A period so brief precludes any possibility of family life or child rearing, any sense of permanency or stability. The entire story of quest and retribution, instigated by royal treachery, is at this point turned on its head. Everything that we thought we understood before encountering Auberon's forest becomes something else. What first looked like a tale of personal loss (initiated by the death of his father) and political deception (Charlemagne's treachery) suddenly appears a manipulative pretext to get Huon into the forest as quickly as possible and into the clutches of Auberon.

The enchanted forest thus mediates between the familiar and the unfamiliar, and "betweenness" becomes our mode of reading: Huon both conquers the forest and is conquered by it; he avenges Charlemagne's treachery only to further the emperor's mission of conquest; he is "saved" by Auberon in order to die and essentially take his place, become him, merge identities. At the end of the story Auberon reveals to Huon exactly what his fate will be: "D'uy en .iij. ans a Monmur en vanrez, / Si averez toute ma roialteit, / Et avuec ceu avrez ma digniteit: / Coronne d'or en vous chief porterez" (vv. 10743–46) [Three years from now you will come to Monmur and you will have all of my kingdom and with it my rank and privileges: a golden crown you will wear on your head].

As unexpected as this speech is when it comes, it should not surprise us. Fairies in medieval literature often prefigure death or a passage into the other world. In Marie de France's *Lais*, for example, the fairy lover of Lanval comes to his rescue after the queen's accusation of sodomy only to whisk him away, never to be seen again, at the conclusion of the tale. Auberon seems to come from this same genetic stock: his beneficent offer to Huon is not really a gift at all, it is a command. Huon must go to Monmur, Auberon's abode, to take up his place, thus freeing Auberon himself to travel to Paradise—so far, so good—but where is this paradisiacal Monmur but in the Middle East, the land of dreamed conquest and sovereignty. Furthermore, Monmur is presented as a metonymy of "betweenness" itself, a space that mediates between the world of the living and the world of the dead. Auberon can pass from one world into the next, as we learn at the end of the text, but what of Huon? Will he ever be able to do the same? In traveling to Monmur to take up Auberon's place, he will presumably be lost to the living, dead for all intents and purposes, accessible only to the fairy. Auberon has effectively seduced and captured his beloved and, like his fairy homologue in *Lanval*, he will spirit him away forever.

In other words, all of Gériaume's warnings about Auberon were completely accurate. Remember that as they leave Jerusalem and approach the forest for the first time, Gériaume cautions that any congress with the fairy will lead to disaster:

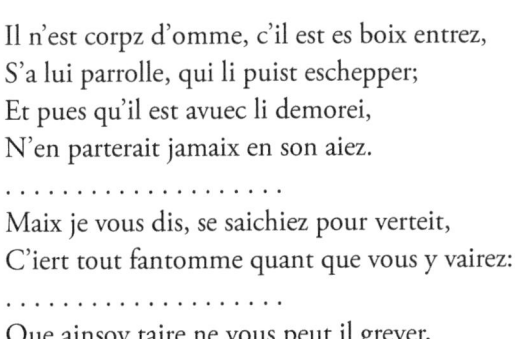

Il n'est corpz d'omme, c'il est es boix entrez,
S'a lui parrolle, qui li puist eschepper;
Et pues qu'il est avuec li demorei,
N'en parterait jamaix en son aiez.
. . . .
Maix je vous dis, se saichiez pour verteit,
C'iert tout fantomme quant que vous y vairez:
. . . .
Que ainsoy taire ne vous peut il grever,
Et a responder trestout perduit avez. (vv. 3156–59, 3178–79, 3184–85)

[There is no body of man who, if he has entered that wood, if he has spoken with him, can ever escape him. Once he has lived with him, he will never be able to leave him in his lifetime. . . . But let me tell you, and in all truth, that everything you see is a phantasm. . . . So keep silent, and he cannot do you any harm, but in responding you will have lost all.]

Gériaume may sound alarmist, but he is right. Don't engage with the other; dialogue will only result in the colonization of your being; your authority will be compromised and your subjection complete.

In their first encounter, Auberon is dressed in a brilliantly striped tunic, carrying a magic bow and arrow that can never miss its mark. Around his neck he wears an ivory horn, a gift from the fairies that can cure all ills. Another such horn assuages hunger and thirst, and yet another has the attractive quality that anyone who hears it cannot help but sing along. These are all illusions, as Gériaume never tires of saying: Auberon cannot really hurt you unless you consent.[8] Sure enough, Huon's men are swept up by a raging river and storm when they refuse to engage with Auberon, yet, having been forewarned, they survive. Despite all this proof, however, Huon begins to change his mind when he hears that Auberon is fully human and a Christian to boot: "Je sus ung hons comme ung aultre charnez, / Si croy en Dieu qui en croix fuit penez" (vv. 3338–39) [I am a man like any other born of flesh and I believe in God who was hung on the cross].

Gériaume does his best to dissuade him. He claims that Auberon represents the pre-Christian era, a fusion of the proto-Christian with the proto-Muslim: in other words, a stand-in for the Holy Land itself—pagan, then Christian, then fallen again to non-Christian, or "fairy," forces.[9] Auberon is, in Gériaume's terms, just a vestige of a bygone era that must now be overcome. But Huon relents, convinced by the fairy's obsessive references to "he-who-was-hung-on-the-cross" and his foreknowledge of every aspect of Huon's life and quest (vv. 3432–78). This Christianization of the fairy world is one of the most original traits of the text, and it seems to reflect directly upon the Crusading ventures of the previous century: all of these lands are "Christian" because they were once Christian. What is most frightening, alien, and strange to the Christian viewer—what seems most otherworldly and inexplicably fairylike—is then simply claimed as always already Christian, having once been Christianized, then lost. Strangeness and unfamiliarity are merely a veneer that can be rubbed away; like the initial aggressivity of Auberon, it might seem dangerous but is not. Furthermore, though Huon is in the Middle East to get his token mustache, molars, and murder, he is never really very far from home. Again, like in the dream of Dorothy in the *Wizard of Oz*, he keeps meeting people from his past in the most unlikely places—his uncle in Tormont, his cousins in Brindisi and Dunostre, his father's friends and vassal in Palestine. The exotic is apparently more easily domesticated than expected.

Kibler and Suard, the editors of the most recently published edition of *Huon de Bordeaux*, claim that Auberon's initially aggressive reaction to Huon's silence can be explained away as passionate friendship rebuffed and turned to hate.[10] Not speaking to Auberon was what kept the fairy in his place and made him incapable of meddling. In other words, as in many fairy tales, we learn that the subject *had to consent* to be tormented, *had to give himself over to* possession by the other. Huon learns in the enchanted forest episode that commerce with the alluring and powerful other—the fairy Auberon—is precisely what will get him what he needs: passage across the Red Sea and access to the emir's lands. Here the fairy tale joins forces with history. The erotic and alluring, when grafted onto the hostile and unfamiliar, offers one explanation for Western Christendom's enduring and infinitely deferred desire to effect cultural and religious reintegration of East and West, Muslim and Christian. And that erotic and alluring element surfaces in two key encounters: one with Auberon and the other with Esclarmonde, the daughter of the emir, who gives up family, heritage, and religion for him.

After his first brush with the fairy, Huon finds himself more and more attracted by Auberon's ways, and he admits to Gériaume:

Or somme nous del nain asseürez;
Maix je vous di en fine loialteit
Qu'ains ne vy homme de si grande biaulteit.
Dieu, comme est biaulz, qui bien l'ait regardér!
Moult bel me samble, saichiez de veriteit,
Comme il sceit bien de Dammedieu parler. (vv. 3409–14)

[Now we are safe from the dwarf, but I tell you in all truth that I have never seen a man of such great beauty. God, how beautiful he is, if you really look at him! It also seems to me quite beautiful, make no mistake about it, that he knows how to speak of God so well.]

Shortly thereafter, Auberon begins his tracking of Huon, a classic stalking motif:

> —Sire, dit Hue, dite que vous voullez.
> Moult me merveille pour quoy me porsievés."
> Dist Auberon: "Hue, vous le savrés:
> Je vous aym tant pour vous grant loialteit
> Que plux vous ayme q'omme de mere nez." (vv.3485–89)

> ["My lord," said Huon, "tell me what you want. I am perplexed as to why you should be following me." Auberon answered: "Huon, you will understand shortly: for your great loyalty I love you more than any man of woman born."]

Auberon is immediately grateful to Huon for recognizing him in his otherness. As a result, he expresses his love, and a charm offensive follows: yes, he admits, he is beautiful;[11] yes, he can read the minds and hearts of men; can travel instantly to anywhere he wants to go; can conjure palaces and luxury; has the adoration of all animals and knows the secrets of paradise; will never grow old until he wills it and has a seat already reserved in heaven![12] Huon and his men are invited after this confession into a palace that has materialized before them, where they are wined and dined to satiation. Auberon sits on Huon's right during this banquet, watching him intently, before unveiling his magic wineskin and revealing that it can produce an endless supply of wine, enough to satisfy all mankind, but that only a man of absolute loyalty can drink of it.[13] When Huon takes the cup and drinks, showing no sign of hesitation, Auberon gives it to him, then explains the moral provisions. There is no mistaking it: this is a gift with strings attached:

> Que se tu garde aussi ta loialteit,
> Et que tu vuelle per mon consoille ovrer,
> Je t'aiderai*t* loialment san faulcer;
> Maix jai si tost mensonge ne direz.
> Que tu ne perrde dou hanep la bonteit
> Et de mon corpz trestoute l'amisteit. (vv. 3700–9)

> [If you remain loyal and continue to follow my advice, I will help you loyally without fail. But the moment you tell a lie, you will lose the good graces of the cup and all signs of friendship from my body.]

Auberon then produces his ivory horn, worth more than the city of Paris itself, and hands it over to Huon with a similar list of restrictions.[14] When Huon has passed the tests and taken control of these magic objects, he has already ensured his success, but he is also henceforth a marked and compromised man.

Huon de Bordeaux thus comments tellingly on thirteenth-century anxieties about religious identity, sexual identity, linguistic and ethnic identity, and the rights that accompany them all. How can one be both Christian and enchanted? How can a Christian man accept the love of another man who has chosen him from many and who proclaims that his love goes far beyond the love of any woman? What is the status of Christians who come from Outremer but have no French-speaking ancestry left in the homeland? Could Auberon be read as a Christian expatriate, one of the crusaders who stayed behind to exploit the land in which he found himself? Or does Auberon instead represent the converted pagan, Islam domesticated, marked physically for his moral and confessional failings? Why does Auberon insist that Huon take his place, merge with him, become in turn the enchanted tyrant? All of these questions lead me to assert that *Huon* should be read as a classic tale of "betweenness" or mediation that has undeniable historical credentials imbedded in its fictional shell.

Roger Kennedy, in a book on history and psychoanalysis, titled one of his chapters "Dreaming History."[15] Dreaming history is said to be an almost inevitable and desirable response to the trauma of historical events. A text that dreams history may not entail compiling, sifting, classifying, verifying, and judging events—those markers of the true historical method—but instead it creates fantasy from trauma and turns dry allegory into art. *Huon* accomplishes all of this through the intertwining strands of its narratives. It is both a disguised travelogue of the pilgrimage route from Paris to the Holy Land and a fantasy narrative recalling the mythological and exotic East; it is a dream narrative about Carolingian revenge and restitution, but it reasserts justice by letting male bonds override heroic acts as the key to individual success and happiness; and, finally, it is an occluded tale of conquest and colonialism that ends in a fantasy restitution of Islamic lands to Christian masters. Those lands, however, turn out to be shadow lands, on the border of the real and the fantastic, lands that can only be attained at the price of death and invisibility to the world.[16] No Christian actually gains any long-term possession of lands in the Middle East in *Huon de Bordeaux*,[17] and the only Christian land alluded to in

Outremer is Auberon's land of *féerie*, the fantastical realm of Monmur. As Anne Berthelot points out, this fantastically wealthy place has much in common with those of the legendary Prester John, serving to familiarize and "inoculate" the lands of Islam for Western Christian readers.[18]

Muslims who will not convert might be massacred after each of the major battles in *Huon*, but there are no political reversals as a consequence, no religious inroads established that would challenge Islam in anything but a very localized way.[19] The tale turns instead on the specter of Western and Christian insufficiency. Despite the robotic repetition of New Testament dogma about the crucifixion, especially from the mouth of Auberon, the West is only ever victorious in a puny and unheroic way.[20] Christian masculinity is established through male bonding and competition rather than through spiritual perfection; heroes are chosen through their looks and through homosocial seduction rather than through dedication to higher ideals; and Christian kingship, in the person of Charlemagne, is seen as weakened beyond redemption.[21]

Huon de Bordeaux is therefore best described as a vaguely dangerous, if charming, text of compensatory dreaming and wish fulfillment. The damages and expenses of world travel and conquest are minimized by reference to endless Islamic wealth, on the one hand, and a self-perpetuating Christian cornucopia, in the form of Auberon's magic golden cup, on the other. This cup, which simultaneously associates Islam with *féerie* and claims that magic as Christian, is another typical example of doublespeak, a not so innocent attempt to mediate between two extreme positions.[22] *Huon de Bordeaux* gives us just enough information to justify Western Christian presence in the Middle East, then softens this ideological message by yoking it to a fantasy narrative. Historical grounding is either abandoned altogether or refigured as symbol. Auberon's cup will offer unlimited riches to its Western inheritor—and we all know what that means in the postcolonial era. Western desire to possess is portrayed solely in terms of sexual attraction, that is, sex as a metaphor for possession; fairy and Muslim desire are read as a cry for Christian liberation;[23] and politics are reduced to just a ploy for settling personal wrongs. By tale's end, Auberon is in Huon, in the sense of possession of the man; Huon is in Outremer; the East is inscribed within the West; and pagan tribute is safely within the hands of Charlemagne. *Huon* may not be history, but it is surely historical, and the dream world that it sketches is troublingly recognizable, even today.

4

Ringing True

Shifting Identity in *Le Roman de la Violette*

KRISTIN L. BURR

From the outset, twists and turns characterize Gerbert de Montreuil's *Le Roman de la Violette*. Over the 6,652 lines of the thirteenth-century Old French romance, the hero, Gérard, is confronted with falsified proof of his beloved Euriaut's infidelity, loses his land, and nearly beheads Euriaut before instead abandoning her in a forest. He then learns that he has accused his lady wrongly, sets out to find her, comes to the aid of several other women, twice forgets Euriaut altogether, rescues her from death at the stake, recovers his land, and at long last weds his beloved. While the focus remains consistently on Gérard, Euriaut too undergoes her share of trials and tribulations.[1] Left in the forest and humiliated, she must fight off the advances of the Duke of Metz, who finds her and wishes to marry her. She must also preserve her honor at the Duke of Metz's court when the scoundrel Méliatir attempts first to seduce and then to rape her. As a result of Euriaut's physical struggle with him, Méliatir decides to kill her. When he instead accidentally stabs the Duke of Metz's sister—Euriaut's bedmate—Méliatir opts to frame Euriaut, conveniently setting the stage for Gérard to rescue her.

The repeated reversals of fortune, most of which are outside of the protagonists' control, force both Gérard and Euriaut into the role of Other. They remain firmly within the courtly world and, indeed, their worth is validated by the desire that members of the opposite sex feel for them. Yet at the same time, the lies told by others and attempts to manipulate Gérard and Euriaut lead the two to seek to marginalize themselves by transforming their identities. In short, they are no longer the traditional hero and courtly lady at the heart of romance but instead make themselves outsiders, alien to the court even as they are part of it. As the couple's identities shift before they eventually return to conventional roles, one item proves to be crucial to the process. Easy to overlook because it appears in only one extended episode and Gerbert devotes little attention to it, a love token in the form of a ring given to Euriaut by Gérard plays a central role in the tale. I contend that the ring has three main functions. First, it facilitates the couple's happy ending. Second, it confirms the true character of both Euriaut and Gérard. Third, and finally, even as the ring reaffirms the identity of each protagonist, it simultaneously reinscribes the pair into their anticipated gender roles. An examination of the trio of functions in turn demonstrates that Gerbert imbues what may seem to be a minor detail with much deeper significance. The simple item enables Euriaut and Gérard to be reintegrated fully into the courtly world: by the romance's conclusion, they are no longer Other.

The ring's most obvious role is to reunite the separated lovers. The jewelry is first mentioned slightly past the midpoint of the tale. During one of the relatively few episodes highlighting Euriaut, we learn that the lady is given a lark while at the Duke of Metz's court. She feeds the bird on her lap—a practice that, the narrator tells us, will lead to much pain for Euriaut (vv. 3892–3903). At this point the ring appears, described very briefly: it was a gift from Gérard, we discover ("La puciele ot un anelet, / Que donné li ot ses amis," vv. 3904–5), and was worth a great deal ("L'aniel, qui fu de riche pris," v. 3912). Although Euriaut usually wears the ring on her finger, it has tumbled onto her lap. She does not notice, but the lark does. Undoubtedly attracted by the stone's shininess, the bird manages to get the ring over its head before flying off.

This loss may appear to be small compared to everything else Euriaut has been through—after all, she has already been accused of promiscuity, menaced with death, and left to her fate in the forest. Here neither her life nor her honor is at stake. Nevertheless, she displays the same grief as when Gérard abandoned her. Pulling on her blond hair, she voices her sorrow:

"Ha! fait elle, sainte Marie!
Com jou ai le cuer esperdu
De mon aniel que j'ai perdu,
Que donné m'avoit mes amis!
Lasse! en com grant dolour m'a mis

Mon cuer cis oysiaus! Maus fus l'arde!
Voir, je ne m'en donnoie garde
Que je deüsse enui avoir;
Mais je sai bien de fi pour voir
Que joie me fuit et esqueule;
Mais c'avient une, n'avient seule.
Par devant oi assés anui,
Cis oysiaus le m'a acrut hui;
Or sera mes maus plus greveus.
C'est bien voirs c'au maleüreus
Rechiet tout adiés la saiete.
Je doi molt haïr l'aloëte,
Qui en a porté mon aniel.
Ha! dous amis, vostre joiel
Me sont piech'a bien eslongié.
Ja mais ne seront alegié
Mi souspir ne ma grans destreche." (vv. 3922–43)

["Ah," she said, "Saint Mary! How my heart despairs because I have lost the ring given to me by my beloved! Alas! This bird has left my heart in such great sadness! May it burn in hell! Truly, I did not anticipate that I would have such hardship. I surely know it's true that joy is fleeting and escapes me. Misfortunes never arrive alone. I have already suffered greatly, and this bird has made it worse today. Now my affliction will be even more grievous. It's true that the arrow repeatedly strikes the unfortunate. I should hate the lark who took my ring. Ah, sweet friend, your jewel is long since far from me. Never will my sighs nor my great distress be alleviated."][2]

Euriaut's anguish occupies more verses than does the bird's act, and with this long lamentation the composer draws our attention to several facts at once. First, Euriaut has lost the tangible sign of her faithfulness to Gérard.[3] Although aspersions have already been cast upon her honor and she has consequently been exiled, the ring is visible proof both of Gérard's original love and of Euriaut's worth. Without that symbol, she no longer has anything to bind her to Gérard and to represent her blamelessness. She has lost the concrete sign of who she is and has become an outsider in her world, both literally and figuratively. Second, the monologue reminds the audience of Euriaut's innocence and of the tribulations she has endured since the cruel Lisiart's accusation of impurity. Gerbert frequently uses this strategy, as we will see again later. Through Gerbert's words, Euriaut insists upon the truth: despite appearances, and regardless of her suffering, she is faithful. Finally, by asserting that misfortunes never come alone, Euriaut creates a link between what has already occurred—her repudiation by Gérard, the Duke of Metz's attempts to wed her, and now the bird's thievery—and the next scene: immediately after Euriaut's expression of despair, the tale turns to Méliatir. Euriaut's wish that the bird burn in hell finds an echo in the narrator's assessment of Méliatir, who is perfidious and arrogant and deserves to come to a bad end: "Dex! c'or fust il ars en un fu!" (v. 3956) [God! May he be burned in a fire!]. This is the villain who will endeavor in vain to seduce and then rape Euriaut, only to succeed in having Euriaut condemned to death by framing her for the murder of the Duke of Metz's sister. Like the bird, Méliatir creates trouble for Euriaut, though the audience must wait to learn exactly how. The worst is yet to come.

So, too, is the best. When the lark pilfers the shiny ring, it sets into motion the chain of events that will lead to Euriaut's rehabilitation and to the happy ending. Just as Euriaut has been imprisoned, awaiting trial, the romance returns to Gérard. Out hunting one day, Gérard—who has entirely forgotten Euriaut, thanks to a love potion that has transferred his affections to another lady, Aiglente—hears the lark's song. The lovely sounds immediately call to Gérard's mind, of course, *fin'amor*. Unfortunately, this love is directed toward Aiglente rather than toward Euriaut, and Gérard's feelings inspire him to sing. As Francine Mora points out, in this instance lyric, so closely bound to love, does not help Gérard recover his memory, as it does the first time he forgets Euriaut.[4] On the contrary, it serves to further distance him from his true love. In a stroke of good luck (or rather, masterful authorial manipulation), the lark perches before Gérard finishes his song, and Gérard's sparrowhawk immediately flies off in pursuit, bringing its catch to Gérard. Our hero takes the lark after giving the sparrowhawk the chance to pluck and begin to eat its prey and, lo and behold, espies the ring with the red stone around the lark's neck. The "choc visuel," as Mora terms it,[5] lifts the veil from Gérard's eyes. The narrator explains:

> Gerars souvent l'aniel esgarde,
> Lors li souvint et se prist garde

Que chou fu Eurïaut s'amie.
On alast bien liue et demie,
Anchois k'il se fust remüés.
D'ire et d'angoisse est tous müés,
Plus noirs que terre tous devint,
Quant d'Eurïaut li resouvint.
Erranment est queüs pasmés;
Au revenir s'est molt blasmés.
"Hé! las! fait il, che m'est avis
Que c'est dolours que je suis vis,
Quant j'ai perdu chou que j'amoie."
Tant est dolans, tant se gramoie,
Che samble bien k'il soit dervés. (vv. 4227–41)

[Gérard looked frequently at the ring, then he remembered that it belonged to Euriaut, his beloved. One could have traveled a league and a half before he moved. From ire and anguish he became blacker than earth when he recalled Euriaut. He quickly fell in a faint, and when he came to, he reproached himself: "Alas!" he said, "I grieve to be alive when I have lost the one I loved." He was so sorrowful and disconsolate that he seemed to be mad.]

His grief takes the form of gestures, as he faints and then wrings his hands, striving to show his despair (and then wondering aloud why he waits to kill himself, as he is a miserable wretch) to the point that he nearly goes insane (vv. 4242–52). His awareness of having been someone other than Euriaut's faithful *ami* takes the form of a very visible expression of distress, which leads his host to ask what is wrong. Gérard quickly explains, continuing to manifest his sadness by tearing at his bliaut (vv. 4266–67) before avowing to seek Euriaut until he finds her.[6]

Like the parallel scene with Euriaut, this episode highlights the heroine's merit, particularly in contrast to Gérard's culpability (minimized by the fact that his forgetfulness is chemically induced). It therefore binds the couple together and brings about their reunion, with Gérard setting out in search of Euriaut, whom he will rescue from burning at the stake. A moment that causes such profound grief in both hero and heroine, paradoxically, is at the root of their happiness. In addition, Gerbert makes an important distinction between types of love. The lark, while associated with traditional *fin'amor*, here evokes false love, or at least love created by false means.[7] The violent end to which it comes therefore does not signify the end of love, crushed by superior force, but the limitations of "unnatural" love. The love potion at the root of Gérard's desire for Aiglente can be effective only temporarily, for it has no power in the face of true love.

Gérard's reaction to seeing the ring points to the token's second main function in the romance: it serves to confirm and reassert identity. Both Gérard and Euriaut experience what we might term an identity crisis. In Euriaut's case, the trouble begins when Lisiart imposes a false identity upon her. As soon as the villain reveals the existence of the violet sign on Euriaut's breast, he marks her as unfaithful. The woman Gérard has described as "la plus biele / Qui soit dame ne damoisiele, / La plus sage et la plus cortoise / Qui soit entre Miés et Pontoise" (vv. 208–11) [the most beautiful lady or maiden, the wisest, the most courtly to be found from Metz to Pontoise] is transformed. She becomes what Gérard's kin calls a deceitful woman ("desloiaus," v. 1002) who should die. While Gérard himself never calls Euriaut faithless—and indeed she is not, since Lisiart knows of the birthmark only by spying on Euriaut in her bath—his behavior reveals his feelings. After promising Euriaut that she will get what is coming to her, Gérard leads her into a forest. He prepares to behead her, explaining, "Honnis sui par vostre folie" (v. 1031) [I am shamed because of your folly]. Gérard's words point to the inextricable lives of the two: Euriaut's alleged act brings shame to Gérard. The false identity created by Lisiart has consequences not only for Euriaut—a fact glossed over in Gérard's statement—but also for Gérard and his real identity. Euriaut escapes death when she warns Gérard of a serpent about to attack him; astonished that a woman on the verge of decapitation might protect her executioner, Gérard chooses to abandon Euriaut in the forest rather than kill her. Still, the identity that Lisiart has forced upon Euriaut brands her so thoroughly that Gérard cannot accept that the heroine's alarm of the serpent's presence could be an accurate reflection of her identity as a faithful lover.[8] He cannot see her as anything other than an outsider in his courtly world.

The poet reminds his audience repeatedly that despite Euriaut's condemnation, she is not the inconstant woman Lisiart accuses her of being. As Kathy Krause explains, the outfit Euriaut dons to make her appearance at court includes a brooch belonging to Florence of Rome and a belt adorned with precious stones given to Aude by Roland, which ally the heroine with other faithful women. They also protect her neckline and hips, two highly sexualized areas of the female body.[9] Euriaut herself underscores her innocence after Gérard has left her in the woods, albeit through unexpected means. Finding the maiden in a faint under a tree, with the slain serpent nearby, the Duke of Metz very reasonably misreads the scene and concludes that the serpent has killed the young woman and then met its own demise. His interpretation is proven wrong when Euriaut regains consciousness. Having quickly become smitten with the lovely heroine, the Duke of Metz expresses his desire to wed her. In response, Euriaut recounts what she swears is her true story: she is a prostitute in love with a thief who stole the nice clothes she wears and who was captured, and she now desires nothing more than to take up her profession again (vv. 1191–1216). Krause notes that Euriaut has appropriated Lisiart's story, but with the goal of rebuffing the duke.[10] Our heroine's strategy does not work, for the duke brings her back to Metz in the hope of marrying her nonetheless, against the wishes of his men. The duke's continued pursuit of Euriaut suggests the depth of his love, as Krause suggests,[11] for the man is enchanted by Euriaut, whom he at first mistakes for a fairy. At the same time, Gerbert intends to highlight the fact that stories and disguises aside, nothing can conceal Euriaut's genuine worth. She attempts to identify herself as an outsider, yet she remains within courtly norms.

The same scenario holds true slightly later, when Méliatir attempts to seduce Euriaut. The heroine assures him that she does not merit his attentions: "Avoi! sire, a molt grant vilté, / Dist elle, seroit a haut homme / De jesir a moi, c'est la somme; / C'onques ma chars ne fu veee" (vv. 3966–69) ["Come now! Sire, it would be a disgrace," she said, "for a noble man to lie with me, that's all there is to it. Never has my flesh been withheld"]. She insists simultaneously on Méliatir's worth and her unworthiness, asserting that she has never refused her body to any man and desexualizing herself with her use of the word "flesh." Once more the audience is reminded of the contrast between Euriaut's words and her actions. By claiming promiscuity, she has underscored her sexual purity. Unfortunately, her approach does not deter the base Méliatir.

While Gérard's predicament differs greatly from Euriaut's, he too undergoes an identity crisis. After overhearing Lisiart reveal that he obtained his knowledge of Euriaut's birthmark by dishonest means, Gérard sets off in search of his beloved. As David King notes, with his land and title lost, Gérard is no longer an appropriate partner for Euriaut; he must reestablish his worth.[12] He has in essence become an "outsider within"—a faithless partner to the woman he loves—and must find a way to reassume his place as a loyal *ami*. On his journey, Gérard undertakes a series of feats that demonstrate his chivalric valor and test his devotion to Euriaut. In the first instance, he defeats a cruel lord who wishes to force a maiden into marriage and has dispossessed her of her land.[13] Although the woman in question, Aigline, hopes that Gérard will wed her, she does not attempt to prevent him from leaving.[14] Next, severe illness causes Gérard to forget both Euriaut and his own identity. His mind and his body are intimately entwined: his anguish and grief at having lost Euriaut lead to his physical sickness. When he then rejects food and drink, his body is so transformed that no one would recognize him (vv. 2266–84). This material transformation brings about further mental deterioration: "De nule rien ne se ramenbre, / S'amie et lui meïsme oublie" (vv. 2285–86) [He remembered nothing at all, forgetting his *amie* and himself]. He has lost all that defined him: his land, his title, his noble appearance, his beloved, and even himself. Gérard is, temporarily, a man without an identity. Fortunately, a young woman named Marote cares for him and, as she sings of a heroine named Euriaut, Gérard recovers his memory. After exhorting him not to test the woman he loves, Marote bestows on Gérard the very sparrowhawk that will catch the lark and the hero departs.[15]

It is at his next stop that Gérard is confronted with his most serious challenge. In Cologne, Gérard assists Duke Milon in defeating the Saxons. Watching the combats, the duke's daughter, Aiglente, and her maid, Flourentine, both fall in love with Gérard. Faced with a persistent Aiglente, Gérard employs a strategy much like Euriaut's, adopting an identity designed to squelch Aiglente's desire. He claims to have forcibly wed a wealthy widow for her money and, his motives discovered, to have lost his land in court and been obliged to leave (vv. 3275–88). Now, he says, he wishes for nothing more than to return to his lady. When Aiglente invites him to return her feelings, he insists to Aiglente that loving her would be disloyal to his marriage:

> Avoi! puciele, mar le dites;
> N'escondi mie, ne n'otroi.
> Par cele foi que je vous doi,
> Mon mariaige fauseroie.
> Sachiés de fi que fols seroie,
> Se pensoie si hautement;

On poroit dire apertement,
Que plus seroie qu'esragiés. (vv. 3346–53)

[Come now! Maiden, wrongly you say that; I do not rebuff you in the least, nor do I grant it. By the faith that I owe you, I would betray my marriage. Know most certainly that I would be foolish if I set my sights on someone of your high stature. One could say openly that I had gone more than mad.]

Gérard's assertions of poverty and dishonorable conduct parallel Euriaut's claims of promiscuity and disreputable behavior.[16] In both cases the professions intend to make the protagonists unworthy of further attention: Gérard would be a poor suitor for a duke's daughter because of his lack of wealth and his willingness to go to any lengths to obtain it, just as Euriaut would not be an acceptable wife for the Duke of Metz—or much of a conquest for Méliatir—because of her past as a prostitute. Both Euriaut and Gérard have tried to place themselves outside the bounds of courtly norms. In the same way that Euriaut's protestations do not diminish the desire that the Duke of Metz and Méliatir feel for her, however, Gérard's affirmations come to naught. Aiglente has her governess concoct a love potion that causes Gérard to transfer his affections from Euriaut to Aiglente. At this point he has a new identity imposed upon him: he becomes the perfect courtly lover, attentive to his beloved and moved to sing by her loveliness—except, of course, that he is not the ideal lover, because he has betrayed his true sweetheart.

Whether identities are imposed upon them or they seek to create their own fictitious personalities, Euriaut and Gérard lack any real power to define themselves through much of the romance. They are either at the whims of another or the stories they tell are incapable of dissuading the desire they inspire. The episode with the ring alters their powerlessness. The token—and its loss and recovery—reaffirms who Euriaut and Gérard "really" are: two faithful lovers. Moreover, the object brings back into alignment the words and deeds of the pair, which have been at odds. Euriaut has been cast as a fickle woman unable to constrain her desire, and she then claims that role for herself, yet it is not an accurate picture of the heroine. Similarly, Gérard has insisted that he pursues women only for their money, and he is then placed in the role of a submissive courtly lover, despite the fact that neither representation reflects Gérard's character. In other words, both Euriaut and Gérard transform their identities—consistently incorporating elements of truth, as Suzanne Kocher asserts[17]—or have their identities transformed for them. Identity is not stable, and whether it is imposed or self-imposed, it does not necessarily reflect reality.

What Euriaut and Gérard say clashes with who they are. This same tension exists between their behavior and their words. If Euriaut denies herself to no man, as she tells Méliatir, one would assume that she would welcome his advances; in the same way, if money is Gérard's primary motivation, Aiglente's wealth should help him to forget his supposed wife. Indeed, Aiglente plays up her financial desirability as she attempts to win Gérard's love. When the ring appears—or rather, disappears—however, actions, words, and identities align once more. Euriaut laments its loss precisely because she is what she claims not to be: a steadfast lover who will not betray her beloved even when she has been abandoned by him. Both what she says and what she does testify to her character. The same holds true for Gérard. When he beholds the love token, Aiglente's enchantment is broken, and Gérard once more claims to be who he actually is: a lover in search of the lady he has mistreated. From this point on in the romance, neither Euriaut nor Gérard pretends to be someone else, nor do any other characters successfully impose a new personality on the two. The ring has definitively determined the identity of each protagonist.

At the same time that the episode with the ring fixes the lovers' fidelity, it also reinscribes the pair into traditional gender roles. Never do Euriaut and Gérard truly take on the conventional personality characteristics of the opposite sex, yet both temporarily move toward more of a middle ground when activity and passivity are examined. Euriaut is no Lïenor, the heroine of Jean Renart's *Le Roman de la Rose ou de Guillaume de Dole*, a wager romance that was an important source for the *Violette*. Lïenor ambitiously sets out when her honor is falsely impugned and very actively works to prove her innocence. Euriaut does nothing of the sort; her situation goes from bad (being accused of infidelity by Lisiart and being abandoned in the forest) to worse (warding off the Duke of Metz's marriage proposal and Méliatir's rape attempts) to catastrophic (being accused of murder and sentenced to burn).[18] Were it not for Gérard's eventual arrival, Euriaut would die at the stake. Her ostensible inaction has led John Baldwin to view her as the conventional passive lady, a "nearly abject pawn of men."[19]

Nonetheless, Euriaut displays what one may term "active passivity." At one point Gerbert's heroine relies on physical force to preserve her honor: she uses her fists and feet as she struggles to avoid being raped by Méliatir. More often, though, she employs other, subtler means of protecting herself. She consistently defends herself through her words, reminding her listeners repeatedly of her innocence on all counts. At times her strategy involves claiming to be what she is not—when she asserts her lax morals to the Duke of Metz and Méliatir—and at others she turns to God. About to be set ablaze, she utters the longest credo prayer found in Old French epic or romance.[20] Besides the anticipated elements, she evokes the handless Onestasse, rewarded and made whole once more by God. She thereby insinuates that, like Onestasse, she is worthy of God's protection so that her body becomes undamaged again.[21] After Gérard leaves her, Euriaut is never as passive as men—particularly Lisiart, the Duke of Metz, and Méliatir—would like her to be. She resists the categories in which they try to place her. Without Gérard there to champion her, she must take on the role herself, or she risks becoming the woman Lisiart has accused her of being: a lady unfaithful to her beloved.[22] The persona she adopts allows her to remain true to herself and to Gérard.

Gérard too finds himself in an unexpected role while he is separated from Euriaut. To be sure, he generally remains very active: his chivalric qualities would otherwise be called into question. He must encounter success on the battlefield to merit Euriaut's love. Still, two key instances of passivity for Gérard mark the period during the pair's separation. The first is when he falls so ill that he forgets both himself and his lady: the malady prevents him from continuing his search for Euriaut. During this time he is physically incapable of activity. Confined to his bed (v. 2267), full of despair, and undernourished, Gérard undergoes a visible transformation: he grows pale, loses weight, and his body becomes greener than the leaf of an elder tree (vv. 2273, 2283–84). His physique no longer marks him as a hero. Gérard himself recognizes both his inactivity and its significance once Marote speaks Euriaut's name in her song. He links his love and his material state:

Que ki sa bonne amor oublie,
Son sens et sa force afoiblie.
N'est merveille se j'afoibli,

Quant cheli ai mise en oubli,
Ki par s'amour me fait valoir. (vv. 2322–26)

[Whoever forgets his true love weakens his mind and his strength. It is no surprise that I grow weak when I have forgotten the one who makes me worthy with her love.]

The recollection spurs Gérard to leave his bed and to start anew his quest to find Euriaut. Shifting from his past forgetfulness to the future tense, he swears that nothing will cause him to stop searching for Euriaut until he finds her, assuming that she is still alive (vv. 2330–34). The memory of Euriaut shakes Gérard from his passivity and leads him to become active once more.

The second episode, of course, is when he drinks the love potion prepared on Aiglente's orders and becomes enamored of her. This case we might deem one of "passive activity." From the beginning of the episode with Aiglente and Flourentine, Gérard is cast in the role of the object of the women's affections, and one who has no say in the matter. The two repeatedly argue over which one will successfully seduce Gérard, never once taking into account Gérard's opinion. The women are far more concerned with themselves. Aiglente boasts of her superior wealth and beauty, and although Flourentine concedes those points, she insists that should Gérard nonetheless prefer her to Aiglente, she will be overjoyed (vv. 3010–58). Only the arrival of Aiglente's father puts an end to the disagreement. Gérard is marginalized in the scene, despite being at the center of the dispute. Once he has swallowed the potion and pledged his devotion to Aiglente, he actively carries out the typical tasks of a courtly lover: displaying his prowess in combat, singing of his beloved, and hunting. Despite this form of activity, he is rendered passive because he cannot continue on his quest for Euriaut. In drinking the love potion, Gérard has literally internalized a liquid that makes him figuratively Other by placing him in the position of Aiglente's *ami*. His will plays no part, and he can be only the man Aiglente wishes him to be.

The means by which the ring passes from Euriaut to Gérard, however, heralds the return of the conventional attributes of female passivity and male activity. Scholars have observed that the symbolic value of the sparrowhawk and the lark is so obvious that one need not dwell on it:[23] just as the powerful hawk overcomes the lark, so too will Gérard triumph over false love and reconquer Euriaut (and his land). Mireille Demaules remarks as well that the literal hunt proves to be the end of Aiglente's metaphorical hunt of Gérard.[24] The sparrowhawk's victory over the smaller bird and Gérard's reaction to it also draw attention to an important difference between this scene and Euriaut's lamentation at losing her ring: Euriaut relies heavily on words to express her anguish, whereas action characterizes the episode with Gérard. In the same way that the hawk aggressively pursues and kills the lark, so does Gérard display his emotion through his actions rather than through speech. While he does give voice to his distress, there are relatively few lines to his monologue, and his host realizes that there is a problem not because of what Gérard says but because of what he does. Seeing the young man's anguish, he cannot help but inquire about the cause: "Sire, fait il, je voi sotie; / Que maintenés si grant dolour, / Que toute vous taint la coulour. / Comment vous est il avenu?" (vv. 4258–61) ["Sire," he said, "I see folly, that you show such grief that you have changed color. What has happened to you?"]. Gérard's physical reaction, more than the words he utters, testifies to the depth of his sentiments and the profound loss he feels at realizing that he has forgotten Euriaut.

As soon as the sight of the ring breaks Aiglente's spell on Gérard, the hero once again takes on a more traditional role. He becomes entirely active. He announces his decision to leave in search of Euriaut, protects his lady from death at the stake, defeats Lisiart in combat, and reasserts his rights to his land. At the same time, Euriaut plays an increasingly passive role; she no longer needs to invent stories to defend her honor, as she has Gérard's sword to do so for her.[25] The episode with the ring thus reestablishes the expected balance between activity and passivity, reinscribing Gérard and Euriaut into their anticipated places and leading to the long-awaited happy ending. They are back inside the courtly roles they occupied at the romance's opening.

Although the ring appears infrequently and Gerbert devotes relatively few lines to the episode relating its loss and eventual recovery, the object plays a key role in the tale. It brings about the marriage of Euriaut and Gérard, and it underscores the couple's fidelity—particularly that of Euriaut, as Gérard recognizes when he attributes his final bliss to his beloved's faith and loyalty: "Mais vo fois et vo loiautés / A sauvees nos amistés" (vv. 6625–26) [But your faithfulness and your loyalty saved our love]. It also confirms the identity of both hero and heroine, and it reestablishes the traditional roles of Euriaut and Gérard in terms of passivity and activity. All the while, it points to the fluidity of identity and boundaries, as Euriaut and Gérard are often simultaneously within and outside of courtly expectations. By the tale's end, both Euriaut and Gérard are fully reintegrated within the court, no longer cast as Other through stories imposed on them by self-interested characters or told by the pair themselves. In many ways, this single piece of jewelry provides thematic and stylistic unity to the romance and encapsulates Gerbert's art. The ring is a symbol of love and fidelity, but it is no mere token.

5

Inside Out and Outside In

(Re-)Reading the Other in the Guillaume Cycle

SARA I. JAMES

We associate the epic poem with the characters who typify it: Roland, Beowulf, or Guillaume d'Orange, whose exploits and characteristics fill lines of verse. Most scholars agree that such characters contribute to a common cultural understanding, to a bond that may be described as "national." But how strong is this bond, when the dividing line between hero and enemy, insider and outsider, Self and Other, is unclear?

Léon Gautier was among the first to study the chanson de geste with sufficient breadth and depth to pronounce upon its significance.[1] But notions of "nation," "nationhood," and "nationality" can be problematic—especially when dealing with poems characterized by Gautier as French but recalling Charlemagne and his Franks. Michèle Gally sees the epic as key in developing cultural identity: "Sa véracité ou son authenticité, que proclament à l'envie les conteurs, se fonde sur le lien de nécessité que le poème épique tisse avec une société qui le reçoit comme sa mémoire originelle et l'expression de la conscience qu'elle prend d'elle-même"[2] [Its truthfulness or authenticity, which the narrators proclaim at will, is founded on the necessary link the epic poem creates with a society that receives it as its original memory and the expression of its own self-awareness].

This statement, while preferring the term "société" to "nation," rightly implies a group's psychological need for poetry that addresses questions of common traits, values, and ideals. However, the chanson de geste does not traffic solely in the binary world of black and white, good and evil. It presents its audience, medieval and modern, with insiders who become outsiders, outsiders who become insiders—and insiders who are outsiders who then become yet another kind of insider. This dynamic neither undermines nor compromises the strength and richness of the heroic ideal: the Other is within.[3]

Gautier himself acknowledged the tremendous variety of characters in chanson de geste who did not conform to a heroic ideal, yet illuminate it; the Other is thoroughly and variously depicted in the chanson de geste. This should surprise no one: all societies create boundaries between what is familiar and what is not: "A culture which 'discovers' that which is alien to itself thereby fundamentally reveals that which it is to itself."[4] This essay explores the alterity and identity of two particular characters from the Guillaume cycle: Rainouart and Orable/Guibourc. Their Otherness is significant both in its complexity and ambiguity, and in its implications for how an epic "center" may exist in relation to such Otherness.

Works on alterity have often focused on post-Renaissance travel literature, or on postcoloniality.[5] Epic studies of the Other have done so with regard to a specific type, such as the Saracen.[6] Yet in most if not all chansons de geste, militant religious opponents are not the only category of characters who fall outside the "heroic" mold, generally accepted as Christian, Frankish, male, and noble. There are many types of Others, including characters of both genders, various races and ethnicities, different religions, classes, physical appearances, and degrees of humanness. It is thanks to such characters that we can more fully understand the criteria of belonging and exclusion constantly negotiated by poet and audience in their attempts to construct a collective identity, a Self: "To obtain that vision, one must not view the object itself but its reflection in a distorting mirror. The figure only becomes 'known' to us through the transformation of an already encoded representation which is subject to the distortions of perspective."[7]

Certainly, the non-Christian character is necessary to Christians' ordering of their universe, to their sense of identity. Therefore, it is reasonable that the more one vilifies—or even simply sets apart—the Other, personified most frequently in epic by the Saracen, the more one asserts the Self. Yet there are also Saracens whose physical beauty, nobility, and knightly prowess are praised; their religion is the one point of difference, and they are worthy opponents. This is a crucial point regarding epic alterity: as Raymond Corbey and Joep Leerssen make clear, "the articulation of cultural identity in these terms [Self and Other] does not by definition imply a denigration of the Other."[8] This is perhaps one reason why the chanson de geste is so rich and varied, featuring so many heroes in combat, in competition, and sometimes in collusion with numerous exemplars of Otherness. The image of the Other is complex even in a work as ideologically "pure" as the *Roland*.

Since the Saracen is the Other par excellence, Rainouart and his sister Orable/Guibourc make fascinating case studies. As Saracens, they are Other; to their native group, however, they are insiders, all the more so given their lofty status. Both become outsiders to their native group through conversion, acquiring again high status, this time among the Christian Franks. They are, indubitably, the Other Within.

First, a brief summary of these two characters and their exploits. Orable/Guibourc comes first in the narrative, appearing in *La Prise d'Orange* as Orable, queen of Orange, daughter of the powerful Saracen king Desramé and wife to king Thiebaut l'Aufriquant (also a Saracen). Following the typical actions of an enamored Saracen princess, she helps the Christian invader Guillaume d'Orange and his men overthrow her own family and people. She converts to Christianity, takes the name Guibourc, and remains in Orange with Guillaume, battling the Saracen hordes on their doorstep. In *La Chanson de Guillaume* (and another version of the same story, *Aliscans*), Guibourc is shown rallying her husband after a crushing defeat, urging him to return to the battlefield and conquer the Saracen enemy, providing him with men, supplies, and practical advice. This includes urging Guillaume to seek military aid from Louis, Charlemagne's heir, who is king thanks only to Guillaume's defense of his throne.[9]

Rainouart appears in *La Chanson de Guillaume* and *Aliscans* when Guillaume, who has gone to Louis's court at Laon, there sees an oafish giant dressed in rags, his head shaven by the master cook as a cruel practical joke. This comic appearance is deceptive, however, for Rainouart is of royal blood, the son of the Saracen king Desramé (and therefore Guibourc's long-lost brother). Kidnapped as a child and sold into slavery, he has ended up in Louis's kitchens. Moved by an unshakeable faith and devotion to the Christian cause, he begs to join Guillaume's troops, even though he is untrained as a knight, able only to lay about fiercely with his fists and his *tinel*, a crude club. After showing his deadly worth on the battlefield, he reveals his identity, is reunited with his sister, and weds Louis's daughter, Aélis.

Rainouart's Otherness is multiple: a Saracen giant, assumed to be low-born and uncomprehending, both marked and mocked by those who surround him. But his apparent status as Other is misleading. Under his ragged, comic appearance, he is extremely handsome—his good looks, like his good manners, have suffered from his mistreatment and surroundings.

> Mout estoit biax, mes l'en l'ot asoté.
> En tote France n'ot nus de sa bonté,
> Ne si hardi, si preuz ne si osez;
> Mes une teche l'avoit mout empiré:
> Ja tant n'eüst une chose amembré,
> Ainz qu'il eüst une traitie alé,
> Que meintenant ne l'eüst obl'ïé.
> Se ce ne fust, je vos di por verté,
> N'eüst tel home en la crest'ïenté.[10]
>
> [He was most handsome, but had been rendered a fool. / In all of France there was none like him for goodness, / Bravery, prowess or daring; / But one flaw had damaged him greatly: / No sooner would he remember a thing / Than, before he'd gone very far, / He'd forgotten it. / If it weren't for this, I tell you truly, / There wouldn't be a man to match him in all Christendom.]

This is an intellectual variation on the epic formula lamenting a noble Saracen's irreligion, when the poet cries out that if only such a fine specimen were Christian, there would be no one to match him. Orable herself is the object of such a complaint in *La Prise d'Orange*, when we first see her: "Et dame Orable, une roïne gente, / Il n'a si bele desi en Orïente, . . . / Dex! mar i fu ses cors et sa jovente, / Quant Dex ne croit, le pere omnipotente!"[11] [And the lady Orable, a noble queen, / There is none so beautiful from here to the Orient, . . . / God! Cursed is her body and her youth, / When she doesn't believe in God, the omnipotent father!]. All her royal blood and beauty cannot mitigate the great flaw of paganism.

But paganism is not Rainouart's great flaw. Despite his Saracen birth, he is as fervent a convert as his sister Guibourc; he is of the right faith and, almost as important, of the right class.[12] Furthermore, although *asoté* to the point that he cannot remember anything from one moment to the next, he is aware of his true rank, and of the responsibilities and respect accompanying it:

> Fiex de roi sui, si doi firté mener,
> Or mais vaurai ma force demostrer;
> Trop longuement m'ai laissié asoter.

Dehait ait fruis qui ne veut méurer
Et honis soit ki n'a soing d'amender.
Nés sui de rois, bien m'en doit ramembrer;
Li bons se preuve, sovent l'oi conter.[13]

[I am the son of a king, and so should conduct myself with pride, / But I must put my strength to good use, / Far too long have I let myself be addled. / Fruit that doesn't mature sickens and dies / And shamed is he who doesn't want to better himself. / I am born of a king, well must I remember it; / I've often heard tell, the good will out.]

While his devout faith and noble birth are unquestioned, Rainouart's life in the kitchens "others" him as a potential hero. Furthermore, his actions once he has joined Guillaume's troops do nothing to disprove his apparent status as outsider. He can neither ride nor use a sword. His one weapon, his *tinel*, is a crude instrument he carries everywhere, washes obsessively, kisses, caresses, and generally fetishizes in a way that must have seemed amusing even to a medieval audience that had never heard of Freud.[14] Joan B. Williamson has written:

> Rainouart is like a wild man, uncivilized in the eyes of his brother knights, for he refuses to accept a horse, key article for any noble combatant. Furthermore, the only skill he needs to be taught is that of *désarçonnement*, which seeks to save the life of a horse when attacking its rider, thus emphasising the animal's value, whose importance has so far been a concept completely alien to Rainouart's experience.[15]

As a Christian of royal blood, Rainouart expresses Otherness through his alien ways and habits. One possible model for the character of Rainouart is the holy fool, the village idiot blessed with a special connection to God. Guillaume even refers to his newfound brother-in-law and savior as "Un joefnes hon que Deus m'ad amené"[16] [A young man whom God has brought to me]. At times he behaves like a large, severely disabled child, lashing out when wounded. Yet he can also engage in debate, attempting to convert his kin to Christianity and showing extreme distress when their refusal forces him to fight them to the death. Given such traits, Rainouart could indeed be what some folklorists would call "liminal," in the sense that he is not completely marginalized by his oddness, but rather is empowered by a compensatory ability, such as his strength and goodness.[17] He is praised by narrator and hero—who give voice to the dominant discourse—and married into the Frankish royal family, his rank and faith finding their proper level.

Rainouart is also Other Within—but how and why? Theoretically, his Otherness cannot be religious or political, given his devout faith and proven loyalty. His size and clumsiness cannot make him Other through making him ridiculous: physical oddities, comic behavior, and brutish force also characterize Guillaume, hero of the cycle. Furthermore, Rainouart's birth is beyond reproach: if anything, as son of a king, he ranks higher than Guillaume, a mere count. So why continue to identify—though not define—him as Other? On a purely practical level, doing so distinguishes Rainouart from other heroes, but the texts cannot support an interpretation that would do so at the expense of his assimilation.

If Rainouart's religion is not in question, his race (sometimes linked to religion in epic) is unclear. Could this be a marker of Otherness? Underneath the soot and grime that obscure his fine features, his skin color is not stated. It may indeed be white, like his sister Guibourc's, or it may not. French epic was hardly consistent when describing the appearance of Saracens, often related to each other. Modern readers may infer whiteness from the text's reticence, but the text does not support this: many chansons de geste describe skin color for Saracens of all races.[18]

In considering medieval alterity, it is not always easy to accept that the prevailing discourse in such cultures may have expressed criteria different from our own, and possibly more tolerant. John Boswell has pointed out that certain ancient societies accepted homosexuality and found race irrelevant, while religious heterodoxy was still taboo.[19]

Although not Other by race, Rainouart's sister Guibourc, formerly Orable, is—we presume—Other by gender. Yet again, the texts do not support this view. Though some critics have commended Guibourc for her "masculine" traits,[20] her strength, initiative, and resolve do not seem to pose a problem in the chanson de geste. The poets routinely praise Guibourc as a noble lady unparalleled in all of Christendom, a sentiment echoed by that most traditionalist of epic scholars, Gautier, who saw in epic heroines the reflection of the medieval women who played an active role at all levels of society.[21]

Guibourc began her literary life as the Saracen queen Orable. The Saracen princess, a stock character familiar to every epic scholar, traditionally boasts great beauty, knowledge of the occult, cunning, and resourcefulness. She also shows an alarming speed and willingness to offer these fine qualities in service of the Christian Franks—who are seeking to conquer the princess's land, people, and family.[22] With such credentials, Guibourc provides a particular insight into what constitutes assimilation, and how it is represented.

While it is true that Guibourc is but one character within a large epic corpus, she enjoys a singularly lengthy and varied career, offering a window into medieval mentalities about religious, cultural, and familial belonging. According to Philip E. Bennett, in spite of her apparent integration, "Orable-Guibourc remains the essential Other to both the Christian and pagan societies represented in the texts, and especially to their male representatives."[23]

The Saracen princess is indubitably Other through her religion. However, the Other may be converted, especially if female, and a converted Saracen princess brings many assets to the French hero. These assets include great wealth, land, knowledge, courtly accomplishments and, most important, the fervent convert's willingness to offer all to the newly adopted cause. Once Guibourc has converted and left Orable behind, she becomes a great heroine, on a par with her equally strong, pious, aristocratic mother-in-law, Ermenjart.[24]

The trope of the Saracen princess, of which Guibourc in her Orable incarnation is the chief exemplar, raises intriguing questions about gender and genre. We have seen that this "double Other" may be read as "masculine." Other critics have descried excessive submissiveness or sexual incontinence. However, the texts themselves rarely support such a reading.

Ascribing "romance influences" not so much to the epic genre as to its critics,[25] Sarah Kay has rightly demonstrated how the Saracen princess in epic performs as an informed individual, acting both politically and morally. As Kay points out, issues of class and status have far more bearing on a character's scope for action than does gender, representing "female characters as persons in the same way as male characters are persons, that is, as the site of an ethically informed will."[26] In other words, eight centuries before Dorothy L. Sayers's polemic on the subject, many epic poems responded to the question "Are Women Human?" in the affirmative.

Racially undistinguished from her new clan, temperamentally similar to her mother-in-law, the Christian Ermenjart, Guibourc seemingly presents the acceptable face of converted paganism. And yet *is* she assimilated?

She has no children by Guillaume, which in itself is a curious point; although she raises his nephews as her own sons, there is no indication that she physically bears a new generation of Gui-warriors. Peggy McCracken has shown that the adulterous queen in Old French literature is childless, possibly because the issue of legitimacy is too touchy a subject to entertain even in fiction.[27] While it is impossible to claim what, if anything, the poet intended Guibourc's childlessness to signify, we do know that distinctions and significations in romance are not the same as in epic. Tellingly, in Guibourc we have a heroine without children, viewed far more favorably than her sister-in-law Blanchefleur, who has a child. A matriarchal role is one thing—whether or not the woman has given birth to the child in question seems to matter much less, if at all.

Guibourc certainly does adopt a matriarchal role in the Guillaume cycle, along with a brood of nephews. As Guibourc, she is so much part of the Christian world, and more particularly the Narbonnais family, that she raises their children as if they were her own. Vivien's thoughts in his last battle, in fact, are for his aunt who has raised him with such care and, ironically enough, for the very purpose of dying in battle. Dying, he asks only to be remembered to Guibourc, his foster mother: "Sez que dirras dame Guiburc ma drue? / Si li remenbre de la grant nurreture, / Plus de quinze ans qu'ele ad vers mei eüe. / Ore gardez, pur Deu, qu'ele ne seit perdue!"[28] [Do you know what you will tell Lady Guibourc, my dear friend? / Remind her how greatly she nurtured / Me for more than fifteen years. / Take care, for God's sake, that she not be lost!].

And yet, this view of Guibourc as traditional female nurturer is not as simple as it seems, as Bennett has noted:

> Despite the perception of alterity which raises fear and suspicion in the mind even of Guillaume's sister, the Queen of France, in both *La Chanson de Guillaume* and *Aliscans*, Guibourc's principal role in these poems, as in many others of the cycle, is as nurturer, supplier of arms and indeed of warriors and women. What is notable in these apparently contradictory roles is that they mark Guibourc as double-gendered: the only unambiguously feminine role she takes is to raise Guillaume's nephews Vivien and Gui, supplying them also with arms, in Gui's case with arms of Saracen origin.[29]

Guibourc serves as an example of how someone supposedly far removed from the epic ideal can become part of that ideal, in a genre whose heroes and heroines abound in inconsistencies and ambivalence. She, like Rainouart, presents ways of exploring the cycle of invasion, appropriation, and assimilation, so often incomplete, with traces of resistance, of lingering, not fully assimilated, at the borders of the "center"—what Bennett refers to as "persistent alterity."[30]

Which brings us ultimately to the question "What is the 'center' in French epic?" Edward Said has examined the extent to which Western notions of the Other—especially the Oriental/Muslim/Saracen Other—are defensive constructs, observing: "It is perfectly natural for the human mind to resist the assault on it of untreated strangeness; therefore cultures have always been inclined to impose complete transformations on other cultures, receiving these other cultures not as they are but as, for the benefit of the receiver, they ought to be."[31]

Converts such as Rainouart and Guibourc "ought to be" identified by unequivocal markers of assimilation. These markers should both draw a line under their former, pagan, Other selves and reinforce their new identities as members of an idealized "center." However, the Other in chanson de geste is often far too complex for such simple binarism.

The epic hero stereotypically incarnates the culture's supposed Christian, Frankish, male, noble center. Yet Guillaume d'Orange, Maugis d'Aigremont, and Huon de Bordeaux, to name but three, all conform to the above criteria while simultaneously destabilizing notions of centrality, conformity, idealized and homogeneous leadership. Maugis is a sorcerer, raised by a fairy; Huon, also surrounded by enchantment, is an exile from Charlemagne's court, mistreated by the king supposed to be the inspiration and figurehead of the *geste du roi*. As for Guillaume, though admired and loved, he is far from perfect. He treats Rainouart thoughtlessly when he owes him his life, land, and honor: at the end of *Aliscans*, Guillaume and Guibourc plan a celebratory banquet, but

> Li quens Guillelmes fist forment a blasmer,
> Quar Renoart a mis en oublïer.
> Ne l'en menbra, si vint aprés souper.
> Defors Orenge fu Renoart le ber,
> De mautalant cuide vis forsener;
> A soi meïsmes se prent a dementer:
> "Li quens Guillelmes nel deüst pas penser,
> Qui ne me deigne o lui ensemble mener

Ne a sa table n'a son mengier mander;
Et si ai fet par moi l'estor finer,
Et ses neveuz ai fet desprisonner;
Toz mes parenz ai fet por lui finer.
Or m'en irai a mon pere acorder,
Si ferai Turs et Sarrazins mander.
Venrai Orenge essillier et gaster,
Et Gloriete par terre cravanter.
A Saint Denis me ferai coroner,
A Looÿs ferai le chief coper
Por sa cuisine que il me fist garder."[32]

[Count Guillaume was greatly to blame, / For he forgot all about Rainouart. / He didn't remember him, and went off to his supper. / Outside Orange stood Rainouart the good and noble, / It seemed he'd go mad with rage; / He thinks to himself: / "Count Guillaume ought not to have even thought it, / Not taking me in with him / Nor sending for me to eat at his table; / And it was indeed I who finished off the battle, / And had his nephews freed; / I have killed all my relations for him. / I shall go make peace with my father, / And send for Turks and Saracens. / I shall come to assault and lay waste to Orange, / And bring Gloriette to the ground. / At Saint Denis I shall be crowned king, / And cut Louis's head off / For having made me keep his kitchen."]

Here we see Rainouart plotting apostasy and treachery in return for an unintentional, though serious, snub. After meeting some knights and terrifying them with his ranting and threats, he is eventually calmed by Guibourc, who comforts and praises him, bringing him into his rightful place in his new family. It is remarkable that such deliberate and specific plans, to overthrow not only Guillaume but also Louis and all of France, are not criticized; the poet treats Rainouart neither as an evil traitor to church and lord nor as a raving idiot. It is Guillaume, the hero, who is blamed from the first for his thoughtlessness. Rainouart has proved himself through demonstrating religious faith, political loyalty, and courage in battle; he has put to death those of his kin who rejected his pleas for them to convert. The poet joins in condemning those who do not recognize that Rainouart's efforts are greater and worthier of praise than those of heroes born to Christian, Frankish allegiance.

Furthermore, Guillaume's failure to behave as a grateful and appropriately generous overlord recalls two points. First, Rainouart's earlier comment that one must constantly strive to better oneself seems suddenly apposite. Those born to nobility do not always behave as they ought, even in epic. Second, Guillaume's behavior reminds us of an even greater failure of feudal duty—that of the king himself.

Guillaume is treated with customary neglect by his own lord, Louis, to whom he has applied for men and aid after the first, disastrous battle of the poem. Guillaume demonstrates that he has spent his all against the Saracens, losing his beloved nephew Vivien in the process. He points out Orange's strategic location as a Frankish, Christian outpost against the Saracens, and Guibourc's vulnerable position as she is left alone with her women to guard the castle and town against all comers. The king, however, can reply only that "N'en sui ore aisez; / A ceste feiz n'i porterai mes piez"[33] [It is not convenient for me right now; / I shall not set foot there at this time]. After being shamed by shouts of support for Guillaume from his assembled nobles, Louis agrees to go with thirty thousand knights.

But the worthless king has an even more worthless queen: Blanchefleur, Guillaume's own sister, who objects to her husband's support for her brother. She declares that it is all a foul trick by Guibourc, who, as a former pagan, knows witchcraft. She accuses Guibourc of plotting to poison the king and put herself and Guillaume on the throne.[34] Guillaume threatens to cut his sister's head off for such slander. Blanchefleur is spared, but roundly blamed by all, including her daughter, Aélis, and her mother, Ermenjart. Ermenjart further shames the assembled court by declaring that she will arm herself, raise troops, and ride out to her son and daughter-in-law's aid. These two insiders accept Guibourc and confirm her status, while rejecting their own blood relation, born Frankish and Christian, as unworthy.

Blanchefleur's misreading of Guibourc's place is certainly an example of identity misrecognition in medieval French narrative; it is clear that Guillaume and his family value Guibourc far more highly than they do Blanchefleur.[35] Just as the true leader of the Franks is Guillaume and not the vacillating Louis, so is Guibourc the heir to Ermenjart's position as matriarch of heroes. Blanchefleur, like her husband the king, shows herself to be less than she ought to be, insiders though they are.

Here, of course, is the crux of the matter: Christian Franks accept and defend a former Saracen as one of their own, confirming her transition from outsider to insider. Meanwhile, the king and queen—meant to be the figureheads of the collective, the "center" of both a culture and its epic tradition—become the outsiders within. Their failure to uphold any meaningful collective ideal, such as feudal support, family loyalty, and solidarity against outside threats, should give us reason to question the existence of any "center" in the chanson de geste. As Julia Kristeva notes, "Strangely, the foreigner lies within us: he is the hidden force of our identity, the space that wrecks our abode, the time in which understanding and affinity founder."[36]

Rainouart and Guibourc exemplify the complexity of identity and alterity in the chanson de geste. Insiders in their native land, they become outsiders through their contact and willing engagement with the Frankish Christians who were once Others to them. Assimilated religiously and politically, they are once again high-status insiders—but still the Other Within.

In their constant shifts—insider, outsider, insider—Guibourc and Rainouart, our Others Within, do justice to the richness and complexity of both the chanson de geste and the culture that produced it. Whether inside or out, the Other is sometimes appropriated, sometimes assimilated, and often feared—but never inherently lesser.

6

Ami et Amile and Jean-Luc Nancy

Friendship versus Community?

JANE GILBERT

Examining Old French chansons de geste with an eye to the Other Within yields an anomalous picture. On the one hand, almost every category of important character can be considered an internal "outsider." Heroes and villains are often similarly strange in the eyes of other characters, and are regularly both rebarbative and sympathetic. They alike manifest the overreactions central to the narratives and tend to be comparably heedless of the welfare and opinions of others in pursuing their own ends. Women and kings, for their part, move within the baronial collective without being entirely of it; their behavior, too, is frequently construed as outrageous. Only those who could be qualified, in Greimasian terms,[1] as adjuvants speak for and out of wider collective interests, and they are marginalized: by secondary status (such as Oliver in the Oxford *Chanson de Roland* and Bernier in *Raoul de Cambrai*), by speaking from a different ideological perspective (Turpin in the Oxford *Roland*), by humorous treatment, or by ethnic or social distancing (Rainouart in the *Chanson de Guillaume*, Bernier again). Those who act for one group against another generally damage the interests of both, as in the internecine cross-generational feuds of the *Geste des Lorrains*. The constitutive excess noted by François Suard in his concise introduction to the genre means that the chanson de geste is peopled predominantly by Others Within: figures who, while not blatantly misfits, do not slide smoothly into some communitarian ethos.[2]

On the other hand, chansons de geste have a famously strong collectivist element. An example is the way they interpellate their audiences in the first person plural. "Carles li reis, nostre emperere magnes" [Charles the king, our great emperor], begins the Oxford *Chanson de Roland*,[3] where the narrator joins the characters in referring to men, religion, and cause as "ours." Such a strategy speaks of a desire to build, if only momentarily, a community extending from text to audience and back again. This collectivist rhetoric is commonly understood as an effort to establish, at least fictionally, one of the genre's ideals: a homosociety in which all who matter will be of one sort, harmonious sameness will rule, and discordant difference be banished to the margins.[4] It has long been recognized that chansons de geste imply a basis in shared values, though what those values are is less established. Many of the historicizing political readings to which the works lend themselves emphasize their engagement with the "warrior class" of feudal barons in its internal conflicts and struggles against encroaching powers.[5] Other interpretations consider Christianity to be the determining element, while some accentuate geopolitical links with northwestern Europe or with Italy.[6] Still others pinpoint propaganda for a struggling Capetian monarchy, or for Norman or Angevin expansionism.[7] It is fair to assert, then, that the collectivist impulse in chansons de geste could legitimize collectives crystallizing around different principles: ideological, geopolitical, dynastic, and so forth. The sense of values shared is an effect of the process of interpellation—which does not preclude the independent manifestation of such values. Its power to energize such collectives was, presumably, one of the genre's attractions. Certainly it has been so since the nineteenth century.

I shall examine here the relations between this well-documented collectivist impulse and the observation that any identifiable chanson-de-geste character role is what we might term an "irony of the community."[8] Highlighting the ironic presences in the texts allows us to rethink the conception of collectives as primarily homogeneous totalities. In its application to secular societies, this conception owes much to nation-state thinking projected back onto the Middle Ages in which that thinking found many of its inspirations; it is, in short, more medievalist than medieval.[9] The challenge, then, is how we, today, can think about a past collective made up largely of Others Within. In pursuing this question, I focus on *Ami et Amile*, a text whose identical heroes have been influentially read as paradigmatic of the genre's homogenizing tendencies. I shall investigate their close friendship in the light of seminal work on community by Jean-Luc Nancy,[10] then turn to the wider implications for the chanson de geste. Finally I shall suggest what chansons de geste may bring to a reading of

Nancy, and thus to Nancy's project of philosophical intervention in the modern world.

Ami et Amile is generally dated to around 1200. It survives in full in only one manuscript, the thirteenth-century BnF fr. 860,[11] where it is preceded by a rhymed *remaniement* of the *Chanson de Roland* (the so-called Paris version) and by *Gaydon* (the continuing story of Thierri d'Anjou after his championship of Charlemagne at Ganelon's trial), and followed by *Jourdain de Blaye* (the story of Ami's grandson) and *Auberi le Bourguignon* (the tale of a relative of Charlemagne's counsellor Naimes). These texts notably share an exploration of biological and symbolic kinship inside and outside institutional frameworks: friendship and fidelity, guardianship and formal or informal god-kin, marriage and seduction, and uncle-nephew or parent-child relations. They also include the genre's commonplaces of exile and revenge, lordly ingratitude and mismanagement, extreme loyalty and treachery. By the late twelfth century, versions in hagiographic and in romance frameworks also circulated in French.[12] In this essay I accentuate the significance of *Ami et Amile*'s self-presentation as a chanson de geste. Whether or not the poet reacted against other realizations, the chanson de geste frame imposes a distinctive set of aesthetic, ethical, and political concerns and priorities orienting the implications of this particular retelling.

Ami et Amile relates how the lives of the eponymous pair intertwine. They are born on a single day, share a miraculous resemblance, and bind themselves in sworn companionship. Serving together at Charlemagne's court, they attract the attention of Charlemagne's steward Hardré and of his daughter Belissant. Both target the heroes. Hardré seeks to kill them and, when his plot fails, offers in marriage his niece Lubias, accepted by Ami; Belissant seduces Amile, whom Hardré promptly accuses of treason. Fearing the ensuing judicial combat, Amile appeals to Ami, who secretly fights in his place and wins. For betrothing himself to Belissant, the prize of victory, Ami is afflicted with leprosy and rejected by his own wife. After much suffering, he turns to Amile who, on angelic advice, kills his own sons in order to bathe the leper in their blood. The cure successful, the children are miraculously resuscitated. Ami and Amile leave on pilgrimage and die at Mortara, in Italy, where their tombs are known to pilgrims.

Commentators on *Ami et Amile* tend to focus on the heroes' resemblance. This is signaled throughout the text in numerous other details besides the physical, most obviously in their names: "Amile" could almost be a declension of "Ami," which itself means only "friend," overdetermining our understanding of the couple. Their explicitly miraculous similarities figure an unbreakable, divinely ordained bond open to different interpretations. The two friends may be considered not merely to share a privileged relationship but also to constitute a privileged unit. For some commentators they are ultimately One, each permitting for the other a completion that escapes frustrated human subjects.[13] In strictly hagiographic versions of the story this completion is, indeed, marked as God-given from the start, and the friends' bond is not of this world.[14] Some scholars read the chanson de geste *Ami et Amile* in the hagiographic mold, and maintain that the providential friendship imposes a divinely authorized exemption from earthly rules. The friends' transgressions would therefore be indices of a special relationship with God, whether on a joint or an individual basis.[15] However, it is significant that the text is distinctly not a saintly vita, and its presentation as chanson de geste brings secular questions also to the fore. Therefore the pair's extraordinary attachment is often interpreted as the paradigm of a social ideal espoused by the genre, in which elite male bonding is society's integrating principle and discordant "others" are easily differentiated, clearly inferior and essentially subservient.[16]

Both these approaches tend to conclude that the heroic friendship is presented (if only eventually) as a shining exception in an imperfect world. I propose a different understanding of the friends' exemplary status: one that focuses on their relationship not as encapsulating ideal harmony, whether secular or sacred, but as epitomizing tensions felt to underlie wider social relations throughout the text. Looking at the study of twins, psychologist René Zazzo contended that observers' fascination with similarity and union had led to their overlooking both the more important differences that distinguish twins from each other and the relationships they maintain with each other and with the outside world.[17] I wish similarly to refocus attention on Ami and Amile to emphasize those things that distance them from each other and that disturb their relationship, emblematized by the extra syllable *-le* that, appended to *ami*, repeats and dislodges friendship. My interest is not in differences of character but in the alienating and self-alienating effects of their mutual commitment. These I read as paradigms of the highly conflictual social model found in *Ami et Amile* and much more widely in chansons de geste, characterized as they are by prominent discord within the social body.

A first objection to characterizing the friendship as an ideal union rooted in simple homogeneity is that it is replete with difficulties for the heroes themselves. Their fictional lives are dominated by the fact that for each, the other's death is an insupportable prospect. The narrative not only demonstrates this overriding commitment but also establishes the inevitability that the heroes will be required actually to act it out. From the moment the two jointly enter society, they become embroiled in increasingly compromising situations which ultimately lead each to commit terrible deeds in order to preserve the other's life. Whether the definitive catalyst is Hardré's jealous aggression, Ami's marriage with the traitor's niece, Amile's fornication with his lord's daughter, or Ami's adulterous betrothal, the narrative weaves unlikely events into a taut series of causes and effects. To save the guilty Amile from dying in judicial combat, Ami fights Hardré illicitly, and hence arguably murders him, before rejecting an angelic warning of leprosy and continuing with a bigamous betrothal. Amile must murder his child-heirs and gruesomely exploit their bodies so as to avert Ami's death—even though Ami himself prefers to die (v. 2904). Each hero chooses his own social and moral isolation over the other's physical annihilation. Each's choice cannot but affect the other, however, and as the plot thickens, neither hero can do anything that does not somehow become also the other's deed. Amile's sexual guilt is uncannily echoed in Ami's condemnation for his bigamy; Ami's questionable homicide in combat reverberates in Amile's killing of his innocent sons.[18] Sameness here, I submit, contributes not to homogeneity but to a distinctness or singularity (to borrow Nancy's terms) accompanying the heroes' intensifying bond. Each one's deed is not the other's, and their acts remain noticeably different, yet each seems to bear and to accept responsibility for the other's deed (vv. 2830–42) even when he himself might have acted differently (vv. 996–1003, 2869–76). Each one acts for and toward the other, who is originator and addressee. The trouble that the two cause to themselves and to each other surfaces in the anguish with which each reacts to angelic messengers urging them to refrain or to act. Amile's final assertion that the two have deserved joint execution acknowledges this co-existence and co-responsibility but does not declare union. It moves between singular and plural first persons to claim the act and its consequences now for Amile alone, now for Ami also:

Or en venéz, si verréz mon torment
Et mon martyre et mon duel qui est grans.

> Quant les avronz enterréz richement,
> Puis noz copéz les chiés de maintenant
> Car deservi l'avommez. (vv. 3163–67)

[Now come, and you shall see my torment and my suffering and my grief which is great. When we have buried them nobly, then cut off our heads at once, for we have deserved it.]

Having ascribed the positive and miraculous part of the previous episode, Ami's cure and return to society (his disease being conceived as a social as much as a physical phenomenon, vv. 2979, 2999), to "Jhesu le Pere qui touz les biens consent" (v. 3162) [Jesus the Father who authorizes all good things], Amile then submits his own action to the common framework of human norms. He does not claim for it a superior meaning beyond the heroes' friendship or use this moment to sacralize the friendship itself. The projected joint death is not the occasion for a vision of union beyond the grave but an expression of surrender to the reality of singularity. The collective posited here is grounded in an estrangement that is shared but does not unite.

This account of the friends' togetherness draws on what Nancy calls "l'être-en-commun" [being-in-common] or "la communauté," a term I shall render by the English "communialty" for reasons explained below. Nancy opposes communialty to several superficially similar notions: to specular, fusional models of being; to the atomism implied by such modern notions as individual, society, and social bonds; and to the myth of an "immanent" community, a lost golden age in which "la communauté se tissait de liens étroits, harmonieux et infrangibles" [in which community was woven of tight, harmonious, and infrangible bonds].[19] Communialty presents human existence as so radically relational that it challenges conventional analytical categories, and Nancy's rhetoric strains accordingly. Perhaps his simplest expression, "*toi partage moi*" [you shares me], shares a paragraph with his most cryptic, "toi (e(s)t) (tout autre que) moi" [you (are/and/is) (entirely other than) I], a formula that he urges us to read "selon toutes les combinaisons possibles" [in all its possible combinations].[20] You me, you and me, you is me, you and anyone but me, you is quite different from me, you wholly other than me. But not "you without me" or vice versa; and not "you are me." The human unit—insofar as it makes sense to speak of one—is "l'être singulier" [the singular being], but not an "individual": "Là où l'individu ne connaît qu'un autre individu, juxtaposé à lui à la fois comme identique à lui et comme une chose—comme l'identité d'une chose—, l'être singulier ne connaît pas, mais éprouve son *semblable*: 'L'être n'est jamais moi seul, c'est toujours *moi et mes semblables*'" [Whereas the individual can know another individual, juxtaposed to him both as identical to him and as a thing—as the identity of a thing—the singular being does not know, but rather experiences his *like*: "Being is never me alone, it is always *me and those like me*"].[21] Nancy distinguishes a similarity produced by and productive of true otherness (*le semblable*) from the similarity of specular logic (*le pareil*): "Le semblable n'est pas le pareil. Je ne *me* retrouve pas, ni ne *me* reconnais dans l'autre: j'y éprouve ou j'en éprouve l'altérité et l'altération qui 'en moi-même' met hors de moi ma singularité, et qui la finit infiniment" [The like is not the same. I do not rediscover *myself*, nor do I recognize *myself* in the other: I experience the other's alterity, or I experience alterity in the other together with the alteration that "in me" sets my singularity outside me and indefinitely delimits it].[22] The multiply-similar Ami and Amile can be interpreted as *semblables* rather than—as they are often read—*pareils*.

Human beings, "les êtres singuliers" [singular beings], come into being in a communicative relation (*la communication*) which can be assimilated neither to social bond (*le lien*)—"un motif du rattachement ou d'un ajointement par l'extérieur" [any notion of connection or joining from the outside]—nor to fusion (*la communion*)—"[un] motif d'une intériorité commune et fusionnelle" [any notion of a common and fusional interiority].[23] Ami and Amile illustrate such an anomalous condition. On the one hand, their sworn *compaingnie* is distinct from the domain of social *liens*. Even allowing for the relative weakness of social structures in medieval literature, the text gives no evidence for institutional status to the friendship. This accords with other chansons de geste, where *compagnonnage* is a—if not the—primary human relation although, or even because, it is not bound by rules or contract, is in fact not "une réalité sociale constituée" [an established social reality] (its literary position outside the strictly social domain proves nothing about historical reality).[24] Their friendship nevertheless carries enormous weight in the eyes of the other characters as well as of the heroes themselves. On the other hand, the privileged connection between the pair is never transparent. Ami dreams that Amile is fighting a lion which turns into Hardré (vv. 866–75), an event that could be read as Nancy's *communion*. Prophetic dreams in chansons de geste, however, conventionally highlight partial knowledge and its frustrations, and they produce anxiety, not reassurance.[25] The communialty between the friends is therefore to be distinguished from the complementary forms of institutional bond and of mystical union.

In building our model of communialty in *Ami et Amile*, we must include the friends' relationships, as a pair and individually, with other characters. The providential friendship complicates these interactions. The pair always provokes attention, positive or negative. The suggestion that a character's presentation as "good" or "bad" depends on whether that character when confronted with the heroes manifests desire or animosity is attractive but not really sustainable. Hostility dominates, and not only because the text represents it as a form of inverted desire, so that Hardré, Lubias, and Belissant are similarly linked to the heroes by a combination of love and harm.[26] Even before the heroes' first meeting, the pattern is set. Each searches for a man who, he has heard, resembles him greatly (vv. 93–94, 152–53), and each progresses through encounters with uncomprehending onlookers whose surprise is tinged with mild antagonism (vv. 134–35, 159–60). Even the generally "good" Belissant is disturbed by the sacrifice of her children: "plorant, criant, trestoute eschevelee, / por ses anfans a grant dolor menee" (vv. 3185–86) [weeping, crying, her hair all dishevelled, she lamented greatly for her children]. God resuscitates the children before their mother reaches them; but Belissant's reaction contrasts with the relatively unperturbed response of the wife in the story's Middle English version, given even before she knows of the resuscitation.[27] Communialty's jointed disjointedness and communication's painful misunderstandings are evident throughout *Ami et Amile*.

We can therefore see in the relation between Ami and Amile themselves a *mise en abyme* of the wider collective: "la limite extrême, mais non externe, de la communauté" [the extreme though not external limit of community].[28] I borrow here from Nancy's description of the loving couple in which, he argues, communialty is realized with a peculiar intensity that makes it exemplary of, even as it distinguishes it from, the common run (Nancy is countering the romantic view of the couple as embodying an ideal communion inaccessible to society).[29] The model for human relationships that *Ami et Amile* supplies is one in which discrete entities infringe on each other in ways that are inevitably, inseparably positive and negative. This corresponds with reasonable accuracy to the world of the chanson de geste, where no one can act without impinging on others and where institutions are thought of in terms of human emotion; *toi partage moi*. However, neither social bonds, affective links, nor encroachment produces full integration, and thus arises "la propriété paradoxale du personnage épique" [the paradoxical property of the epic figure] highlighted by Suard: "constamment associé à d'autres, il est condamné à la solitude" [constantly associated with others, he is condemned to solitude];[30] the paradox is perhaps more apparent, because more unfamiliar, to modern eyes. The same communialty and *communication* found in *Ami et Amile* mark other chansons de geste. To take only one famous example, *Raoul de Cambrai* highlights the tragic disjunctions that prevent Raoul and Bernier, the text's *couple épique,* from both wanting peace at the same time, and that make Aalais's maternal curse on Raoul irretractable.

Having discussed what Nancy's essay can bring to an understanding of chansons de geste, one may in turn argue that a theory of communialty based in the chanson de geste can focus difficulties with Nancy's analysis. To take one aspect: while Nancy insists that communialty involves the recognition of real disagreements between singularities, he downplays the potential for conflict it must logically encapsulate. In implicitly promoting adherence to his version of communialty as a safeguard, if not against quarrelling, then at least against its escalation into violence or oppression, he in effect substitutes an idealized community for his own communialty. The chansons de geste are truer to his analysis in foregrounding bloodshed and ferocity even where they condemn them. Their gory destructiveness and dark energy show up ironically the abstraction of parts of Nancy's argument, such as the following crucial passage:

> La communauté est révélée dans la mort d'autrui: elle est ainsi toujours révélée à autrui. La communauté est ce qui a lieu toujours par autrui et pour autrui. Ce n'est pas l'espace des *"moi"*—sujets et substances, au fond immortels—mais celui des *je,* qui sont toujours des *autrui* (ou bien, ne sont rien). Si la communauté est révélée dans la mort d'autrui, c'est que la mort elle-même est la véritable communauté des *je* qui ne sont pas des *moi.* Ce n'est pas une communion qui fusionne les *moi* en un *Moi* ou en un *Nous* supérieur. C'est la communauté des *autrui.*[31]

> [Community is revealed in the death of others; hence it is always revealed to others. Community is what takes place always through others and for others. It is not the space of the *egos*—subjects and substances that are at bottom immortal—but of the *I*'s, who are

always *others* (or else are nothing). If community is revealed in the death of others it is because death itself is the true community of *I*'s that are not *egos*. It is not a communion that fuses the *egos* into an *Ego* or a higher *We*. It is the community of *others*.]

The warfare, killings, and menaces that fuel even the less combat-ridden chansons de geste bring Nancy's rather bloodless rhetoric into vividly imagined concretion. Differences can and will emerge in viciousness, and accepting alterity must mean acknowledging this. The appeal for forbearance can be made only on the basis of this acknowledgment.

One may similarly question Nancy's view that conflict arises primarily between would-be immanent communities, intimating that demolishing the myth of immanent community will reduce such clashes. Nancy depicts warfare *within* the collective as absurd and illegitimate, to the point where naming a particular conflict "une guerre intestine"[32] [intestinal warfare] appears a positive step toward ending it. For chansons de geste, contrastingly, civil war represents the primary, essential form of conflict. Internal enemies are more interesting than external ones, unless the latter are constructed along lines of similarity as well as difference, creating a stimulating tension. Thus the oft-remarked resemblances between Saracens and Christians in the Oxford *Chanson de Roland* are, in my view, evidence not of embryonic or senescent states of community formation but of the predominance of communialty for thinking human relations. Feud, another of the genre's great themes, occurs not between stably separate, internally consistent communities but between shifting groupings of kin and allies. If people are not like us, how are we to fight them? Most interesting of all are "friends" and "companions," where these terms are understood with the freight of disjunction, suffering, and infringement that I have examined in *Ami et Amile*. Hence the preoccupation with friction within the *couple épique* and the close family as well as with other kinds of *ami*: lords, allies, and relatives.[33] Although Nancy downplays it, internal conflict is the corollary of positing a group based on the *semblable*, that being in whom and of whom I experience "l'altérité et l'altération qui 'en moi-même' met hors de moi ma singularité" [alterity in the other together with the alteration that "in me" sets my singularity outside me].[34]

This is not to argue that communities are wholly absent from chansons de geste; on the contrary, they prompt a further observation concerning Nancy. In "La communauté désœuvrée," the term *la communauté* means three things: (i) the disjunctive common humanity that resists both (ii) the drive to immanence and the constitution of (iii) any bounded community. Nancy thus attempts to reclaim *la communauté* from its associations, variously, with the *communautarisme* that haunts contemporary French politics, with Soviet-era communism, and with Christian brotherhood. In order to distinguish it from the other senses, I have translated the first sense of *la communauté* as "communialty," an obsolete word whose meaning the OED gives as "community; fellowship." Nancy's text, however, slides between senses so as to suggest that communialty is the unacknowledged but inescapable condition of particular, actual communities, which ought therefore to accept their hankering after immanence for the constitutive fantasy it is: "La communauté assume et inscrit—c'est son geste et son tracé propres— en quelque sorte l'impossibilité de la communauté" [community acknowledges and inscribes—this is its peculiar gesture—the impossibility of community].[35] In later work he abandons the polyvalent use of *la communauté*, preferring such terms for communialty as "être-en-commun" [being-in-common], "être-ensemble" [being-together], "être-avec" [being-with].[36] His new vocabulary achieves theoretical clarity at the expense of a productive ambiguity. For "community" importantly has a bounded sense as well as the unbounded one that Nancy seeks to impose. Bounded communities distinguish between insiders and outsiders, even if relations between them are friendly and even if boundaries are permeable and shifting. The slide established in the essay "La communauté désœuvrée" between bounded and unbounded communities corresponds to a real association. If it is vital to appreciate the element of estrangement within any apparently consistent community, it is equally crucial to recognize the tendency to form bounded groups—however temporary, contingent, and internally heterogeneous—that is inherent in communialty's fragmenting nature. Moreover, alienation and disjunction, which Nancy deems central to communialty, are not stably divisible from antagonism and exclusion. Communialty includes at its core the potential for both group formation and group hostility. These tendencies may be illustrated by Nancy's comment on the "dangers" that led him to abandon the term "communauté," whose use in *La Communauté désœuvrée* he later considers to have contributed toward empowering a late twentieth-century "reviviscence de pulsions communautaristes, et parfois fascisantes" [revival of communitarian and sometimes fascistic urges].[37] With their preference for rendering conflicts as struggles between *semblables*, chansons de geste show that human grouping is not fundamentally opposed to the kind of overlapping relationality, the *partage*, that Nancy wants to salve the intercommunal wound. Conflict and violence in these works are not only destructive of the social fabric nor radically alien to it; they also constitute the social fabric, for good and ill.[38]

This point is distinct from but connected to Nancy's argument about immanence, to which I now turn. As already quoted, Nancy affirms that communialty is to be distinguished from the community that "fusionne les *moi* en un *Moi* ou en un *Nous* supérieur" [fuses the *egos* into an *Ego* or a higher *We*]. This cannot fail to recall the collective *nous* with which chansons de geste often interpellate their audiences. My suggestion is that whereas we moderns tend to read such a *nous* as indicating a self-consistent community, a fortiori when it issues from a premodern past, the same supposition does not orient medieval audiences of chansons de geste. Their collectives are not immanent communities but communialties, in which "[les] *je* . . . sont toujours des *autrui* . . . , ne sont pas des *moi*" [the *I*'s are always *others,* not *egos*]. It is a truism that modern modes of what we call subjectivity, individuality, singularity, and personhood are not identical to medieval ones, though this appreciation of historical difference is not always extended to the corresponding matter of group formation. In fact, chansons de geste do occasionally, and in specific circumstances, refer to the formation of communities comparable to those Nancy criticizes. A character may attempt to channel the power of the collective for his or her particular ends, for instance speaking authoritatively for others in council or initiating fighting that entangles many. An example of the first is Hernaïs d'Orléans in the *Couronnement de Louis*; of the second, Thiébaud de Bourges in the *Chanson de Guillaume*. The "community" that these figures attempt to actualize can validly be called a "sujet collectif" [collective subject] or "un *Moi* ou . . . un *Nous* supérieur" [an *Ego* or . . . a higher *We*]. Although not always ascribed to traitors or troublemakers, the move to embody such a community sooner or later attracts comment expressive of a wider perspective, thus restoring the element of *autrui*. As Oliver comments in the Oxford *Chanson de Roland*: "Vostre proëcce, Rollant, mar la veïmes!" (v. 1731) [Your prowess, Roland, in an evil hour we saw it!].

Chansons de geste thus draw on the myth of immanent community to explain civil war. They turn to a different aspect of that myth in the effort to prevent it, notably calling for the formation of a Christian community that will fight as one against the infidel. *Girard de Vienne* ends with the indecisive combat between Roland and Oliver, opposing champions in an inter-Christian war halted by an angelic summons to direct their energies into crusade. Such solidarities, however, remain wishes to be fulfilled beyond the text's narrative ken. Similarly, at the end of *Ami et Amile*, the miraculous restoration of the heroes' physical similarity brings the text to a rapid close; their withdrawal from earthly society, pilgrimage, and joint deaths hint at full union with and in the divinity—but if this occurs, it is outside the text's own order. Immanent community certainly functions in numerous chansons de geste as an incitement to ideological violence. Nevertheless, violence in the chanson de geste is not primarily produced by or productive of groups that function harmoniously because watertightly "same" and opposed to a "different" other.

If we take Ami and Amile's friendship as the image in miniature of the chanson de geste collective, then it is evident that the way of being-together that the genre foregrounds is not a harmonious union, homosociety, or immanent community based on the erasure or expulsion of difference. Nancy's model of non-totalized, non-totalizing communialty[39] stimulates us to reexamine the collectivist urge of chansons de geste, and to find a place in that collective for the Others Within who observably compose it. A communialty such as that of Ami and Amile can be made up only of Others Within, a not inadequate alternative term for Nancy's *êtres singuliers* [singular beings] or *semblables* [likes]. Nancy critiques the immanent community, whose location in the lost past (or as yet unattainable future) he considers to be a myth constitutive of modern societies.[40] Medievalists, whose specialist period is prone to be co-opted to embody that myth, can be grateful. Like other modern theorists, he further moves us beyond the polarity of "individual" and "society" which, notwithstanding notably exciting work in the 1970s and 1980s, is recognized to be ill adjusted to medieval relations between the person and the collective. Nancy encourages us to reconceive what preceded this post-Enlightenment discourse. We can utilize his work without diminishing the many differences between his thought and agenda and those of the chansons de geste. Conversely, attentiveness to chansons de geste collectives exposes ways in which Nancy's analysis of the *communauté désœuvrée* is obscured by the political and ethical "work" that he calls on it to do.

7

The Devil Inside

Merlin and the Dark Side of Romance

FRANCIS GINGRAS

With the reorganization of vernacular genres in the twelfth century, romance emerges as a form in which otherness is not always estranged. The clear opposition between right and wrong that characterized the chanson de geste, bluntly stated in the *Chanson de Roland* where "paien unt tort e chrestiens unt dreit" [pagans are wrong and Christians are right], tends to be replaced by a densification of characters who have their own share of flaws. The increasing complexity of characters, concurrently good and bad, is probably best represented by Merlin, usually introduced as the son of a devil and a virgin. With this strange character, otherness stands at the very origins of the Arthurian world, for it is through Merlin's sorcery that Uther Pendragon can take on the form of his rival and then conceive Arthur, "the once and future king" of so many romances. The Arthurian world thus rests on fiction from its beginning. This magical conception will thereafter often serve to question the status of romances,[1] those fictitious tales that developed between the twelfth and thirteenth centuries, especially around King Arthur and the Round Table.[2] The founding myth with its heroic elements, notably through a herculean model, is set aside in favor of a reflection on the status of fiction as well as on the questions that intrusion of otherness brings up.

The tale of Arthur's conception through the intervention of Merlin's magic can be found in Geoffrey of Monmouth and in Wace's "translation," where the birth of the future king is the result of subtle plays with "semblance" and "form." The uncertain bases upon which rests the origin of Arthur, "le bon rei, le fort, le seür" (v. 8735) [the good king, the strong, the resolute], do not worry Geoffrey and his translator, who do not offer any negative comment of the scene, focusing instead on the king's great popularity, which they both recognize as largely deserved. Merlin's intervention could seem like a way to duplicate the supernatural component of his own conception. Though I have written elsewhere that the sorcerer creates, in his own image, a fatherless son,[3] it would be more accurate to suggest that Merlin creates a son with multiple and uncertain fathers: Gorlois, the legitimate spouse playing the role of the apparent father; King Uther, playing the masked father; and Merlin, the adoptive father, who plays a crucial role in the future king's upbringing.

Historical Truth and the Myth of Origins

These two tales of origin echo rather than confront each other. The narrative treatment they initially receive in Geoffrey of Monmouth's *Historia Regum Brittaniae* clearly distinguishes them. Merlin's conception is told in direct discourse by the mother, the incubus's victim, who relates the visit of "quidam in specie pulcerrimi iuuenis"[4] [someone in the form of a most handsome young man]. The nature of this presence is then explained, still in direct discourse, by the clerk Maugantius, summoned by the king, whose reaction is described as "admirans" [astonished] by the otherwise very discreet narrator. Wace, who reprises the discourses' attributions in his translation,[5] further specifies the incredulity of the king, who "si demanda s'estre poeit" (v. 7437) [asked if it could be true]. The clerical discourse must answer this incredulous astonishment—Wace presents Maugantius as "un clerc ki mult esteit savant" (v. 7436) [a learned man who was very wise]—a discourse that relies on scriptural authority: "in libris philosophorum nostrum" [in our philosophers' books] for Geoffrey; "trové avum, dist-il, escrit" [we have found it written, he said] for Wace. The Anglo-Norman translator even succeeds in maintaining the prestige of Latin in the clerk's discourse, since he has him declaring that these creatures "*incubi demones* unt nun" (v. 7445) [are called *incubi demones*]. Through this allocation of speech, Geoffrey of Monmouth, loyally followed by Wace, distances himself from a tale of origin that appears to be grounded in *fabula* rather than *historia*.

In his *Vita Merlini*, Geoffrey remains somewhat discreet as to the conception of the central character, allowing the bard Taliesin—who speaks, Geoffrey specifies, "under Minerva's dictation"—to evoke

> At cacodemonibus post lunam subtus habundat,
> qui nos decipiunt et temptant fallere docti,
> et sibi multociens ex aere corpore sumpto
> nobis apparent et plurima sepe sequuntur.
> Quin etiam coitu mulieres agrediuntur
> Et faciunt gravidas generantes more prophano.[6]

[But there is a place under the moon that abounds in evil demons who deceive us and are taught to try to mislead us, and who, having taken on aerial bodies, often appear to us, with numerous and frequent consequences. Moreover, they approach women in sexual intercourse and make them pregnant, thus conceiving in an impious way.]

The link between Merlin's conception and Taliesin's theoretical presentation is never directly established in the *Vita Merlini*, which remains silent as to the prophet's origins. Nevertheless, Taliesin's description of the demons recalls several points of Maugantius's speech, which specifies that the *incubi* were sublunary spirits (*inter lunam et terram habitant spiritus*). The distance created by a general discourse (only indirectly relating to Merlin's conception) reported by a legendary bard (acting as the prophet's double) allows Geoffrey to present the primal scene of the Arthurian world as a "sacrilege" (*prophano*) without any intervention from the narrative voice.

By comparison, the tale of Arthur's conception is claimed much more directly by the narrative. Initially recounted by Merlin, the metamorphosis permits Uther Pendragon to take the appearance of Igraine's legitimate spouse in order to quench his desire for the Countess of Cornwall and thus conceive Arthur. It is repeated by the narrator in similar terms that highlight the role of the potion (*medicaminibus*) and the transformation's vocabulary (*transmutatus est; mutatus est*). Wace's translation even underlines the supernatural part of the transformation by declaring that "Merlin fist ses enchantemenz" (v. 8727) [Merlin performed his enchantment].

The two tales of conception in which the supernatural intervenes thus distinguish themselves from the outset by their narrative modalities. The former, concerned with Merlin's conception, creates such doubt that the tale itself is never fully taken on by the narrator. The latter, detailing Arthur's conception, allows, on the contrary, a game of reprisal: announced by the protagonists, it is then related in much detail by a narrator who concludes with the future grandeur of the king rather than with the troublesome nature of the conception.

In a perspective that looks to unite both didactic and pleasing aims, Godfrey of Viterbo between 1185 and 1187 writes a universal history that devotes an entire chapter to England and mentions the conceptions of both Merlin and Arthur. Merlin's is once again related through a dialogue between the king and Merlin's mother. The sovereign inquires as to the possibility of a woman conceiving without a man's participation: "Quaeritur a matre, quo spermate, qua novitate, / Filius a matre potuit nasci, sine patre?"[7] [The mother is asked: "Solely because of semen, by some novelty, could a son be born to a mother, without a father?"]

The mother simply answers that the father was an incubus, without giving any more details: "Rettulit illa, patet incubus esse pater"[8] [She replied: "It is clear that the father is an incubus"]. Here again, the narrator remains in the background, though he alludes to this maculate conception by presenting the fatherless child as "phantasmatis arte creatum" [created through the art of imagination]. The "phantasmatic" nature of the incubus would find itself at the core of theological and medical debates of the thirteenth century. Some, such as William of Auvergne, bishop of Paris, associated the incubus with a *phantasma* as early as 1230, before the Montpellier doctors' argument that "incubus est phantasma in somnis"[9] [an incubus is a fantasy during sleep]. Godfrey of Viterbo's formulation is prudent and even ahead of its time within the history of debates on the "reality" of incubi and on their capacity to procreate. It anticipates the doubts that Caesar of Heisterbach and Vincent of Beauvais will formulate at the beginning of the thirteenth century, by relying specifically on the tale of Merlin's conception.

The Cistercian Caesar of Heisterbach establishes a link between the tale of Merlin's conception and the founding myth that seemingly lends supernatural origins to the ancestry of every British sovereign:

Legitur etiam Merlinus propheta Britannorum ex incubo daemone et sanctimoniali femina generatus. Nam et reges, qui usque hodie regnant in eadem Britannia, quae nunc Anglia dicitur, de matre phantastica descendisse referuntur.[10]

[We also read that Merlin, the Britons' prophet, was born from an incubus devil and a holy woman. Indeed, we found that, to this day, all the kings that have ruled Britain, which is now called England, are descended from a fantastic mother.]

To depict the problem of the nature, human or diabolical, of beings thus conceived, Caesar of Heisterbach relies on what is read (*legitur*) or reported (*referuntur*). The monk shifts the English's supernatural origins back on the side of the *phantasticus* as, in answer to his novices' queries, he explains that the *incubi* are formed by demons that collect a human seed "scattered against nature," requesting it in order to acquire a body so as to be rendered visible and sensible to human beings.[11] The presence of human seed in explaining the demons' capacity to generate is repeated throughout the thirteenth century by Albert the Great as well as by Bonaventure and Thomas Aquinas.

The gap between the tale of Merlin's origins and its scientific explanation is patent for Vincent of Beauvais, who evokes Merlin in his *Speculum Historiale* to recognize both his prophetic abilities and the alleged circumstances of his conception, mentioning that "professa est de spiritu in specie hominis illum concepisse"[12] [It is taught that he was conceived by a ghost in the form of man]. Here again, the "professa" filter steps in, and with "spiritu in specie hominis" the vocabulary remains relatively imprecise regarding the father's nature. The Dominican Vincent of Beauvais goes back to Merlin's conception to explain that the spawning demons are nothing but mere illusions: "Sed nec ipse demonum concubitus videtur esse verus et naturalis, sed magis phantasticus" [But if sexual intercourse with a demon seems real and natural, it is indeed more of a fantasy]. The *Actor*, as Vincent refers to himself, even suggests a theory of optical nature in order to explain diabolical intrusions into the imaginative faculties. Through a process similar to specular reflection, the devil himself forms the seductive image that is then projected onto the human imagination, much as a mirror reflects an image coming off another mirror.

While the uneasiness concerning Merlin's conception appears somewhat general, historians' attitudes toward Arthur's conception are much more mitigated despite the theological problem that Uther Pendragon's metamorphosis creates. For Geoffrey and Wace, the narrative voice fully assumes the tale it reprises, almost word for word, from Merlin's explanation given through direct discourse. Only Vincent of Beauvais avoids the supernatural intervention, merely mentioning in his *Speculum Historiale* that the king fell in love with the duke's wife and that he ended up conceiving with her the famous Arthur as well as a girl named Anna.[13]

Most writers prove as discreet as the Dominican scientist. The great majority of French Arthurian romances of the twelfth and thirteenth centuries remain mute as to Merlin's and Arthur's conceptions. One finds a certain number of allusions to Arthur's genealogy, meaning that Uther Pendragon is presented as King Arthur's father (*le pere au roi Artus*) and Igraine as his mother, but the details of the events surrounding his genesis are never revealed. The same discretion is reserved for Merlin in verse romances, which ignore him altogether most of time, or at best associate him with topographic indications. In these instances, he plays an essentially onomastic role, as is the case with the Esplumoir Merlin in *Meraugis de Portlesguez*,[14] Merlin's stone (*le perron Merlin*) in *Escanor*,[15] or the Nouquetren, where he had resided for quite some time according to the romance *Fergus*.[16] Even in the *Lancelot-Grail* prose cycle, mentions of Merlin and Uther Pendragon are mostly allusive,[17] with the obvious exception of Robert de Boron, who centers an entire romance on the prophet and King Arthur's conception. Through the development of these episodes by Robert de Boron and their resumption by certain prose and verse writers, the different modalities of the correlation between history and fiction begin to emerge.

Between History and Myth

Known through a textual fragment in octosyllabic couplets and its rendition in prose transmitted through forty-six complete manuscripts, Robert de Boron's romance *Merlin* uses these two episodes at the core of the narrative. In the Micha edition,[18] the first twenty-three chapters are dedicated to Merlin's conception and its consequences, and twenty-five are concerned with the episode of Uther's infatuation up to Arthur's baptism (the last thirty-nine, if we go up to Arthur's royal consecration). Thus, more than half of Robert de Boron's romance is dedicated to the development of two episodes that amounted to a few lines in Geoffrey of Monmouth. However, with this development, the text tends to blur the boundary between history and myth. By making his own the story delegated elsewhere to direct discourse, Robert de Boron inflects the reception of what he seemingly wished to inscribe under the banner of *historia*.

The gap between the text's historic legitimacy and its medieval reception is perceptible in the single verse manuscript of *Merlin*, where the fragment of 504 verses was copied without interruption from *Joseph d'Arimathie*, after the author himself gave his text a title, laying claim to the name of *history*: "Et pour ce que la chose est voire / L'apelon DOU GRAAL L'ESTOIRE" (vv. 2683–84) [And because this thing is true we call it the *History of the Grail*].[19] Yet this title, which positions history not as the source but as the nature of the tale, is not retained by the rubricator, who instead inscribes in the incipit's margin: "Ci commence li romanz de l'estoire dou graal" [Here begin the romance of the history of the grail].[20] In doing so, he reestablishes the story's primary status as a source-text and labels the text that follows as subsidiary to history: the romance is an implicit translation and formatting of an original tale.[21]

The uncertain status of Robert de Boron's tale is directly linked to the myth surrounding Merlin's conception. The author represents the problem posed by the tale's transmission when, following the birth of a hairy, fatherless child who immediately possesses the ability of speech, the midwives begin to spread the news. The question of the news' circulation is particularly developed in the β version, where the oral transmission dovetails with a scriptural one:

> Quant eles oïrent ce si s'esmerveillierent molt et disent: "Ceste merveille ne puet estre celee. Nous irons l'aval au peuple." Lors vinrent as fenestres et apelerent les gens et lor dient que des ores mais est il bien tans c'om face justice de la feme. Si en firent faire letres et envoïerent partout pour les juges que il soient illuec dedens .XL. jours pour faire justice. (§ 25)[22]

> [When they heard that, they wondered greatly and said: "This wonder can not be hidden. We will bring it down to the people." Then they came to the windows and called the people and told them that henceforth it is high time to do justice to that woman. They thus wrote letters and sent them everywhere so the judges might come in the next forty days to dispense justice.]

In a few lines, the text materializes the tale's circulation: the news travels through windows and *descends* toward the people, before vying for a juridical legitimacy through writing. The veracity of the tale of Merlin's origins takes a juridical turn through the accusation of the mother, saved from the bonfire by her son, who reveals that the judge is in fact the illegitimate child of a priest.

For Merlin, this is not a case of answering slander by slander; it is an opportunity to have the truth triumph, and what he reveals about the judge is immediately verified by the magistrate's mother. Following this shock, although he can be content to have saved his mother, Merlin's love of justice leads him to admit that he is the son of a demon. Thus, truth is reestablished and rumors concerning his mother's loose morals are denied, but at the price of a terrible revelation about the prophet's paternal ancestry. Following this episode, Merlin asks Blaise, his mother's confessor, presented as a "molt bons clers et molt soutis" (§ 37, lines 2–3) [very good and very subtle clerk], to write his story: "Ensi devisa Merlins ceste œuvre et li fist faire a Blayse et molt s'esmerveilla Blayses des nouvelles que Merlins disoit. Et toutes voies li sambloient eles vraies et bones et beles" (§ 40, lines 1–3) [So Merlin told this work and had it done by Blaise, and Blaise was most amazed by the news Merlin was telling. Anyway, it seemed to him to be true and good and fine]. The first of an important series of *mises en abyme* in the story's structure, Merlin's dictation to Blaise corroborates the text's veracity. The fiction's truth (news that seemed true) is immediately distinguished from the Truth revealed by Merlin himself, who vies to separate the *Book of the Grail* from the Holy Scriptures, telling Blaise: "Mais il ne sera pas en auctorité, por ce que tu n'iés pas ne ne puez estre des apostoles, car li apostole ne mistrent riens en escrit de Nostre Seingnor qu'il n'eussent veü ne oï et tu n'i mez riens que tu en aies veü ne oï, se ce non que je te retrai" (§ 16, lines 96–101) [But it [this book] will not be authoritative since you are not and cannot be one of the apostles, because the apostles did not put anything in writing about Our Lord unless they had seen or heard it, and you do not write about anything you have seen, but only about what I have told you]. In Robert de Boron's romance, the tale depicting the Arthurian world's problematic origins reaches a particular status between history and myth, being neither a full-fledged fiction nor a historical episode on the same order as *L'Estoire dou Graal* which is tied to the truth of the Gospel thanks to Joseph of Arimathea.

Another text that situates itself, much like *Merlin*, between the absolute truth of Holy History and the more problematic one of Arthurian history is *Le Haut Livre du Graal* (also known by the name of its protagonist, *Perlesvaus*), which creates a place for the tale of King Arthur's origins. The telling of the king's conception is delegated to a priest who must explain why the castle's enclosure has "fondus tresqu'en abisme" (*HLG* 726.19)[23] [melted down to the abyss]. The priest's narration follows closely what Geoffrey of Monmouth and Wace relate, though he adds a commentary on the deceitful faculties of Merlin, "qui si fu engignos" (728.16) [who was so crafty]. There is no detailed description of Merlin's conception here, yet the priest hints at the prophet's partially diabolical character when he explains how Merlin's body was not in his coffin in the Tintagel chapel:

> "Seigneurs," fait li provoires, "en cel sarquieu fu mis le cors de Merlin, mais onques ne le peut om metre en la chapele, ainz covint le sarquieu demorer par defors; et sachiez tot de voir que li cors ne gist mie dedens le sarquieu, kar tantost con il i fu mis, en fu il ravis et portez ou de par Dieu ou de par diable, nos ne savons liquel." (*HLG* 730.6–732.1)

> ["Gentlemen," said the priest, "Merlin's corpse was put in this coffin, but nobody could ever put it in the chapel, so it was decided to leave the coffin outside; and you should know that, truly, the body did not lie in the coffin because as soon as it was put there, it was stolen and taken away, whether by God or by the devil, we do not know which."]

The religious man's avowal of ignorance leaves a doubt as to the true nature of Merlin, which resurfaces, at least indirectly, when dealing with Arthur's conception. This, as the priest specifies, was made possible "par l'art de Merlin" (730.1) [through Merlin's art]. He states once again that "fu li rois Artus conceüs en pechié" (732.4–5) [King Arthur was conceived in sin], establishing an explicit link between the exceptional circumstances of Arthur's genesis and the site's collapse.

The etiologic character, gained here by the tale of Arthur's genesis, draws a comment from the narrator, who associates the transformations undergone by the Arthurian landscape with the qualities of the Knights of the Round Table:

> Josephes nos tesmoigne que les samblances des illes se muoient por les diverses aventures qui par le plaisir de Dieu i avenoient. Et si ne plout mie as chevaliers tant la queste des aventures s'il nes trovassent si diverses, kar quant il avoient esté en une forest ou en une ille ou il avoient trové aucone aventure, se il i revenoient autrefoiz, si troveroient il reces ou chastiaus et aventures d'autre maniere, que la paine

ne li travaus ne lor anuiast, et por ce que Dieus voloit que la tere fust confermee de la Novele Loi. (*HLG* 732.17–734.2)

[Joseph testifies to us that the islands' appearances changed according to the different adventures that were happening, thanks to God's will. And the quest for adventures would not have pleased the knights as much if they did not find the places so different, because when they had been in a forest or on an island where they found some adventure, when they came back some other time, they would then find hideouts and castles and other kinds of adventures, so the difficulty and labor would not bore them, and because God wanted the land to be confirmed by the New Law.]

Similar to the fluctuating appearances that allowed for the king's conception to take place,[24] then, are the islands' appearances, "les samblances des illes" which "se muoient por les diverses aventures." The tale, even when corroborated by its historical source Joseph—and, ultimately, by its true guarantor, God, who willed the adventures—remains a "semblance" that calls for both an annotation and a theological justification (here the instauration of the New Law by Arthur's knights).

The same reflection on the "semblance" and on Merlin's and Arthur's problematic conceptions are found at the core of the *Suite du Roman de Merlin*, also called *Suite Huth*, the sequel to Merlin's tale that appears to delight in multiplying tales of troublesome origins (Mordret, Tor). By reprising at length the tale of Arthur's conception at the beginning of a text expected to establish a link between *Merlin* and the *Lancelot*, the author interrogates the status of truth and lies, of interiority and exteriority,[25] of above and beyond,[26] of revelation and secret.[27] The tale is told twice: first for the benefit of Arthur, intermingling direct discourse details with a third-person narration reserved for summaries, then for Igraine with the king in the role of an informed reader. Arthur feigns discovering the tale for the first time: "Li rois fait samblant qu'il soit trop courechiés de ceste parole" (*SRM* 29.11–12) [The king pretends to be utterly shocked by these words]; "Li rois fait semblant que il tiegne la chose a moult grant miervelle" (*SRM* 30.1–2) [The king pretends to find this thing a very great wonder]. The role of semblance in the king's conception and its deceitful character are mentioned on more than one occasion: "Adont li conte par quel decevanche il jut a li premierement" (*SRM* 20.9–10) [And then he tells him through which deception he first slept with her]; "Et tout ensi que vous en avés esté decheus, fu vostre mere decheue par samblance le nuit que vous fustes engenrés" (*SRM* 22.27–30) [And in the same way you have been deceived, your mother was deceived through a false appearance the night you were conceived].

In a tale where Merlin is designated, exceptionally for the Arthurian corpus, on several occasions as the son of the devil,[28] the tale of Arthur's origins—which underscores its political[29] and ontological[30] values—is provided by Merlin, who can alter his appearance at will (*SRM* 22.27–30) and who, to prove his tale's veracity to Igraine, appears "en sa samblance vraie" (*SRM* 30.47–48) [in his true semblance]. This provides a clear example of the paradox that lies within the books of the Grail, of the fundamental otherness and strangeness constitutive of Arthurian romance. Better yet, by establishing a link between the origins and downfall of the Arthurian world, the writing of the *Suite Huth* provides its own justification and praises active reading: that which looks to discover "la samblance vraie" behind the prophet's numerous transformations. Merlin thus becomes the perfect representative of this protean genre. Through their paradoxical nature, Grail romances epitomize the otherness of fiction intruding within history. These issues are not specific to Grail romances: they are developed in other Arthurian romances. However, in these (mostly verse) romances that do not deal with the "high matter" of the Grail,[31] the role of fiction gains a different legitimacy, regardless of (or rather playing with) Merlin's troubled origins.

The Art of Fiction

While generally discreet regarding Merlin's conception, and very discreet regarding the pretense that allows for Arthur's conception, the verse romances that allude to it do so in an indirect manner or sometimes through a clear mode of deception. This is the case in Heldris of Cornwall's *Roman de Silence*, which grants its eponymous heroine a scene where, in Merlin's presence, she exposes the circumstances of Arthur's conception. As expected, she insists on the mutations of form, but she adds a new element by introducing herself as a descendant of Duke Gorlois (Gorlains) of Cornwall, who died by Merlin's hand. While the genealogy is credible—through her mother, Silence is the granddaughter of Duke Reynald of Cornwall—the murder accusation is but a pretext. Both the reader and Merlin are well aware of it, since the narrator specifies that "Silences dant Merlin enguie" (v. 6158) [Silence lies to Sir Merlin], but also that "Merlins ne se fait gaires morne, / Qu'il set ja bien u li viers torne" (vv. 6159–60) [Merlin is not really worried, because he already knows how things will turn out].[32] Silence's accusations are refuted by the immediate context—she is addressing an overly bloated Merlin, who ate and drank without moderation[33]—and by the incongruousness of her denouncing the change of appearance, since she is dressed as a knight at this point. Merlin's position clearly points to the tale's conclusion, which the narrator's restrained expression "set ja bien u li vers torne" overtly highlights. He must reestablish the truth amid the tissue of lies created by Silence's false declarations (diversely justified) and by the inflammatory—and poorly named—Queen Euphemia.

This succession of truth and lies is presented by the author as the actual substance of his story when he alludes to a hypothetical Latin source, which he promises to follow loyally while still playing with the truth for the benefit of his text: "Jo ne di pas que n'i ajoigne / Avoic le voir sovent mençoigne / Por le conte miols acesmer" (vv. 1663–65) [I am not saying that I will not add quite a few lies to the truth so the tale can be better]. The tale's ornamentation contains a considerable quantity of lies, or fiction. The play that exists with the myths of the foundation of the Arthurian world retold by a disguised minstrel provides a perfect illustration of such a notion.

The play with the tale of Arthur's genesis can be found in another work relatively marginal to the Arthurian corpus, *Le Chevalier aux Deux Épées*, written in the first third of the thirteenth century. In this verse work, Meriadeuc's coronation offers an occasion to fix the representation of an ancient world, thanks to the advent of the king the text designates as "li rois noviel" (v. 12316), in perfect symmetry with "li rois Artus" who opened the preceding verse (v. 12315).[34] This idea of succession is materialized through the coat worn by the queen depicting the king's conception:

S'estoit portrais tous li mantiaus:
Comment Merlins Uter mua
Sa face; et comment il sambla
Le conte Gorloÿs de chiere
Et de vois; et en quel maniere
L'avoit por son seignor tenu
Ygerne; et comment engendrés fu

> Li boins Artus a Tingaguel;
> Et comment ele fist puis duel
> Des nouviels ki la nuit vinrent,
> Car son seignor por ocis tinrent
> Cil ki de l'estor escaperent. (vv. 12188–99)

[The coat was fully illustrated: how Merlin transformed Uther's face; and how his face and voice looked like Count Gorlois; and how Igraine had mistaken him for her husband; and how the good Arthur had been conceived in Tintagel; and how she was afterwards plunged into mourning by the news that came that night, since her husband was considered to be dead by those who had escaped the fight.]

By insisting on both the metamorphosis and the murder that allowed for the birth of the famous king, the new queen's coronation robe denounces through its very fabric the basis on which the Arthurian rule was founded.

Another ill-conceived court succeeds this one, founded by Bleheri's son, homonym to the *famosus fabulator* mentioned by Gerald of Wales,[35] who avenges the murder of his father by Gawain, the king's cherished nephew. The murder of Bleheri (who also happens to be the source evoked by the first two continuations of *Perceval*)[36] signals the end of the time of Arthurian heroes, a fact once again highlighted in *Le Chevalier aux Deux Épées* by the coat depicting Arthur's exploits: "Et furent ou mantel portrait / Et les proeces et li fait / K'Artus fist dusqu'au jor de lores" (vv. 12203–5) [And on the coat were depicted the prowesses and feats that Arthur had accomplished until that day]. This "jor de lores" takes on a dual meaning through the aptly named Queen Lore, who celebrates both her nuptials and her coronation on this very day. The pun is relayed through the succession of verses with the third-person feminine pronoun that immediately follow, beginning with "Et ele avoit les treces sores" (v. 12206) [And she had blond braids], even though its antecedent, "La dame ke on devoit / Coroner" (vv. 12177–78) [The lady that was to be crowned], is found twenty-eight verses before it. The narrator once again rhymes the name of the heroine with a temporal adverb at the close of his tale, associating the passing of time with the names of his new heroes.

The tale of Arthur's conception is evoked again in a late thirteenth-century romance, *Claris et Laris*, where a mysterious voice reveals to

Brandalis that he has missed his opportunities to free Laris, who was prisoner of Tallas, King of Denmark, by not asking Merlin how to liberate his friend. The voice identifies Merlin as "cil qui le roy Artus fist" [he who made King Arthur], juxtaposing the king's advent with his conception, both ensured by the prophet:

> C'est cil qui le roy Artus fist,
> C'est cil qui l'espee tramist
> Au perron dont fu receüz
> Et par Bretaingne retenuz.
> Merlins fist la roonde table,
> Merlins fu mestre connestable
> Roys Pandragon veraiement,
> Merlins set bien confaitement
> Li roys Artus fu engendrez. (vv. 22245–53)[37]

[He is the one who made King Arthur, he is the one who put the sword in the stone, thanks to which he was accepted by and committed to Britain. Merlin made the Round Table, he was really master constable to King Pendragon, Merlin knows well how King Arthur was conceived.]

Though the reference to the conception is but mere allusion here, Arthur clearly appears through the discourse of a voice seemingly from nowhere, recalling one of Merlin's creatures. The origins of the king are as mysterious as the voice that takes on the task of revealing the secret of his birth.

It is remarkable that such an allusive game regarding the origins of the Arthurian world is found in a story that assumes wholeheartedly its status as fiction. While numerous twelfth- and thirteenth-century authors strive to blur the boundaries between history and fiction, the author of *Claris et Laris* declares without reservation that he has no claim to historical truth:

> Le voir dire ne m'est pas sains,
> Martyr seroie, non pas sains,
> Car en voir dire apertement
> N'a fors que tristece et torment;
> De ceus qui or sont maintenant,
> Ne puis faire conte avenant,
> Se je vueill dire verité.

Pour ce me vient en volenté
De dire, qu'on ne m'en repraigne,
Des aventures de Bretaigne. (vv. 79–88)

[Truthtelling would not do me any good: I would be a martyr, and not healthy, for in telling the truth openly, there is nothing but pain and torment; I could not tell a pleasant story about those who live nowadays, if I were to tell the truth. That is why I have had the wish to tell—and no one should criticize me for it—the adventures of Britain.]

This choice of fiction over history appears as a form of victory for the devil inside the history of the kings of Britain. The strange tale of origins that historians and Latin writers have regarded with suspicion has become, in less than a century, the perfect fabric for romance—and this narrative universe is more and more openly a world where semblance and deception are a game both writers and readers are willing to play.

Since the first historians opened up a space for exploring the characters of Merlin and Arthur, the stories of Britain have rested on shaky ground. The malaise that surrounds Merlin's conception and, to a lesser degree, that of the British kings, offers an opportunity to adopt a singular position for both truth and fiction. The level of truthfulness granted to the tale in its various retellings allows the demarcation of specific narrative spaces for historians and romancers alike, and allows romancers to characterize their choice of prose or verse according to their relationship with truth. However, these tales-within-a-tale—whether embroidered in a coronation robe or indirectly evoked by a mysterious voice—are a clear demonstration of how the genre established itself on the porous boundary that exists between history and fable. By associating the genesis of the Arthurian world with what psychoanalysts justly refer to as "family romance," Britain's historians opened the way for a new form that finds itself, to paraphrase a title that lived its glory days in the seventies,[38] at the origins of the novel.

8

Melly and Merlin

Locating Little Voices in Paris BnF fr. 24432

JAMES R. SIMPSON

In Jehan de Saint-Quentin's version of the exemplary verse narrative *Merlin Mellot*, a peasant gathering firewood in the forest for market is unable to keep up with his neighbor who returns fully laden to town.[1] Despairing, he laments his situation and is answered by a voice that identifies itself as Merlin, promising to help him on condition the peasant will honor his newfound patron by helping the poor with his new wealth and by providing an annual report on his good works. Delighted, the peasant agrees and returns home to find himself miraculously made rich by a found treasure. As the years pass, the peasant, whose name is revealed to be Renier, asks more favors for himself and his family: noble marriage for his daughter, high ecclesiastical office for his son. He himself becomes the local provost. However, Renier cares nothing for the poor and grows arrogant and disdainful of his protector as he tires of the annual meetings. Honoring him initially as "my lord Merlin" (in Jehan's version "mon seigneur Merlin," vv. 55, 91, 94, 98), the peasant's language becomes increasingly disrespectful, sliding from "sire Merlin" (v. 110) in the second year to "Merlin" *tout court* in the third and finally "Mellot" (vv. 156, 157) with the diminutive *-ot*, the nearest and neatest English equivalent being "Melly." Weary of his insolence and ingratitude, Merlin curses Renier. The peasant's wife and children die, and he himself is stripped of office and wealth, perishing in poverty shortly after.

Merlin Mellot (perhaps more illuminatingly rendered as *When Merlin Became "Melly"*) survives in two versions.[2] The earlier and more elegant—cast in suavely worked octosyllabic couplets thought worthy of Gautier de Coinci—is contained in the first *Vie des Pères*.[3] Jehan's later version, which will be the principal focus here, is cast in alexandrines grouped in monorhymed quatrains. This text survives in one manuscript: Paris BnF fr. 24432, a mid-fourteenth-century miscellany of eighty-six pieces.[4] The various items, the majority attested elsewhere, include pious and religious works, as well as comic and satirical materials.[5] *Merlin Mellot* appears alongside twenty-one exempla in the same form, most of which are dedicated to the Virgin Mary.[6] The identity and status of their author, who names himself as Jehan de Saint-Quentin at the end of *Le Dit du chevalier et de l'escuier* (v. 221), has been a matter of some discussion, Edmond Faral being of the opinion that he was a *clerc* rather than a jongleur.[7] This view is contested by Joseph Morawski on various grounds: the echoes of chansons de geste, the use of proverbs, the somewhat lurid cast of some of the tales, and the absence of traces of clerical culture or reference to Latin sources.[8] B. Munk Olsen suggests that Jehan may in fact designate himself as a *clerc* in *Le Dit du petit juitel*, although this depends on his own reconstruction of a corrupt verse in the manuscript. Such features and indications render it unclear which literary domain Jehan is most at home in.

Perhaps reflective of the crossroads position of its author, *Merlin Mellot*'s focus on the values we should rightly accord matters worldly or spiritual is apparent from the outset, with the tale's prologue bewailing the overweening folly aroused in some by worldly wealth lent to them by God (vv. 1–4). In keeping with this premise, when Merlin takes pity on Renier, he asks him whether, if rescued from poverty, he will serve God and love the poor (vv. 47–48). Significantly, the first gift Renier receives from Merlin is a direction to a hoard of coins (vv. 50–52), a discovery or *inventio* that, in parallel with Christ's parable of the talents (Matthew 25:14–30; Luke 19:12–27), figures the importance of divine grace as both a miraculous favor and a call to embrace with wholehearted sincerity the economic and spiritual munificence of charity: the sense that to be invested with love entails a duty to express and share it. In response to the peasant's effusive thanks and protestations of faithful devotion, Merlin instructs him to return in a year to render an account of himself and his estate ("De toi, de ton estat, le conte me rendras," v. 60), an obligation in which value and expression go hand in hand.

In keeping with this volume's exploration of interiority and alterity, Jehan's version of *Merlin Mellot* highlights a nexus of issues associated with religious and social attitudes, as well as material and textual cultures, in a manner that draws together a range of different but complementary

Others Within. Its unfolding dialogue between socially mobile peasant and small, hopping voice shapes into a rich vignette of relations between voice, subjectivity, and the body foregrounded in the internalization—successful or otherwise—and expression of religious values. The central and recurring contrast between spiritual and worldly treasures highlights the possibilities for change and conversion that go with giving vibrant testimony to precious truths taken to heart. Moreover, Renier's rise and fall is indexical of differences within medieval Christianity, not least with regard to those whose status was more precarious or marginal.[9] In this respect medieval peasants found themselves not entirely part of Christendom, subsisting as "little people" relegated to a dehumanized marginality of provincial superstition and illiteracy.[10] Accordingly, the role of Merlin reminds us that integrating what was revered in rural corners into the collective currency of a broader church could be problematic, as is apparent from various studies of local cults.[11] In this context, the growing popularity of the cult and name of the Virgin as a singular, transcendent focus offered the possibility that individuals in different places could both unite against the scepticism and insults of outsiders and offer fewer hostages to fortune in terms of their own observance.[12] Accordingly, while medieval Jews were extensively scapegoated as "doubters or offenders" against Mary, *Merlin Mellot* explores the problems associated with "enemies within" whose spiritual allegiance was superficial.[13]

Such concerns are directly apparent in *Merlin Mellot*'s handling of its ungrateful protagonist. Unlike in the majority of Jehan's works, where Mary appears as an intercessor and protector, Renier is assigned as spiritual patron and gatekeeper a figure associated with profane narrative and the pagan arts of prophecy whose name just happens to begin in much the same way as the Virgin's, a coincidence underscored by the work's alliterative title. At another level, Merlin acts as a cipher for Jehan's incorporation of tropes and voices associated with other genres. However, if any talismanic invocation is to be diminished and trafficked here, it will not be that of Mary. This dialectic between valuing and debasement is also apparent in the thematicized treatment of precious objects. Merlin's injunction to Renier to turn his new wealth to charitable use appears thus as the kernel of a transformative dynamic with the potential to make itself felt beyond the individual tale. Its account of the capacity of riches to betoken something beyond base coin forms a counterpart to Jehan's didactic mobilization of his unlikely characters in a manner that reflects beyond his particular œuvre, thereby perhaps also serving to enhance the aura of BnF fr. 24432 as a trove of spiritual and literary treasures.

Internalizing Voices in Jehan's *Merlin Mellot*

A key means of foregrounding the relation to Others Within in the versions of *Merlin Mellot* lies in their borrowing and internalization of other literary voices. Thus, the playful relation to chivalric literatures evident in the octosyllabic version of *Merlin Mellot* contained in the *Vie des Pères* can be gleaned from the narrator's sardonically pithy rebuke of human vanity: "cuidons bien que par nos bobans / valoir mex que ne fist Rolans" (vv. 18278–79) [in our foolish pride we think ourselves more worthy than Roland]. Here the rhyming of the derisive "bobans" with the name of a great epic hero sets the tone for a cautionary tale in which the peasant lauds his daughter in terms that call to mind Enide's father in Chrétien de Troyes's romance, with his reprisal of the popular song line "C'est mes solaz, c'est mes confors" (v. 18617) [She is my solace, she is my comfort]. Jehan's monorhymed quatrains seem bound to a less suave, more insistently repetitive aesthetic.[14] However, here Jehan seems to exploit an ostensibly pedestrian form as a springboard for elegance and spry humor. Contrasting with the more abrupt "once-upon-a-time" introductions to his other tales, the tale's opening reflection on worldly vanity segues into an apostrophe of Fortune down from whose wheel the narrator glides neatly into the body of his narrative ("De ceste proverbe ci *descendrai sur* .ii. hommes," v. 15, my emphasis). By this move, Jehan neatly allies and identifies himself with the birdlike Merlin.

The centrality of expressive speech is apparent from the fact that Merlin singles out the peasant as an object of charitable pity and concern because his prayer-lament (vv. 31–40) is principally structured around anxieties for his family and for his ass (v. 33). In that sense, Merlin accords the *asnier* the possibility of wealth that would make him a new Saint Nicholas, the patron to whom the peasant initially addresses his prayer: "Diex! Que porrai je faire, sire saint Nicolas?" (v. 31) [O God, o Saint Nicholas, what will I do?]. Indeed, this identification seems to present a means by which the marginal figure of Merlin (found in the forest in the manner of the *Lai de l'oiselet*) can be legitimately internalized or translated into the cult of saints through the potential good deeds of his protégé. Thus, Merlin's sympathetic identification with the peasant implies a parallelism: both figures are in their own ways marginal or external to Christian community and culture.

However, as a sign of things to come, neat transitions and the bonds of fellow feeling are shortly counterpointed by a series of jarring notes. Renier's ornamenting of his effusive gratitude with a superficially pious evocation of the miracle of Cana—"Je vous commant a Dieu, qui de l'yaue fist vin" (v. 56) [I commend you to God, who made wine out of water]—raises a question about the genuineness of his own miraculous conversion, a caution hinted at in Merlin's understatedly ominous farewell: "or y parra comment te maintiendras" (v. 57) [we'll see how you get on]. The oafish peasant's flat-footedness is likewise apparent in the infuriatingly enigmatic laugh with which he greets his wife on return home from his forest encounter: "Le vilain li a ris, qui n'en fu pas rentiers. / Quant elle le vit rire, a poi que n'est dervee" (vv. 64–65) [The peasant laughed and wasn't shy about it. / When she saw him laughing, she nearly went mad].[15]

The questions apparent in the tale's opening scenes pave the way for a drama of spiritual transformation, but one that goes in the opposite direction to what might have been hoped. In that regard, Merlin's comment on the ultimate resurgence of Renier's base nature, "Ton fel cuer orgueilleus plus celer ne se pot" (v. 169) [Your vicious and prideful heart could no longer conceal itself], is also foregrounded through animal imagery. If *asnier* is to ass as *chevalier* is to *cheval*, this is not to say that the peasant is necessarily an ass any more than a knight is a horse. However, the ass is one externalized expression of the peasant's nature, a thing advancing before him: "ton asne devant toi" (v. 163) [your ass before you]. Likewise, in his pride Renier dismisses his neighbor as a "vilain mastin" (v. 108) [peasant cur], a construction that in context leaves one wondering which one is in apposition to the other. This insult returns in both Merlin's cursing of the peasant's dog-in-the-manger hard-heartedness—"la seconde annee fu ton cuer si mastin" (v. 167) [the second year, your heart was hardened like a cur's]—echoed in the narrator's concluding comparison of the uncharitable to dogs (vv. 213–16).

Jehan's mapping of the relation of human to animal counterpoints comparable ambiguities he reveals in the construction of human community. Merlin's instruction that the peasant serve God through charity toward the poor (vv. 46–48) responds to and redeems Renier's vision of the family as an additional burden that disadvantages him relative to his unmarried, childless neighbor ("cil qui n'ot nulz enfanz," v. 25). In that sense, the central problem in the tale of individuals caught up in an economic competition centered on the town may reflect changing attitudes to social cohesion. At one level, our peasant appears as a classic embodiment of rural precarity. As Miri Rubin notes, in earlier rural communities, the consequences of having a substantial proportion of the population at subsistence level almost necessarily fostered an awareness of interdependence, the "poor" in this context being the small freeholders who found themselves without the support and protection of these communal networks.[16] However, as town-centered trade activity became more prominent in the central Middle Ages, this social landscape atomized and absolute material poverty became a more visible and pressing source of concern.[17] That fragmentation is clearly apparent here through Jehan's picture of day-to-day struggle in which the peasant's neighbor appears first as an economic competitor and then later as a despised inferior.[18]

Jehan's perspective seems not so much trapped in older models of social justice as self-consciously nostalgic. Charity begins at home, the community thereby conceived of as an extended kin network. However, at this point the poem's moral logic seems rather less straightforward:

> Cel an tout coiement belement s'esleverent;
> Mais onques pour ce Dieu ne povre plus n'amerent.
>
> L'anier par couverture, le mois au bois ala.
> Une foiz quant fu riche, chascun forment l'ama:
> Tel ne li apartint qui cousin le clama.
> Au chief de l'an aprés a la vois retourna;
>
> Ainsi est il du monde a la journee d'ui:
> Car le povrë homs n'est conneü de nului,
> Mais quant il devient riche, maint s'en viennent a lui
> Qui lui dient: "Cousin, de vo lignage sui." (vv. 79–88)

[That year they quietly raised themselves up very nicely, but did not love God or the poor on account of it. For a while, the ass-driver kept going to the wood by way of a cover. When he became rich, everyone loved him, and people who were nothing to do with him would call him cousin. At the end of the following year he returned to the voice. That's the way of the world these days: nobody wants to know a poor man, but when he becomes rich, many come to him and say, "Cousin, I'm of your line."]

Given that our peasant is about to be damned for his contemptuous treatment of the poor, it seems inconsistent that the narrator shows him beset with fair-weather scroungers posing as kith and kin. However, one way of construing the narratorial reflection here is as a bird's-eye view of the road traveled in the course of that year from servile but either superficial or short-lived gratitude to complacently weary arrogance. In that sense, the parallelism between false sentiment and false family is readily apparent: the importuning of the latter offers an externalized translation of the former. Jehan's presentation here dramatizes how the base Renier's social promotion places him at a social and discursive crossroads, newly acquired treasure and newly acquired language—albeit of the wrong kind—going hand in hand. What is missing here is the relation between charitable giving and social capital, its surplus dimension of enlightened self-interest.[19] It is precisely this truth the peasant seems unable to grasp, his avarice a misunderstanding of the relation between actual and social capital fundamental to the feudal system as Jehan presents it. The peasant appears to suffer from an imaginative poverty that is caught between past and present, trapped either in the mode of the isolated small freeholder or that of the new urban poor. In that absence of understanding, the narrator usurps the place of the peasant's voice.

In such a complex universe of spiritual, material, and literary interdependence, it pays to tread carefully. However, while Jehan's narratorial "footwork" appears deftly assured, the same cannot be said of the peasant on whom he descends. In keeping with what Morawski attributes to a lack of subtlety, the clod-hopping peasant's riding roughshod over the conventions of deference is compounded by a literal trampling that adds injury to insult: Merlin finds himself forced to perch on a tree branch to escape the hooves of Renier's horse.

Le vilain, qui nul bien ne nul honour ne sot,
Quant l'an si fu passez, au plus tot que il pot
Monte sur .i. cheval, .ii. serjants o li ot:
Au bois s'en est venuz, si apella Mellot.

> Par grant outrecuidance Mellot l'a appellé;
> La voiz saut sur .i. arbre, si à lui a parlé.
> Le vilain li a dist: "Pourquoi es haut monté?"
> "Pour ce que ton cheval m'éust tost defoulé." (vv. 153–60)

> [When the year had passed, as soon as he could, the peasant—ignorantly devoid of any notion of good or honor as he was—got on a horse and took two men at arms with him. He went to the wood and called for "Melly." Out of impertinent pride he called him Melly. The voice leapt up into a tree, and he spoke to it. The peasant said to it, "Why have you climbed so high?" "Because your horse would have trampled me otherwise."]

Here the accent is probably on the rider's poor control of the animal rather than the beast itself: *asnier* rather than *chevalier*, the peasant appears irredeemably flat-footed, whether in his speech or in locomotion. In what may be an element of grotesque overkill, Renier is incapable of merely "trampling" Merlin verbally—for him, there is no such thing as "just a metaphor."

The sense that Jehan's vision of the social universe in *Merlin Mellot* might carry with it an element of nostalgia is reinforced by consideration of the text's literary resonances. The peasant appears at the fringes of a quasi-epic universe of feuding and the economic consequences: he is impoverished through having to support his feudal superior. However, instead of accumulating the social and spiritual capital that goes with the exercise of charity, he allows his relentless self-seeking to cause his undoing. His lack of popularity, his failure to earn the love of the people he manages, is a key factor in prompting his lord, returning home from war, to call in his debts. Here once again the tale's internalizing appropriation of epic overtones plays a crucial role:

> Son seignour terrien un autre guerre guerroia:
> Son meuble y despendi, dont moult li anuia.
>
> Quant sa guerre ot finee, si li failli deniers;
> Ses celiers trouva vuis et trestous ses greniers.
> Lors li fu endité que son prevost Reniers
> Si en avoit asséz, mais n'estoit pas maniers

De faire courtoisie a nului ne bonté.
Le sire respondi: "Du mien est haut monté.
Il n'a pas de mes rentes s'anee a moi conté
Mais je l'avrai tost, s'il me plaist, desmonté."

Le sire le manda, mil livres li requist.
Le vilain respondi, voiant touz, et li dist
Qu'il n'avoit nus deniers, que ailleurs en querist.
Le sire fu dolant quant il le contredist.

Car il li toli tout, meubles et heritages.
Quant ce voit le vilain a poi que il s'esrage;
Car il li toli tout, et rentes et mainnages. (vv. 183–99)

[His earthly lord fought another war and spent his wealth on it, which was a great burden to him. When his war was over, he was short of money. He found his cellars and granaries all empty. Then someone said that although his provost Renier had plenty, it was not his nature to show courtesy or goodness to anyone. The lord replied, "He has done very well for himself on the back of what is mine. He has given me no account of my rents this year, though I could take him down a peg and quickly too if I saw fit." The lord summoned him and demanded a thousand livres. In front of everyone, the peasant answered him and said that he did not have any money and he should look elsewhere. The lord was aggrieved when he spoke against him. For he took everything from him—property and inheritances. When the peasant saw this, he nearly went mad with rage, for he took everything from him—rents and movables.]

At this point in the narrative, Jehan's use of the quatrain form becomes distinctly varied and lively, with syntactic structures continuing across the break and concluding in the following stanza (see notably vv. 188–89). This use of run-on in preceding stanzas adds weight to the lord's reaction. The apparent stop at the end of verse 195 renders neatly the pin-drop silence following the provost's unfortunate refusal, as the narrator's gleeful repetition in the next stanza renders the whirlwind dispossession that follows.

The picture Jehan paints of the moment shows a reduced use of direct speech compared to the earlier exchanges between the peasant and

Merlin.[20] In those exchanges, the peasant's increasingly discourteous address was made dramatically apparent in the lively back-and-forth between the two protagonists. By comparison, the exchange between lord and peasant is viewed from more of a distance. One possible reading here—apart from the consideration that there are some conversations we might be grateful not to be too much in the middle of—is that the audience has heard enough from the uncouth Renier to understand that his blunt refusal might offend not merely by fact but also by a delivery that mirrors his thoughtless insolence to his supernatural forest patron.

Complementing the nods to romance in the *Vie des Pères* version, Jehan's nimble and creative use of epic lends weight to a feudalized view of the economy of salvation in which all worldly goods are ultimately on loan from God. This scene of a village provost refusing to render what his Caesar claims as his due recalls the counsel scenes of works such as the *Chanson de Roland*. The peasant speaks against his lord ("contredist," v. 196) like Roland against Charlemagne—"En piez se drecet, si li vint cuntredire" (*Chanson de Roland*, v. 195) [(He) rises to his feet and comes forward to voice his opposition]—and then, when summarily dispossessed, goes mad with rage like Ganelon.[21] Indeed, the suggestion that the lord look to Renier as his provost could read as an echo of Roland's suggestion of Ganelon as emissary to Marsile.[22] In a work where one of the main protagonists is a disembodied voice with a literary name, the suggestion's emergence as a mysteriously unattributed whisper in the circle of counsellors implies there may be some gleefully Merlinesque ventriloquism at work. Similarly, Jehan's emphasis on the agent of Renier's misfortune being his temporal lord ("seignour terrien," v. 183) belies the measure in which his detailed commentary on worldly interests echoes Merlin's original injunction to the peasant to provide a yearly account of his good works. His summary dismissal and dispossession thereby also reads implicitly as a ringing damnation at a spiritual level, such that where Merlin arguably served as a surrogate for Mary, keeping her safe from profanation, so now Merlin can delegate much of the rougher bailiff work to secular agents. The role of other voices within this concluding crushing is apparent from the additional weight provided by the scene's epic resonances, supplementing the cosmic symmetry of pattern and movement that saw the narrator swing down from Fortune's wheel at the start of the tale.

Jehan's Rough Polyphony

Merlin Mellot's mix of coarse and courteous is mirrored elsewhere in Jehan's works, its gruff music forming a counterpart to the salutary bluntness of tough love characteristic of Marian devotional discourse and its related exemplary material. In such contexts, frankness of expression is not invariably an evil, but may paradoxically carry sincere concern at its heart. In the context of other works attributed to Jehan, *Merlin Mellot* thus offers a neat counterpoint to stories such as *Le Dit de l'enfant qui sauva sa mere*, in which a concerned son urges his mother to confess and pray. Here, speech appears as the goading of the recalcitrant body in service of the interests of the soul (all emphases mine): "Se moriez *sans langue* ce seroit honte à vous" (v. 91) [If you die *without speaking* (lit., without tongue), it will be to your shame]. Right through, the drama is emphatically centered on the dynamic and tone of expression and speech. Initially hectoring, the son's genuine anxiety emerges in his gentleness: "En plorant li a dit, *dolant et corrouciez*" (v. 94) [Weeping he said to her, *aggrieved and angered*]; "Lors li dist *doucement*" (v. 101) [Then he said *gently* to her]; "A tant le premier mot si dist *moult doucement*" (v. 137) [From the first word, he spoke *gently* to her]. The truth of this urging is affirmed in the mother's apparition after her death, again speaking gently, but also calling for him to speak to her: "Quant vint au chief de l'an, trestout certainement / La borjoise revint à son fil proprement, / Plus blanche que fleur; si li dist *doucement*: / 'Biaus fils, *parole à moi*. Je n'ai mal ne tourment'" (vv. 157–60) [When it came to the end of the year, then truly the burgess came back to her son cleansed, whiter than a flower, and said to him *gently*: "Fair son, *speak to me*. I am neither in pain nor torment"].

Here the mother's gentle imperative appears as the exact contrary of Renier: unlike the grudging and ungrateful peasant, she returns with due propriety to her son in obedience with the cycle of the year. This sense of events taking their place in the microcosmic mirror of larger cycles frames the lesson that the sometimes blunt conversations of this world are sweetened by their place in a pattern; what springs from love is part of a necessary preparation for a true reciprocity beyond the mortal coil.

The scenario of desperate appeal in moments of spiritual peril figures throughout Jehan's tales, voice and spirituality struggling with their confinement in the estranging prison of the body. Accordingly, in other tales people are either being strangled, silenced, or bursting out with truths that can no longer be contained, a dynamism underscored in the chant-like pounding of the monorhymed stanza, its insistence a nagging alien presence in the narrative.

In that respect, Jehan's dramatic situations reflect ambiguities and ambivalences in medieval attitudes to the voice, hovering between ethereal, soulful beauty and base braying, between stern intervention and suave persuasion.[23] Mirroring more recent conceptualizations of its "uncanny" (*unheimlich*) dimension, voice appears here as both a remainder of the body in language and—in parallel with psychoanalytical conceptions that have considerable bearing on the medieval texts examined here—an Other within ourselves.[24] In Jehan's vision of duty to the good of the soul, Renier's clumsy mishandling forms an important contrapuntal element, a displaced reminder of what might be characterized as the traumatic unmannerliness of spiritual witness and intervention. If Renier is in some measure like an ass, this is perhaps a sign we should remember Balaam.

Such considerations also have inevitable bearing on authorial stance. As Anna Drzewicka notes, "vocality appears as an invasive cliché in the written sphere, becoming bound up with the writer's function and persona."[25] Such an aesthetic is part of a strategy of outreach, as is apparent in the literary play the *Vie des Pères*'s narrator shares with his audience. In effect, the peasant becomes a problematic scapegoat for the text's own internalization of the romance motifs it puts into his mouth. Thus, although the text incorporates profane literary elements to woo an audience it thereby looks to flatter, it does so at the price of questions begged regarding the ethics of this double operation and its underlying disavowals. How can the subaltern peasantry speak in Christian culture and what does this literature want them to say? When viewed this way, the *Vie des Pères*, although undeniably sophisticated, starts to look a little smug. In that regard, the contrast between its and Jehan's versions of *Merlin Mellot* raises—perhaps quite knowingly—important questions about the role and ethics of moralizing literature. What relations do works of this kind establish between author and discursively impoverished audience? What does it want them to say and what script does it give them to follow? The logic of Jehan's version is readily apparent, its concern—reflected in its extended monorhymes—less to do with literary grandstanding than with getting the penitent to say and feel the right thing. This pricking aesthetic of metrical and spiritual *agenbite* points reassuringly in one direction: it prompts for the one utterance efficacious when all else fails. Yet, in spite of the seemingly greater emphasis on fellow-feeling, Jehan's peasant remains a butt of literary jokes, his braying an irreducibly dissonant note within the noble harmony of Christian community.

Conclusions

> Qui sert Nostre Dame, cele dame d'onour
> Il ne puet en ce siecle, certes, servir meillour.
>
> Jehan de Saint-Quentin dit que l'en doit servir:
> On puet de son service a grant honor venir.
> C'est le tresor de grace por tous ceulz garantir
> Qui la veillent de cuer amer et chierir. (*Du chevalier et de l'escuier*, vv. 219–24)

[Who serves Our Lady, that honorable lady, surely cannot serve a better one in this world. Jehan de Saint-Quentin says that we should serve, and that by service we accrue great honor. This guarantees the treasure of grace for all those who sincerely wish to love and cherish her.]

Jehan's sign-off at the end of *Du chevalier et de l'escuier* makes plain his vision of religious devotion as the cherishing of spiritual treasure. In similar vein, the prologue to *Le Dit qu'on clamme respon* casts Mary as "la tresoriere / de grace" (vv. 5–6) [treasurer of grace], the spiritual focus of a range of tales in which wealth hovers between the literal and the metaphorical. In keeping with this, Renier's failure to give voice to charity and love, a churlishness mirrored in his lazily arrogant refusal to honor his protector and patron by his full name, provides a key cautionary Other within a corpus rich in praise and celebration.

Although comparable constellations of theological and natural historical materials are found in other manuscripts, what is arguably distinctive in BnF fr. 24432 is its concern with the cherishing or profanation—variously through word or deed—of small objects. Thus, narratives take as the focus the Host (*Le Dit de la beguine* as well as *Le Dit du chien et du miscreant*), rings (*Le Dit des anelés*), and even nuts (*Le Dit de la nois*). In similar fashion, *Le Dit du lendit* gestures toward students' customary presentation of gifts to their tutors at the time of the Lendit fair, traditional offerings typically consisting of coins hidden inside a lemon presented in a glass.[26]

Such an insistent focus on objects fits with a popular material culture of tokens, whether in the form of stones from key sites, relic bone fragments, or other items collected in small reliquaries, hidden inside an altar or a house as a concealed *sanctum sanctorum*.[27] Such collections frequently include pieces wrapped in small parchments bearing descriptions, names, or prayers, thereby transforming the mute materials into chorales seeking and imploring intercession or protection.[28] Further exploration both of *Merlin Mellot*'s place in BnF fr. 24432 and the character of that collection more generally might look to both evidence of material culture and studies of the organization of manuscript compilations notably associated with Keith Busby.[29] In that respect, although unusual in Jehan's production, *Merlin Mellot* is certainly not isolated but finds birds of similar feather beyond Jehan's œuvre in the related narrative of the *Lai de l'oiselet*, a version of which survives in BnF fr. 24432 and which likewise explores issues of enrichment, social promotion, and identity in a troublingly dynamic economy.[30] Religious concerns similarly find a cherishing secular counterpart in texts such as *Les Divisions des .lxxii. biautés qui sont en dames*, a work shorter than its title might suggest. Moreover, my emphasis on dissonance and counterpoint in this essay could be set against the less disharmonious, but nonetheless puzzling, doubling evident in the two versions of *Le Dit des planetes* contained in the manuscript (fols. 84r–86v and 263r–65r). For now, suffice it to say that *Merlin Mellot*'s reflection on the (de)valuing of revered names could play its own rough diamond part in shedding light on conceptions of the miscellany compilation as a marshaling of literary voices in a cultural reliquary combining popular and learned, profane and sacred.

9

Sex, the Church, and the Medieval Reader

Shaping Salvation in the *Vie des Pères*

ADRIAN P. TUDOR

Hagiography sits comfortably alongside other types of narrative in the Middle Ages. Saints' Lives, short pious narratives, Virgin miracles, and religious stories of surprising variety constitute a major part of the medieval French canon. A courtly audience seeking stories of adventure, heroes, struggle, contemplation, or quest could just as easily turn to the exploits, trials, and tribulations of a saint or martyr as to those of Roland, Reynard the Fox, or Arthur. Fundamentally, a good story is a good story, a battle between good and evil likewise. The beginning of the thirteenth century was a time when the Church sought to codify the most intimate behavior of the faithful, exerting influence through the power of the confessional. Whether authors responded directly to Church directives or reflected the prevailing atmosphere, a subtle change in the nature of vernacular narratives can be sensed.

The pursuit of identity lies at the heart of many if not most such works of this period. Hagiography is in essence little different as an art form from other texts of this period. Not unlike the most famous and popular secular medieval texts, brilliant hagiography is aesthetically pleasing, morally inspiring, and psychologically realistic. Moreover, it could be argued that, more than any other textual tradition, hagiography manipulates identity.[1] There is at play a profoundly sober proselytizing schema: the skill of the hagiographer is to compose what may be labeled "literature of conversion," the purpose of which is to further the prospect of salvation of both reader and hagiographer.[2] Through the use of examples showing sinners convert into saints, authors discovered fertile ground to explore the Other Within; literary characters and legendary figures here become examples for the faithful to follow. At stake are the lives and souls of living, breathing people. The framework of pseudo-historical narrative allows for mythical figures or fictional characters to live lives of sin but, through an experience broadly labeled "conversion," to become virtuous examples to be copied and venerated.

Given the emphasis on the conversion experience, it is to be expected that authors would often focus on human shortcomings. As a consequence, the theme of sex is unsurprisingly common in hagiographical texts. It is after all humanity's Achilles heel. In the vein of many a writer before now and of the author of the text at the heart of the present study, the use of the word "sex" in my title is in some ways a trick, a hook with which to lure the reader.[3] Despite a discussion of a variety of issues and episodes selected precisely because of their carnal nature, the present study is not really about sex at all. Rather, my intention is to consider how the authors of the Old French *Vie des Pères* manipulated this subject with a view to produce a spiritual text far more interested in the souls of their audience than the actual ins and outs of their conduct. Looking at some instances in the *Vie des Pères* to study sex and salvation, I aim to explore how the theme was exploited in discussions of the Other in a Christian context. Sex in a religious work provides plentiful examples of who or what is accepted and who or what is proscribed, illegal, "other."[4] The Other in hagiography is most logically defined with reference to that which is accepted. In the *Vie des Pères* there is a constant manipulation of literary and spiritual topoi, challenging assumed and imposed identities as a commentary on the process of conversion through intertextual composition. This manipulation of identity is central to establishing the "strangeness" of marginal figures at both extremes of the Christian barometer.[5]

The *Vie des Pères* is a collection of pious tales dating from the thirteenth century. The primitive collection was twice added to, giving a total of seventy-four individual tales and more than 30,000 lines within the framework of a tripartite "collective text." This is a text of extraordinary quality.[6] It clearly enjoyed popularity in the Middle Ages, given the number of surviving manuscript witnesses (over fifty). However, the text fell somewhat out of favor as the medieval literary canon was formalized by scholars in the twentieth century.[7] This can largely be explained by the lack of a complete edition and the text's complicated manuscript tradition.[8]

As a large post-Lateran IV proselytizing collective text, its aim is precisely to shape the identity of its readers, preaching confession through the examples of its protagonists. It may well be that the *Vie des Pères* attempts to offer an alternative to the comic fabliaux. The fabliaux have often been described as negative or counter-exempla; the tales of the first *Vie des Pères* especially would then be counter-fabliaux.[9] The Other is a constant presence, whether in the form of Saracens, Jews, heretics, various and varied sinners, devils, and demons, or simply in the form of the man/woman in the street needing to make minor changes in their lives in order to please the Almighty. We also meet recipients of miracles, saints, angels, hermits, and those living well in the world, all of whom are in their own way also Other. This is a living, breathing, talking, recognizable world.

This, then, is a text with a function. At its heart is a requirement to seek out marginal figures and present them as models for the audience to follow. Men and women of virtue may in fact be wearing a mask behind which less seemly character traits prevail. Sinners may be more worthy than at first appears. As with a number of other vernacular short pious narratives—the most compelling of which are perhaps *Le Chevalier au barisel* (the twists and turns of a reluctant penitent's spiritual transformation from transgressor to sanctity), *Le Tumbeor de nostre dame* (affirmation of an individual's place in society and how this impacts those around him), and *L'Ermite et le jongleur* (a hermit's understanding of his value and role are made clear following his arrogant demand for approbation)[10]—it is the journey rather than the destination that tends to be more attractive to the reader. How that journey can involve sex provides a focus for the present study. This is not to say that sermons and descriptions of paradise were of no interest to the audience of these texts. It is widely accepted, though, that the example is the most appealing element of the lesson.[11]

The *Vie des Pères* does not shy away from sex. A collection of pious tales of this dimension could neither dismiss nor ignore it. The text is at the same time typical and atypical literature of conversion, promoting the sacrament of penance and annual auricular confession, stressing God's infinite forgiveness, while in no way dismissing the value of marital sex. In the eyes of Sarah M. White, this was a time of transition. White argues that sexuality as a theme of personal fulfillment in Old French literature belongs more to the twelfth century than later periods.[12] Eroticism evolved into a motif for interpersonal struggle with the evolution of the fabliaux. It is in this atmosphere that the author of the first *Vie des Pères* in particular composed a number of narratives dealing with individuals facing sexual temptation in a variety of situations.

What we may consider characteristically Augustinian attitudes toward sex are frequently far from obvious: worldly interests are dwarfed by the imperative of attaining salvation. The authors of the *Vie des Pères* appear to have viewed Augustinianism through the lens of Aquinas, Bernard of Clairvaux, individual experience, a sense of pragmatism, and deep personal spirituality. The confluence of cultures in which the text is rooted and examples—if not definitions—of what the authors considered marginal are nowhere more apparent than when considering sex, lust, and their relationship with salvation. Augustine taught that, however difficult it may be in practice, the faithful seeking salvation should always strive to rise above sexual desire.[13] Our text offers a more realistic lesson in this regard: within the strictures of a legally and morally proper wedding bed, sexual desire has its place in the Christian world. However, the *Vie des Pères* depends on a broad range of different sources for its subject matter. To a large extent, this may explain a number of contradictions of substance and in tone. Improper sexual activity is one sin among many that are explored, commented and advised upon, illustrated, and censured. It is the one sin surest to grab the attention of the audience.

Naturally, we witness the worst possible sins in the hinterlands of what can be pardoned in the appropriate circumstances: if ever we are to enter the minds of author and audience and discover their limits, then it is surely here. The *Vie des Pères* does a tour of such sins, as does Gautier de Coinci in his *Miracles de Nostre Dame*. The audience may be shocked and edified by—or may lap up—tales relating wicked murders, infanticide, gluttony, pride, drunkenness, ingratitude, avarice, possession, and usury. The intention was to engage with an audience of mixed backgrounds and to preach confession and conversion. Even in the first third of the thirteenth century this was not necessarily an easy sell. The inclusion of narrative elements that are variously scandalous, exciting, strange, courtly, and fabulous surely helped. In certain manuscripts, Keith Busby has suggested, there was also a "sugaring of the pill" in the form of certain *tituli* which are nothing if not *fablialesque*.[14] And of course, the confluence of literary traditions, themes, and motifs made for multiple fusions of content and form. In the right hands, the subject matter, poetic quest, spiritual intent, and openness of the audience were dynamite. The final twist to this volatile cocktail of sources and intention, already burgeoning with narrative potential, was sexual themes.

The relatively high incidence of *Vie des Pères* tales using sexual themes and motifs is significant but not unusual: fornication, adultery, prostitution, lust, and incest are the staple of moralizing and pious material of all types—sermons, miracles of the Virgin, vernacular literary texts, fabliaux, and so on. James A. Brundage sees nothing strange in an emphasis on sexual sin immediately before and after Lateran IV: this was a period of "the rethinking of doctrine and restructuring of law concerning sex."[15] Things become juicier in the *Vie des Pères* in the small number of oblique references to the potentially more serious sexual sins of sodomy, oral sex, intercourse in unnatural positions, and homosexuality, all of which were classified as *contra naturam*.[16] These are delicate issues because of their close ties with heresy. More common narrative themes are not without their interest, however. These include sexual fidelity, unwanted pregnancy, rape and attempted rape, prostitution, incest, and fornication by religious, hermits, and nuns. We encounter active and resourceful devils urging the characters to cede to desire, and a generally sympathetic divine presence. Taken as a whole, the *Vie des Pères* strongly reflects the interests of the thirteenth-century Church but also understands the concerns of the laity, that is, its readers. The author of the primitive collection—considered by scholars the best tales and widely referred to as the first *Vie des Pères*—comes across as quite a realist, willing to accept the aspirations of those living in the world and the limitations imposed by such a life. This tolerant attitude, whose influence is still felt in the two continuations, is a truly remarkable aspect of the *Vie des Pères*.

Vern L. Bullough labeled not just Christianity but Western culture as a whole a "sex-negative culture."[17] This is a neat formulation which fits our preconceptions like a glove, but taken on its own the expression ignores the complexities surrounding sexuality, Christianity, and marginality. The Church's ambiguous attitude toward sexuality was in no way a new phenomenon by the time the *Vie des Pères* was composed: the eroticism of the Song of Songs had already given rise to numerous commentaries, not least the *Sermones in Cantica* by Bernard of Clairvaux, whose attempts to reconcile the biblical text's apparently open eroticism with sacred teachings were translated into French in the twelfth century. It is not without irony that the same era that saw the development of the *fin'amor* lyric tradition into the fashionably courtly codification of love and behavior also saw the Church rise to new positions of influence. Strengthened by canon law and scholastic thought, legal and ecclesiastical norms concerning all matters sexual were established.[18] According to Gratian, there are only three conditions under which couples can safely partake of sexual intercourse, even in marriage. Brundage summarizes: "Either in order to beget a child, or to avert temptations to marital infidelity, or to accommodate the insistent (and probably sinful) demands of their spouse." Michel Raby concurs: "L'acte sexuel n'était envisageable qu'au sein d'un mariage légitime, et encore qu'à la condition expresse que cet acte soit animé uniquement par l'intention sous-jacente de procréer" [Intercourse was possible only within a legitimate marriage, and then only on the express condition that this act take place solely with the underlying intention to procreate]. All other sexual activity is sinful, including desire and arousal whether intentional or not, both in and out of wedlock. What is more, if such activity were to become publicly known, it "might be subject to criminal prosecution as well."[19] But in practice confusion seems to have abounded, as is evident from vernacular narratives of all traditions. As Raby would have it, "la liste de ces péchés, longue et fournie, constitue bien le miroir incontestable d'une réalité que l'Église n'a jamais su réellement contenir, car nier le plaisir, c'est aussi agir, en quelque sorte, contre la Nature" [the list of these sins, which is long and comprehensive, without a doubt provides an authentic window into a reality that the Church has never really been able to control, because to deny pleasure is also in some way to act against nature].[20]

By the thirteenth century marriage had become a sacrament and fell within the jurisdiction of the Church. As such it became, along with confession, a valuable weapon with which the Church could exert more control over its flock's sexuality in particular and, by extension, its overall behavior. Marriage in addition to confession is a subject regularly encountered in the *Vie des Pères*. Post Lateran IV, the double whammy of sacramental marriage and obligatory annual auricular confession, allied to the relatively new medium of effective preaching, should have placed the Church in a powerful position to police (if not enforce) the carnal habits of the faithful.[21] However, things were not quite as straightforward as Rome may have wished. Definitions of prohibited practices were not available, not attempted, or contradictory, and euphemisms or general terms abounded even in works that aimed to address directly the problem of sexual morality. It is no surprise that there was considerable ambiguity over what actually constituted a sexual sin in the Middle Ages. The term "sodomy," for example, far from being restricted to intercourse *in ano*, was frequently used to refer to any sin *contra naturam*, even though the biblical story giving rise to the term (Genesis 18–19) is anything but ambiguous.[22] The scholarship and knowledge of canon law of the authors of the new literature is one matter; exactly how and when the concerns discussed here became an issue for people reading the *Vie des Pères* and other vernacular texts is quite another. We may never know when old and new canon laws trickled down to the public that enjoyed texts such as ours. It is, however, now broadly accepted that didactic texts were indeed to the taste of audiences in the Middle Ages. The number of such texts surviving and the number of extant manuscripts, the fact that lyric poetry was never far from didacticism, the number and nature of sermons that have come down to us, roles played by preachers and lessons in a variety of other text types, the nature of medieval drama, and much other circumstantial evidence has helped build up a picture of material produced by medieval authors and consumed by medieval audiences.[23] Simon Gaunt, summarizing his chapter on hagiography in his landmark *Gender and Genre in Medieval French Literature*, makes a point too often overlooked by modern scholars. Their interest in vernacular works

> distorts their view of medieval culture. . . . the Middle Ages were deeply Christian, yet all too often students and critics of vernacular literature focus on the chivalric and courtly margins, thereby failing to appreciate the centrality of the dominant Catholic culture. The profane texts students of Old French and Occitan mostly read represent a tiny proportion of the texts produced in medieval France and Occitania. Even in the vernacular the quantity of religious texts which has survived is far greater than their availability in modern editions suggests and vernacular hagiography was at least as popular as other literary genres, if not more so. Modern views of medieval vernacular writing are skewed by the marginalization of hagiography.[24]

The explosion of literacy and the expansion of the new urban middle classes in the thirteenth century combined to provide a useful opportunity for the promulgation of Church teachings. Evelyn Birge Vitz is adamant that it was "only in the thirteenth century"—that is, as the *Vie des Pères* was being composed—"that many teachings of the Church concerning sexual ethics and other matters began to be brought to the laity," and that according to the evidence of narrative works, the faithful in the twelfth century had "only the very dimmest grasp" of the Church's attitude toward sexual morality.[25] The *Vie des Pères* must be placed within a general atmosphere of official concern with sexual matters, stoked by centuries of unease with carnal matters, now translated into concerted efforts to preach to and exert some control over the Christian world.

The stories of the *Vie des Pères* reflect the fact that sexual morality and control over even the most private aspects of daily life were pressing topics during the thirteenth century. Alain-Julien Surdel quite correctly insists that the Church's desire to manage and order the sex lives of the faithful was not necessarily motivated by a need to have power and influence in every aspect of a Christian's life, "mais aussi par un désir sincère de sauver l'homme des pièges du démon: *Diabolus in lumbis*, l'enseignement de s. Augustin est très clair" [but also by a sincere desire to save man from the devil's traps: *the Devil in the loins*, the teaching of St. Augustine is very clear].[26] Notwithstanding, however complex the issue viewed from the twenty-first century, for the preacher-poet who composed the primitive series of tales known as the first *Vie des Pères*, sex is an easy way of attracting the attention of his audience. To put it crudely and perhaps a little unfairly, sex sells. I have yet to come across a more sensitive, subtle, and succinct way of expressing this truism than that formulated by Jean-Charles Payen: "La luxure . . . est la tentation qui trouble le plus les gens du Moyen Âge. C'est elle qui éloigne de Dieu le plus grand nombre d'âmes. . . . c'est elle qui provoque les chutes les plus spectaculaires, suivies généralement il est vrai des remords les plus subits" [Lust . . . is the temptation most troubling to people in the Middle Ages. Lust is what distances the largest number of souls from God. . . . Lust causes the most spectacular falls from grace, generally followed it is true by the most sudden remorse].[27] Forgiveness and salvation are all the more dramatic in stories that include the most evil of sinners making the most unexpected acts of repentance and the most remarkable spiritual recoveries. Forgiveness and salvation shape identity throughout the *Vie des Pères*. The powerful, sometimes brutal reality of our tales is a vital element in the authors' plan, given that the stories and sermons providing the framework within which they operate aim first and foremost to propagate the teaching that no sin is beyond forgiveness. Payen views this as the raison d'être of poetry of conversion: "Les penitents . . . soient de très grands coupables, qui reviennent de loin et ont besoin d'une grâce exceptionnelle, ne serait-ce pour avoir le courage de confesser leurs fautes" [The penitents . . . are persons guilty of terrible things, who return from the precipice and are in need of exceptional grace, if only to have the courage to confess their sins].[28] Gautier de Coinci understood this, as did the authors of *le Chevalier au barisel*, *Sainte Marie l'Egyptienne*, and similar accounts of the "penitent within." By this term I refer to sinners who may see no need for penitence, or who actively fight against it, but whether through divine intervention, the devotion of another human being, or some other event, finally come to terms with the need to confess their sins and do a sincere act of penance. The *Vie des Pères* abounds in such penitents.

There are plentiful examples where accepted norms are either upheld or appear to be challenged, especially in the first *Vie des Pères*. Although sexual themes and motifs may occupy center stage in a given narrative, they are rarely central to the teachings found in the prologues, introductions, epilogues, *queues*, or in-text short sermons. The tales and collective texts are works of hagiographical fiction and plainly distinct from vernacular sermons where, to borrow Michel Zink's words, "lorsque le prédicateur parle, et il en parle souvent, du péché de la chair, seul le péché de l'homme est pris en considération, analysé, condamné, seul sa tentation est décrite. La femme n'est que l'occasion du péché et l'objet du désir" [When the preacher speaks of sins of the flesh, and he speaks of them often, only the sin of the man is considered, analyzed, condemned, only his temptation is described. The woman is merely the cause of sin and the object of desire].[29] The *Vie des Pères* is very much at the convergence of traditions: drawing together examples from patristic sources, biblical stories, sermons, exempla, hagiography, courtly literature, comic texts, and his own imagination, the author of the first *Vie des Pères* offers multiple illustrations of sexual temptation per se and its consequences. The continuations are less fertile ground, but even so sexual intrigue crops up from time to time. A combination of the raw material at the authors' disposal and the scandal factor that is so valuable in moralizing contexts results in few descriptions of premarital sex and adultery—perhaps the most common type of literary sexual sin, certainly in romance—in favor of fornication by holy men and women. The anticlericalism rife at the time of composition feeds into narrative illustrations that are shockingly contrary to the laws of religious celibacy. In *Sacristine*—the tale of the nun who leaves her abbey—the shock value is palpable, dampened only by the fact that this was an extremely well-known story.[30] The same might be said of *Abbesse grosse*, an equally popular story which recounts an abbess's hidden pregnancy and miraculous, secret childbirth.[31] Prostitution also attracts attention, giving rise as it does to the reprehensible sin of sex for pleasure.[32] The important spiritual (and often civil) crimes committed by those indulging in deviant practices would be immediately apparent to the audience of any medieval work, and should appeal to their sense of scandal. A scandalous sinner makes for an attractive narrative character. The audience can delight in following a reluctant conversion as the innermost identity of a prostitute or a wayward abbess is shaped from sinner to penitent to saint.

By my count eighteen tales in the first *Vie des Pères*—whose author had Cistercian sympathies and who was preaching the necessity of confession—have sexual transgressions or transgressions provoked by sexuality as a major theme, and at least another nine make passing references to important sexual issues occupying contemporary theologians. In the continuations, half a dozen (*Image de Nostre Dame, Prêtre pécheur, Femme aveugle, Nom de Marie, Coq, Infanticide*) of some thirty-two tales deal with sexual issues. The fact that these are Virgin miracles, added decades later by authors with ostensibly different sympathies—Dominican rather than Cistercian—does somewhat muddy the waters.

Although sex is a significant part of the plots of the stories, it is rarely described minutely. The author goes as far as necessary to establish a narrative situation without succumbing to pornographic detail. Whether dealing with physical beauty or rape, incest, or any other aspect of sex, words are chosen with care. A small number of examples from a variety of tales should illustrate this. There is a sparsity in the language of the author suggesting that sex is not in itself what is at issue here. Rather it serves as a conduit to a conversion story, in whole or in part. There seems to be no doubt that the author of the primitive text is sincere and deeply spiritual. The coming together of current Church interest in the sex lives of the faithful, the potential that sex offers as a narrative tool, and an aspiration to proselytize with sensitivity and skill results in stories generally light on detail regardless of the erotic situation.

In *Prévôt d'Aquilée* a chaste wife inflames a hermit with no intention of submitting to his desires. She is treating him the same way she treats her husband, through a series of manufactured temptations, enticing him to the limits of his self-control: "Lors dist que il se leveroit / et cele dist que non feroit. / Vers li se trest, si l'enbraça" (vv. 13978–80) [At this point he said that he wanted to get up but she didn't want him to. She pulled him toward her and embraced him] and said "Prodom, atendez. / Levez sus, avec moi venez / jusque ci; quant vos revendoiz, / de moi vostre voloir feroiz" (vv. 13992–95) [Sire, wait. Get up, come with me here; when you return you can do with me as you wish].

The precise nature of her acts is significant only inasmuch as it is important for the audience to know that the hermit is tempted and does indeed wish to give in to his carnal desire. Beyond this the author of *Prévôt d'Aquilée* has no need for salacious description. The emphasis is very much on the hermit, a human being with the same weaknesses as any other human being, including the reader. It is his pride that gets him into this situation in the first place: he is a holy hermit, too aware of his own piety and shocked to discover that his equal is the worldly Prévôt d'Aquilée. The Other inhabiting this hermit's identity is a voice pushing him to ask just who might be as worthy as he. The result of his pride is the testing of his piety, the most interesting part of which for most readers is the sexual episode that he is unable to avoid. At the end of the tale, following the torturous night he suffers, the hermit is not only a humbler individual but also, and essentially, now able to recognize good where before he was scornful. This ability to see good in unexpected places and unusual circumstances marks a significant, and positive, change in how he views himself.

In *Ivresse* a miller finds his wife—or should the emphasis be on the hermit?—in flagrante delicto: "il m'est avis, par m'ame, / que cil ivres gist a ma feme" (vv. 15378–79) [upon my soul, it seems to me that this drunk is sleeping with my wife!]. Although for narrative reasons it is vital to know that the drunken hermit has sex with the miller's wife, the author again resists the temptation of giving a blow-by-blow account.[33] After all, fornication in this tale is just a small part of the longer narrative: what is central is the hermit's daily battle with the devil, and the only mistake that he makes is entering into a covenant with the devil in order to end daily demonic torture. Drunkenness leads to sex and then murder through human weakness. Sex may be a significant chink in a pious individual's armor, but it is not the point of this story. It is important to know that it takes place but not to know every detail. Spiritual works do not always display such discretion. It is a testament to the skill of the author that he has found a way of satisfying his audience's natural desire for scandal while still highlighting the importance of the pious lesson: that even the worthiest character can be undone by the wily devil. In this case the hermit's identity is shaped by the external agency of the devil himself, who cannot bear the sanctity of the hermit.

A little more detail of sex acts is given in *Thaïs*, the story of a prostitute seemingly willing to perform any sex act to procure material reward. This debauchery and obsession with riches is important, given her almost forced conversion and ultimate beatification. From prostitute to saint is not an uncommon journey in medieval hagiography.

An analogous situation arises in *Nièce*. Although a hermit's niece succumbs to selling her body, it is soon clear that she has sex for material benefit rather than for pleasure: "Ilec a toz s'abandona, / si ot de li qui li dona" (vv. 14940–41) [In that place she gave herself completely, taking whatever was given to her]. This detail is important, placing the niece in contrast to the virgin in *Sénéchal* who replaces her cousin in the wedding bed. This is a tale in which there is great sexual intrigue and murder, and in which there is one character at least—the cousin—whose identity will not be shaped by a third party, whoever that third party may be. Of the sex act itself, the enjoyment of which is the cousin's downfall, we learn enough to excite our own voyeuristic nosiness: "nu coucherent en un lit / ou cil aconpli son delit / et fist son talent de la bele" (vv. 12886–88) [they lay naked in a bed where he took his pleasure and had his way with the beauty]. These two tales track human fragility most expertly. The girl who becomes a prostitute and is saved by her loving uncle is not really the main character of the story. It is the hermit's compassion that we are to copy, although the niece's lesson is an important one also. As far as the cousin in *Sénéchal* is concerned, I find it difficult to accept that the author considered her sexual sin the main teaching for his audience. This is a complicated story in which characters are damned—something of a rarity for this indulgent author—and although the girl's discovery of sexual pleasure is to be noted, the emphasis is on the queen's hardships. It would be foolish in such a complicated tale to stress the cousin's sexual sin beyond how it is presented here.

Brûlure and *Malaquin* are more brutal, at least with regard to sex. Both recount how hermits' chastity vows are put to the test. Both result in heroic acts of self-mutilation inflicted only to resist natural sexual desire and opportunity. In *Malaquin* we learn more about the forcible sexual arousal of a holy hermit seduced by three beautiful girls and the bloody ejaculation that saves his chastity. There is a glimpse of how this author and his audience considered feminine sexuality: "Frere, je sui bele et jonete. / Encore n'ai en sain mamelete" (vv. 10900–10901) [Brother, I am beautiful and young, my breasts are still not fully developed]. These Saracen girls are tasked with breaking a holy hermit's resolve in order to satisfy their lord's scepticism about Christianity. Since it is important for the narrative that the hermit is indeed tempted by their advances—to the point of biting off his own tongue so as not to give in to carnal desire—there is logic in the fact that this tale devotes more time to describing the various tactics used to seduce him. The hapless hermit is finally stripped and tied to a bed where one of the women lies naked upon him, making him a victim of his own biology:

> Desus l'ermite tote nue
> la fist couchier et bien li dist,
> ainz que de lui se departist,
> *qu'amont et aval l'esmeüst*
> tant q'a lui conpaignie eüst. (vv. 10951–55, my italics)

[He made her lie on top of the hermit, quite naked, and told her that before she departed from him she should arouse him up and down his body until she had sex with him.]

The use of the expression *qu'amont, qu'aval* has been noted by Brian J. Levy to describe the act of oral sex in short comic narratives. In *Malaquin* it is only too easy to imagine the actions of this beautiful Saracen girl.[34] In the same tale an even more explicit reference to sex acts is suggested: "Cele, qui desus lui se jut, / tant l'eschaufa et tant l'esmut / par besier et par acoler" (vv. 10990–92) [The girl who is lying on top of him arouses and inflames him so with kisses and embraces]. It becomes clear, although not in a vulgar way, that she achieves her objective: "au fere se voloit doner" (v. 10993) [he is ready to give in to the act]. Here is an example of a holy hermit able to remain holy and chaste even when facing the greatest challenge of all. He is rewarded by a miracle and succeeds in converting the initially evil pagan Duke Malaquin. The author is clever: this story begins by opposing the Christian and the Other, and it ends by Christianizing the Other.

In *Inceste*, a tale where a mother's initially chaste caresses of her fourteen-year-old son develop into impure carnal activity, there are few details of their sex acts, but the mother's pleasure is clear: she follows her body, doing nothing to end the incestuous relationship. There are less-than-subtle modifications—distortions?—of identity here. Initially we witness a model family bond. The loss of the woman's husband gives the devil the opportunity he needs to corrupt the mother and, by extension, alter the son's relationship with her.[35] Her active seduction of the son is a sign of weakness, ceding to demonic temptation. The boy just goes with the flow. Events are driven by the devil, by mourning, by human weakness. Apart from the fact that the mother finds the incestuous sex pleasurable, there is little to truly trouble the commentator in *Inceste*. All reverts to "normality" thanks to divine intervention. We are told that before the mother's widowhood this was a loving and recognizably Christian family unit, a model family, no less. The intervention of the devil causes a shift in just who the mother and son consider themselves to be—from mother and son to enchanted lovers—but this distortion (in the eyes of the Church) is overcome. Identities have been manipulated, but temporarily so, with the devil and the Virgin pulling the strings.

In some ways the most detailed—pornographic even—episode of sexual activity is a description of female beauty in *Sarrasine*. A hermit falls in love with a Saracen girl whom he spies upon as she washes. Her beauty mesmerizes him, provoking a decidedly unwelcome feeling of lust. The reader is invited to share the hermit's enjoyment of her physical appearance. Yet just whose identity is being shaped here? Certainly not the girl's; she is a Saracen, after all. The hermit's? Ultimately he undergoes a journey of sin and penance not unlike any other holy person who succumbs to temptation but ends up victorious in his spiritual battle. It may just be that sex here is a tool employed by the author to control, shape, and convince his audience of the need to themselves repent and confess. This is, when all is said and done, his primary goal. Inspired by the teachings of both Church and theologians, this is literature of conversion at play:

> La sarrazine a l'endemain
> vint a la fonteine bien main,
> si ce fu lavee et pigniee,
> et entre .ii. euz fu guigniee,
> onques n'i ot lessié pelet.
> En son chief ot un chapelet
> de flors de pré et de fanueil.

La garce joine ot riant l'ueil
et fu brunete et acemee. (vv. 873–81)

[The next day the Saracen girl came very early to the spring, where she was bathed and combed, and was plucked between her two eyes to leave not a single hair. On her head she wore a garland of wildflowers and fennel. The young girl's eyes sparkled, and she was dark and comely.[36]]

It is worth bearing in mind that sex is rarely the major issue in our tales; rather, the motif provides illustrative material in an exemplary narrative describing sinful behavior, repentance, confession, and salvation. These tales are intended to operate in a similar fashion to exempla: their place is at the intersection between patristic exegesis and popular culture. They are not just another reworking of the *Vitae Patrum* tradition where sexual sin is prominent. Pious tales certainly represent a variation on an extremely popular type of hagiography, but the traditions of the chanson de geste, comic fabliau, and romance are in many ways more intimately connected to the *Vie des Pères* than is patristic legend. Our authors may well be concerned with the spiritual and theological dogma post-Lateran III and IV—as Duncan Robertson neatly points out, pious tales can "rouse the god-fearing reader from his moral sleep"[37]—but they are, it would appear, even more preoccupied with the practicalities leading to an individual's fall, and the circumstances that can lead to salvation.

The *Vie des Pères* offers a fascinating glimpse of how Church teachings on sexual matters were being transmitted by generally indulgent and realistic men, and received by the faithful. By so doing, it allows us to see the relationship between sex, salvation, and the Other in the medieval world. This is a well-defined space populated by recognizable characters for the large part. The appetite for exploring marginality as witnessed in profane texts is clear for all to see here too. The reader encounters characters who are forced into sanctity by the Divine Other, whether in the form of human agency (a hermit, a nun, a pious nonreligious) or an act of God. What could be better than a miracle to force a sinner's hand?[38] But a modest hermit proves just as able in the shaping of another's identity—the saving of a soul through conversion—in some of the most effective tales. There is nothing like a clash of human personalities (as witnessed in *Thaïs* and *Sénéchal*) or intense personal struggle (viz. *Malaquin* and *Brûlure*) or a strong character putting the virtue of another to the test (*Abbesse grosse*) to create drama and tension. The problematic contradictions of pious ideals and human nature are constantly apparent in the first *Vie des Pères*. The collective text brilliantly illustrates that the value of a pious life can be undone by an inability to refuse sexual temptation. Conversely, although the holy virtues of chastity and sexual integrity are the most worthy, sexual activity does not in itself rule out salvation, and a soul stained by carnal sin can in the right circumstances be remodeled and sanctified. For the primitive text in particular, the author is an astute observer of real life who appears to grasp the value of exploring characters inhabiting the margins, and whether their sexual activities impact who they really are in the eyes of God. The author is adept at revealing how the resolution of unfortunate situations produced by sex can bring even the most marginal figure back into the fold. He also seems to recognize that there are occasions where excessive piety may distort who a person is or should be. This author, like Augustine, seems to understand just what it is that makes the faithful tick.

10

Roland's Confession and the Rhetorical Construction of the Other Within

MARY JANE SCHENCK

According to Peter Brooks, "Lateran IV constitutes a revolution in the development of Western society and its members of the highest magnitude. What we are today—the entire conception of the self, its relation to its interiority and to others—is largely tributary of the confessional requirement."[1] In claiming so much for the impact of Lateran IV (1215) with its requirement of annual confession to a priest, Brooks is not unaware that confession had a continuous history beginning in Judaism and acquiring new dimensions throughout early Christianity. Nonetheless, he pays little attention to the earlier period and believes the thirteenth century marked a watershed moment when confession moved from public penance for grave sins and a once-in-a-lifetime requirement for the average sinner to the once-a-year mandate that led to the cultivation of interiority, the very creation of the self. This interiority, he believes, was first expressed in the twelfth-century renaissance literature of troubadours and Chrétien de Troyes. We know that legal historians and other medievalists have long since questioned the idea of a major "renaissance" in the twelfth century, placing more emphasis instead on the continuous post-Carolingian culture. Even earlier, Augustine had differentiated various types of penance: that which converts and heals the individual, daily confession in the Lord's Prayer, beating of breast, and for serious sins the self-imposed withdrawal from communion. The essence of the penitential attitude is an exploration of the self. In the words of Paul Anciaux, "Personal conversion, willing self-accusation and expiation in reparation of the wrong done are all necessary if there is to be a real cure and if sin is to be totally destroyed."[2] This initial posture, both psychic and physical, is the first step that leads to reintegration with the Church through ritual. What occurs in the twelfth century is not a new view of penance but an elaboration of the theology of how elements of ecclesiastical penance, the interior and exterior forms of confession, are to work together.[3] The development of penitential practice in the fourth through twelfth centuries demonstrates that the exploration of self, guilt, or interiority that Brooks has characterized as a "protomodern" moment did not await a shift in confessional practices at Lateran IV.[4] The council not create the practice of yearly confession, nor did it have an enormous impact in this regard. It took two centuries before auricular confession was imposed on the people.[5]

It is true, however, that confession as a sacrament has an intellectual and practical history that becomes more complex throughout the twelfth century and into the early thirteenth. Culturally this is reflected broadly in the writing of penitentials and saints' lives, and in the rise of contritionism and the preaching orders. It was not only the troubadours and romance writers who were cultivating the self or the interior. Confessions in epic and chronicle are other moments of public revelation of private states of mind. The question is the nature of interiority of such scenes, for they may be as much rhetorical performances as psychological moments. Brooks is most insightful when he points to the origins of confession in oral culture and its connection to the "I" of confession that requires a listener: "saying *I* implies and calls to a responsive *you*, and in this dialogic, transferential relation consolation and self-definition are to be found. The form of address to a listener found in confession is similar to prayer."[6]

The terminology of transactional analysis highlights the psychological dimension that is certainly appropriate from a modern point of view. For the texts we are to consider here, however, key rhetorical terms—ethos, logos, and pathos—are even more appropriate because of the influence of oral performance. The way Roland's confessions in the Oxford *Chanson de Roland*, the later Châteauroux version of the epic, and the vernacular translation of the *Pseudo-Turpin* chronicle present rhetorically the relationship between interiority and audience is the subject of this essay. These texts reveal how Roland draws on his interior, especially his memories of achievements and belief in salvation stories, to confess in several senses of the word, revealing the ethos of this Other Within and deploying pathos in unique ways in each heroic text. Whether Roland confesses in the sense of feeling remorse for particular sins or whether he is guilty, even if he does not admit or recognize it, has been at the heart of traditional Roland scholarship, although less so in recent years. *Approaches to Teaching the "Song of Roland"* does not include a chapter on the issue.[7] But confession as admission of guilt is not the question here; the nature of the public spectacle of his death scene and its relationship to interiority is.

In the Oxford *Roland*, the hero's apostrophe to his sword, Durendal, in *laisses* 171–73 precedes the three *laisses* relating his confession. As much a praise song to himself as a paean to Durendal, Roland's address to the sword celebrates its beauty and its accomplishments as well as expressing his sadness and indignation at the thought of it falling into pagan hands. Roland has remained active to the end, of course, lashing out verbally and physically against the Saracen who stealthily attacks him. The verbs used in the preceding *laisse* (170) are strong: "si l'fiert en l'elme, ki gemmét fut a or: / fruisset l'acer e la teste e les os, / Amsdous les oilz del chef li ad mis fors, / Jus a ses piez si l'ad tresturnét mort" (l. 2288–91)[8] [And strikes him on his golden helmet, studded with gold and gems. / He shatters the steel, his skull and his bones; / He put both his eyes out of their sockets / And cast him down dead at his feet].[9] After failing to break the sword against the rock, he addresses Durendal directly, but concentrates less on what he will do to protect the sword than on his knowledge of his own situation—"E! Durendal, bone si mare fustes! / Quant jo mei perd, de vos nen ai mais cure" (l. 2304–5) [Oh, my good sword Durendal, what a fate you have suffered! / Now that I am dying, I have no more need of you]—and his next lines focus on what he, Roland, has accomplished, not the sword: "Tante batailles en camp en ai vencues / e tantes teres larges escumbatues" (l. 2306–7) [With you I have won so many battles in the field / And conquered so many vast lands]. The repeated "I" statements that follow in *laisse* 172 elaborate Roland's victories and make him the instrument of Charlemagne's extensive successes. The person is the physical instrument more than the weapon, the ostensible audience for the lines. As in a drama, the character is speaking to an audience onstage while the real audience sits and absorbs the lesson.

Jo l'en cunquis e Anjou e Bretaigne,
si l'en cunquis e Peitou et le Maine;
jo l'en cunquis Normendie la franche,
si l'en cunquis Provence et Equitaigne

et Lumbardie e trestute Romaine;
jo l'en cunquis Baiver et tute Flandres
E Buguerie et trestute Puillanie. (I. 2322–28)

[With it I conquered Anjou and Brittany
And with it I conquered Poitou and Maine;
With it I conquered Normandy the free
And with it I conquered Provence and Aquitaine
And Lombardy and all Romagna.
With it I conquered Bavaria and all Flanders
And Burgundy and all Apulia.]

Continuing the list (the victory theme, according to Gerard Brault),[10] he tells us how he feels and prays that God will not let the sword be dishonored. Less centered on Roland himself, *laisse* 173 recalls the precious relics of Saints Basil, Denis, and Mary contained in the hilt, and he naturally asserts that they must serve only Christian people.

As an introduction to his confession beginning in the next group of *laisses*, the three preceding ones addressed to Durendal are neither humble nor penitential. Roland did pray for help earlier when he knew he was dying, asking first for his peers to return and then for his own sake (I. 2261), so he is certainly capable of humility. As for the tenor of his words throughout *laisses* 171–73, some would suggest this is an example of Roland's *desmesure*, others that it is the heroic and tragic Germanic element, still others that it is the healthy pride of the Christian warrior who knows he has given his best for God and Charlemagne.[11] But it is the oral, rhetorical quality of both his words and the narration that strikes us. Roland establishes his ethos through this list of victories, and pathos emerges as he worries about the sword falling into pagan hands. What then is the logos; what is Roland arguing for? In what appears to be an apostrophe, the sword is only fleetingly the audience. Who is to be moved by his speech? God, so that He will forgive his sins? Is Roland saying, "Look at all the good I did during my life," so that he will be considered worthy of salvation? Or is it the audience of warriors listening to the poem who will be swayed to carry on the mission, taking great care of relics and fighting until the end? That it is the men and Charles seems obvious in the next *laisse* that leads to the confession.

Roland's final actions—running to the pine tree and positioning himself on top of the sword and olifant with face turned toward Spain—are designed to create a final symbolic triumph over the enemy and guarantee his reputation: "Turnat sa teste vers la paiene gent: / pur ço l'at fait quë il voelt veirement / que Carles dïet e trestute sa gent, / li gentilz quens, qu'il fut mort cunquerant" (I. 2360–63) [Towards the pagan host he turned his head, / Because it was his earnest wish that / Charles and all his men should say / That he, the noble count, had died victoriously]. Clearly the audience consists of those who must be told about his final gestures and confession—which, in this first of the *laisses similaires*, is rendered in only two lines of narrative, not direct discourse. He beats his breast several times and proffers his glove to God: "Cleimet sa culpe e menut e suvent, / pur ses pecchez Deu en puroffrid lo guant" (I. 2364–65) [He confesses his sins over and over again; / for his sins he proffered his glove to God]. But God is not directly addressed, the observer/listener is. Roland is onstage, and the audience admires the gestures of a pious warrior. We are able to understand this visual argument when the narrator explains that Roland positions himself thus because he really, "veirement," wants others to see him this way. In the critical history of this passage, the meaning of the gesture of offering the glove has occupied much attention, some seeing it as a gesture of feudal homage, others arguing over whether the fief rendered is his life, or whether the glove is a token of his desire for forgiveness.[12] The interpretation of each gesture has been amply covered by others, but what should, in any case, be apparent is that the audience must see this as a series of symbols to be decoded. They all, from medieval clerics to warriors to laypersons listening to the recounting, will see/hear according to their particular points of view. The clerics might focus on Roland's piety, the chevaliers surely on the man as model hero, and women would no doubt recall husbands, fathers, and brothers lost to them but gaining eternal life. The pathos is nonetheless muted here because the two narrative lines describe the act of confession, not Roland's emotional state.

The four lines of direct discourse in *laisse* 175 create more pathos by letting us hear Roland's voice as he addresses God. Roland's dying posture is reaffirmed; then he speaks:

"Deus, meie culpe vers les tües vertuz
de mes pecchez, des granz et des menuz

> que jo ai fait dés l'ure que nez fui
> tresqu'a cest jur que ci sui consoüt!"
> Sun destre guant an ad vers Deu tendut,
> angles des ciel di descendent a lui. (l. 2369–74)

> ["Oh God, the Almighty, I confess
> My sins, both great and small,
> Which I have committed since the time I was born,
> Until this day on which I have been overtaken."
> He held out his right glove to God;
> Angels come down to him from Heaven.]

This is a general mea culpa, the ritual acknowledgment of sins great and small, from the time of his birth. It affirms his human condition, binding us to him, but this confession shows no remorse, and in its brevity it is not significantly different from Turpin's in *laisse* 166.

In the last of the death scenes (*laisse* 176), his position on the ground is reiterated, and a new theme is introduced. Roland calls to memory the lands he conquered, fair France, his ancestors, and Charlemagne—an almost exact restatement of the reasons he offers Oliver for why he cannot sound the horn. The pathos is built on Roland's tears and sighs as well as on the irony of this scene's juxtaposition to the conversation with his now dead companion. But, as the narrator says, Roland does not want to lose himself in memories and forget his confession, so he begins this time with an evocation of the grace of God:

> Veire Paterne, ki unkes ne mentis,
> seint Lazaron de mort resurrexis
> et Daniel des lëons guaresis,
> guaris de mei l'anme de tuz perilz
> pur les pecchez que en ma vie fis! (l. 2384–88)

> [True Father, who has never lied,
> You who brought back Lazarus from the dead
> And rescued Daniel from the lions,
> Protect my soul from every peril
> And from the sins which I have committed in my life.]

Thus his confession is preceded by thoughts of God's power, not Roland's prowess, and the biblical examples of Lazarus and Daniel evoke salvation iconography which the audience would surely recognize. Roland avoids the extremes of polarized emotions; he shows no fear facing death, nor joy at the idea of God's mercy. He merely asks for God's protection. There is no preoccupation with his sinfulness, nor anxiety about the final judgment. The audience should be moved by his calm, sure faith and self-possession.

Interpretations of the death scene and Roland's confession have focused on the meaning of the gestures and the issue of whether he feels guilty of a specific sin, or whether he is guilty, even if he does not recognize it.[13] In other words, is his confession merely ritualistic or is he genuinely contrite? Does it manifest the influence of the growing movement of contritionism? As Jean-Charles Payen has explained, this twelfth-century movement developed from early writers such as Grégoire de Nazianze, who wrote that true penitence was a "second baptême par les larmes"[14] [a second baptism through tears]. As the theology developed through the tenth- and eleventh-century prophets, contritionism emphasized dramatic conversion away from sin, accompanied or revealed by the abundant tears of the truly contrite. Neither abundant tears nor conversion are evident in *The Song of Roland*. It was mentioned above that Roland sheds tears that contribute to the pathos of the situation, but in v. 2381—"ne poet müer n'en plurt e ne suspirt" [he cannot help weeping and heaving great sighs]—it is memories, especially of Charlemagne, that provoke the tears, not Roland's feeling of contrition. As Payen comments, none of the three remaining heroes dies repentant. They die true to themselves: "Oliver meurt en bon Chrétien et loyal sujet. Turpin meurt en prêtre et prélat dans l'attitude de la prière. Roland meurt en grand capitaine face à ennemi"[15] [Oliver dies as a good Christian and loyal subject. Turpin dies as a priest and prelate in a posture of prayer. Roland dies as a great captain facing the enemy].

There is no "confession" of a specific sin, and he certainly doesn't show any regret for not sounding the horn.[16] His words are formulaic, and the gestures create a *tableau vivant* of appropriate ritual. The rhetoric of the situation makes of this a performance primarily addressed to human observers/hearers. In a sincere but only formal sense, God is addressed. There is no priest to hear the confession, no intermediary to ask for pardon, and God is not really an interlocutor. Roland doesn't plead or reveal much; he asks for pardon. As with other mea culpas asked for in the *Song*, it is part of the "absolutions collectives"[17] [collective absolution] quickly granted. His list of accomplishments could be seen as Roland trying to sway God, but there is no consciousness expressed about a need to do so. The accomplishments of Durendal and Roland are to be models for other men, not examples he asks to have put in the balance as he awaits judgment. So the audience is witness to what happens; we are not agents or substitutes for the priest, acting for Roland, but observers who should take away the lesson that this is how to die. The rightness of what Roland does and has done is manifest. The angels descend and take his soul to heaven. For Payen, it is not a true confession but "une agonie à la fois logique et dramatique"[18] [an agony at once logical and dramatic]. The rhetorical situation has created a self, constructed of memories, calculated to evoke audience empathy, as the hero argues for and achieves a good death.

In other versions, the ethos of Roland, the logos, and the element of pathos all shift. The later Châteauroux–Venice 7 version of the *Song* offers a few interesting variations on the scene.[19] In this rhymed thirteenth-century version, the sneaky Saracen's attack is recounted through two *laisses*, beginning at 231, and the Saracen speaks twice. After Roland dispatches him with the olifant, the narrator says "Mahon" could not protect him, and that he is bodily taken away by one hundred devils. Roland observes the dilapidated state of the olifant, and then asks for God's mercy for his sins: "Au roi de gloire a li merci crïé / por ses pechiez, qu'il n'en soit encombré!" (III. 4160–61) [From God the glorious he asked pardon for his sins that he not be burdened by them].[20] Then Roland's thoughts return to Durendal. The next two laisses (233–34) open with him attempting to break the sword followed by his apostrophe as in the Oxford version, although with some variation in details, such as which relics are contained (Saints Sophye, Piere, and Doinie [Denis], not Basile, Denis, and Mary of the Oxford version). These differences have an incidental value in demonstrating the "mouvance" of saints' popularity depending on region and timeframe of the poem.

Roland's confession begins in *laisse* 235 with the description of his beating his breast and his words:

a ses deus mains avoit son piz batu:
"Deus, moie cope, par la töe vertu,
des grant pechez don quit estre perdu,
Cist las pechable des l'ore qu'il nez fu,
Tresqu'a cest jor qe ci est conseü" (III. 4208–12)

[With both his hands he beats his breast: "God, I ask pardon, through your power, for the great sins by which I think this miserable sinner will be damned, committed from the hour I was born up to this present day that has overtaken me."]

He tenders the glove, the skies open, the angels arrive. In the next, somewhat similar *laisse* (236), the narrative returns to Roland's attempts to break Durendal, but he is so frustrated that he throws the sword in a pool of poisoned water. His emotions are running high; he is "corroços et dolent" (III. 4229) [angry and in pain]. He positions himself with face toward Spain as in the Oxford version, but here the narrator has prefaced this with a strong interjection, "E, Deus! Quel duel qu'il sofri tel torment" (III. 4240) [Ah God! What a pity that he is suffering so], which heightens the pathos and shifts the emphasis from Roland's reputation to his agony. Roland confesses again, rendering his weapon and body to God and Mary, another variation (III. 4247).

Roland next turns to his memories (*laisse* 237), thinking of Aude as well as his companions and Charlemagne. When he beats his breast, he evokes the power of the glorious one born of the Virgin, who has converted the saints Feron and Policarf; protected the children in the furnace, Mary Magdalene, and Jonah in the whale; punished the people of Nineveh; and raised Lazarus from the dead. This more elaborate list of God's miracles is part of his confession, not of sin, but of faith. The characters and events also cover a wider spectrum of salvation history, from conversion to forgiveness to final judgments. Seventeen lines of direct discourse versus five in the comparable passage in the Oxford text suggest the elaboration of confession to oral performance, and we should note that it is praising God and Jesus by retelling salvation stories, not confessing any sin on Roland's part. As he is dying, he reclines on his shield.[21] The angels take Roland's soul to Jesus: "en paradis le poserent riant / devant Jesu ou a de joie tant: / nel vos puet dire nul clers, tant soit savant" (III. 4288–90) [laughing, they place it in paradise / before Jesus, in whom there is such joy / no clerk, no matter how learned, can do it justice]. The shift from the Oxford to the Châteauroux version does not include a different confession. The gestures and words are almost identical and remain very ritualistic. The details I have pointed to, the two speeches by the sneaky Saracen and the narrator's intervention at the moment of attack (v. 4240), both create a greater sense of pathos and identification with Roland's suffering. Others, such as the reference to the Saracen's god not protecting him and his body being taken by one hundred devils, expand the religious significance and attention given to the afterlife. This is especially true of Roland's address to God when he mentions so many who have been converted and saved, and the happy laughter that greets Roland's soul in heaven. His ethos has shifted to emphasize his faith. In my opinion, these details do not reflect a clerical influence, but popular piety. They incorporate knowledge of local saints, salvation stories known not only through the Bible but also through popular legends, and they create a meaningful message for a broad audience. The logos of these scenes seems directed to the common man who must think about heaven and hell, heresy and fidelity, as much as to the warrior who can emulate Roland in his dying gestures.

The most interesting variation in the death scene appears in the comparison of the two epic versions with the vernacular *Pseudo-Turpin* chronicle. The Latin chronicle is considered to date from the first third of the twelfth century.[22] This well-appreciated work has come down in hundreds of manuscripts and had generated six independent vernacular translations by the early thirteenth century. The Old French translation known as the Johannes version dates from 1206 and was one of the most popular.[23] The final scenes reveals a shift in focus, from Durendal, the exploits of Roland, and the final heroic gestures recounted in the epics, to a salvation theology and personal confession of faith, some fear and trembling at the thought of the afterlife, and ritual gestures, not to show heroic prowess and guarantee reputation, but to assist Roland's petitions for God's mercy. The presence of a witness is also a clear departure from the epic scenes. This is at once more naturalistic—if there was no living witness, who reported what Roland did?—and more overtly ecclesiastical, as befits a chronicle that Cyril Meredith-Jones believes was written to promote the Spanish crusades.[24]

The scenes leading up to Roland's confession are quite different in the chronicle. First, Charlemagne has sent Ganelon to Marsile's camp, where he is corrupted by the wealth offered. There is no question of a feud with Roland, who is not even mentioned until Charlemagne leaves the rear guard in his care. The devastating battle, following a night of debauchery by the French, leaves a remnant of the rear guard fleeing, Baldwin and Thierry hiding in the woods, and Roland standing his ground. After relating this, the narrator offers a straightforward explanation for the defeat. For the pious, a *judicium dei* means Christians are supposed to win because they are right, so the defeat must be explained by a different facet of God's plan, namely, judgment based on sin. Indeed, the narrator says that the French died because they consorted with the pagan women brought into camp as part of Marsile's false peace offerings. There are those, however, who will be rewarded for their good deeds, if they recognize their sin and repent.

> Ci puet en veoir cler que Nostre Sires est si pius qu'il velt bien guerredoner les travaus de cels qui en la fin reconoissent son non, et regehissent lor pechiez par confession. Car ja soit ce que cil eussent fet fornicacion, si furent il ocis por Deu en la fin. (LIV. 8–12)
>
> [Thus one can clearly see that Our Lord who is so holy wants to reward the work of those who finally recognize his name and confess their sins. Because they fornicated, they were killed for God in the end.][25]

The narrator refers also to other great military heroes who were done in by bringing women into battle camps, and he admonishes priests and the religious against drunkenness and fornication which, if not avoided, lead to "la perpetuel mort d'enfer" (LIV. 25) [eternal death in hell]. After this judgmental and apocalyptic blast, he returns to his narrative about Roland.

Here there is no sneaky Saracen, but Roland captures one who is described as "un paien molt noir" (LV. 3) [a very black pagan], ties him to a tree, returns to battle, and then retrieves the Saracen, threatening him with death if he does not point out Marsile. Baligant flees when he sees Roland has killed Marsile. Roland addresses Durendal, making no mention of relics but establishing themes of praise for its beauty and concern for its falling into pagan hands, much as in the epic versions. There is no long list of "I" statements; all he has accomplished, which is characterized less as military conquest than as triumphs for God, he credits to the sword.

> Par toi est ocise et destruite la gente paiene, et la loi crestiene essauciee et la loenge de Deu et la gloire de lui aquise, et par tantes foix ai venchié par toi le saint sanc Nostre Seignor Jhesu Crist, et tantes foix en ai ocis les anemis Deu, et tant Sarrazin et tant mescreant detranchié et destruit. Par toi est la jostise Deu aemplie. (LVI. 24–30)

[Through you, pagans were killed and destroyed, the Christian law exalted and the praise of God and his glory achieved; through you so many times has the blood of Our Savior Jesus Christ been avenged, so many times the enemies of God killed, so many Saracens and so many evildoers slain and destroyed. Through you, God's justice has been fulfilled.]

When he sounds the horn, Charlemagne hears it, but so do Baldwin and Thierry, who return to Roland's side. Roland asks Baldwin, his brother, to get him water, which Baldwin attempts to do. Finding none and fearing the approach of the pagans, Baldwin takes Roland's horse, sword, and olifant and retreats to Charlemagne.

Thierry, the most loyal one, begins to cry and immediately plays the role of confessor. He urges Roland to gird his soul with faith and confession. The narrator then tells us that Roland has earlier that day, as was the custom, taken communion and confessed to the priests before going into battle. Thierry functions to enhance both logos and pathos here. His tears over Roland's dying body sharpen the deep personal emotions of grief and loss; his exhortation to Roland is an important part of the argument of the poem. The fighting and dying are for God, and the ritual sacraments must be respected. We not only have a witness (in both chronicle and theological senses), but we have a lesson, showing the "common practice" of battlefield Eucharists. The rhetorical impact of having Thierry present is to embed Roland's confession in a community, as does the allusion to his participating in Mass earlier in the day. It moves Roland slightly, from his single and singular position as epic hero, to a place of common humanity; he is a soul in need of a proper death.

The confession begins, not with a narrative description of a mea culpa, but with Roland lifting his eyes to heaven and addressing his Savior through twenty-nine lines of direct discourse. He recounts all that he has undergone for Him in this life, attributing his successful battles to God's help, not to Durendal or his own prowess, and he recites a credo:

Sire, come tu deignas nestre de la Virge Marie por moi, et soffrir mort en la croiz, et el sepulcre ester enseveliz, et au tierz jor resusciter et monter es sainz ciels qu'en la presence de ta deîté ne deguerpis onques, Sire, si deignes tu m'ame delivrer de la perpetuel mor d'enfer. (LIX. 8–13)

[Lord, since you deigned to be born of the Virgin Mary for me, and suffer death upon the cross, and be buried in the sepulcher, and the third day rise from the dead to ascend into heaven to be in the presence of your God, do not abandon me, Lord, but deign to deliver my soul from perpetual damnation.]

His ethos is securely fashioned by his faith in God's aid, purpose, and promises of salvation for all who have sinned—"Sire, qui totes felonies de pecheor en quelconques hore il se convertist a toi pardones" (LIX. 15–17) [Lord, who pardons all evil deeds of the sinner who at any time turns to you]—such as the Ninevites, or those who have repented (converted from sin) such as Mary Magdalen, Peter, and the thief. Roland asks for himself that he be pardoned: "tu me faces pardon! Tot ce que je ai mesfet me pardone et m'ame met en perdurable repos!" (LIX. 21–23) [May you forgive me! For all my sins, forgive me and accept my soul into eternal rest!]. From praise of God's power to his earnest cry of faith and belief in salvation, Roland's prayer is more self-consciously theological and penitential than either epic version: "je croi de cuer et regehis de boche que por ce vels tu m'ame mener de ceste vie qu'aprés la mort la faces vivre en meillor vie" (LIX. 26–28) [I believe in my heart and confess with my mouth that because of this, you wish to lead my soul from this life so that after death you may make it live a better life]. We hear his voice as he speaks at length, and in this instance we sense ourselves to be overhearing the confession rather than having it directed at us.

What follows is a description of Roland's anguished gestures and tears, a sign perhaps of the influence in this late twelfth-century text of contritionism: "Rollant prist donc sa pel entre le cuer et les memeles et dist gemissenment, plains de lermes, si com Tierris en fu tesmoing qui puis le reconta tot ensi com il le vit et oï" (LX. 1–4) [Roland took his skin between the heart and the breast and spoke, groaning tearfully, as Thierry was a witness, who then recounted it all as he saw and heard it]. Roland speaks again, a shorter confession of faith, places his hand on his eyes, repeats three times that his eyes will soon see God, and then opens them to stare at the sky while making the sign of the cross on his extremities, and exclaiming that only those who love God will be saved. As he is dying, Roland directs his thoughts to those, lying dead on the battlefield, who sacrificed their lives:

qui de lointiens païs en estranges contrees vindrent combatre a la gent mescreant, et essaucier ton saint nom, et venchier ton precious sanc, et esclairier ta foi. Il gisent ore mort por toi par les mains des Sarrazins, mes tu, beau Sire, esleve par ta pitié lor pechiez et oste des tormenz d'enfer lor ames! (LX. 21–27)

[From far away, strange countries they came to fight the evil people and exalt your sainted name, and avenge your precious blood and evangelize the faith. They lie there dead for you at the hands of the Saracens but, dear Lord, in your mercy absolve them of their sins and take away the torments of hell from their souls.]

There is no recall of sweet France or Charlemagne, only of those who died in the service of their Lord. Roland is referred to as the "blessed martyr," and after he dies, "se parti Teirris d'iluec qui tot vit et oï et verais tesmoing en fu" (LXI. 6–7) [Thierry left there, he who saw and heard all and was a true witness to what happened].

If the tears of Roland signal the impact of contritionism, the extended confession, both of faith and the request for mercy, also shows the growing emphasis by the end of the twelfth century on auricular confession, apocalyptic thinking (devils, fires of *enfer*), and appropriate sacramental behaviors. But can the vernacular *Pseudo-Turpin* which was widely circulated before Lateran IV by at least a decade be used, among other examples such as Chrétien's work, to demonstrate a growing sense of introspection? It hardly seems the right word, for there is none of the vacillation of Chrétien's heroes over the correct action, none of the regrets for past misdeeds that send a hero careening into another adventure to redeem himself. Introspection, second thoughts, remorse, or tragic anagnorisis plays no role. But Roland's confessions do show the knowledge of self as a postlapsarian man who needs God's help. His confessions in the three texts examined are rituals embedded in a theology of individual salvation. In each successive text, his rhetoric evokes greater pathos, and with God as audience in the *Pseudo-Turpin*, one can see a turn inward and a more refined sense of the meaning of his confession. Ultimately, it is not the confession itself that shows greater interiority, but the context of confession revealed in shifts of ethos, logos, and pathos that indicate several ways in which self is constructed for one audience or another throughout the twelfth century.

NOTES

Introduction: Shaping Identity in Medieval French Literature

1. This idea has gained renewed prominence in the assertions of white supremacist groups, eliciting numerous responses from medievalists and stoking a lively and contentious debate about the academy's role in countering the narratives of the alt-right and neo-Nazi groups, as well as about inclusivity. See for instance Carol Symes, "Medievalism, White Supremacy, and the Historian's Craft," *AHA Today*, 2 November 2017, www.historians.org/publications-and-directories/perspectives-on-history/november-2017/medievalism-white-supremacy-and-the-historians-craft; Nell Gluckman, "A Debate about White Supremacy and Medieval Studies Exposes Deep Rifts in the Field," *Chronicle of Higher Education*, 18 September 2017, www.chronicle.com/article/A-Debate-About-White-Supremacy/241234; Josephine Livingstone, "Racism, Medievalism, and the White Supremacists of Charlottesville," *New Republic*, 15 August 2017, newrepublic.com/article/144320/racism-medievalism-white-supremacists-charlottesville; Colleen Flaherty, "Whose Medieval Studies?," *Inside Higher Ed*, 12 July 2018, www.insidehighered.com/news/2018/07/12/medieval-studies-groups-say-major-conference-trying-limit-diverse-voices-and-topics.

2. Donald Maddox, *Fictions of Identity in Medieval France* (Cambridge: Cambridge University Press, 2006), 14.

3. For works cited in this paragraph, see Jeffrey J. Cohen, *Medieval Identity Machines* (Minneapolis: University of Minnesota Press, 2003); Kirsten A. Fudeman, *Vernacular Voices: Language and Identity in Medieval French Jewish Communities* (Philadelphia: University of Pennsylvania Press, 2010); Sylvia Huot, *Madness in Medieval French Literature: Identities Found and Lost* (Oxford: Oxford University Press, 2003); Sharon Kinoshita, *Medieval Boundaries: Rethinking Difference in Old French Literature* (Philadelphia: University of Pennsylvania Press, 2006); Sharon Farmer and Carol Braun Pasternack, eds., *Gender and Difference in the Middle Ages* (Minneapolis: University of Minnesota Press, 2002); Megan Moore, *Exchanges in Exoticism: Cross-Cultural Marriage and the Making of the Mediterranean in Old French Romance* (Toronto: University of Toronto Press, 2014); Virginie Greene,

ed., *The Medieval Author in Medieval French Literature* (New York: Palgrave Macmillan, 2006); Jill Mann, *From Aesop to Reynard: Beast Literature in Medieval Britain* (Oxford: Oxford University Press, 2010); Jean-Marie Fritz, *Le Discours du fou au Moyen Âge, XIIe–XIIIe siècles* (Paris: Presses Universitaires de France, 1992).

Chapter 1. The Medieval *Moi Multiple*: Names, Surnames, and Personifications

1. Jean Dufournet, *Dernières recherches sur Villon* (Paris: Champion, 2008), 17.
2. On these terms, see Richard Glasser, "Abstractum agens und Allegorie im älteren Französisch," *Zeitschrift für romanische Philologie* 69 (1953): 43–122; Rupprecht Rohr, "Zur Skala der ritterlichen Tugenden in der altprovenzalischen und altfranzösischen höfischen Dichtung," *Zeitschrift für romanische Philologie* 78 (1962): 292–325; Marc-René Jung, *Études sur le poème allégorique en France au moyen âge* (Bern: Francke, 1971), 9–23.
3. Chrétien de Troyes, *Cligés*, ed. Stewart Gregory and Claude Luttrell (Cambridge: D. S. Brewer, 1993), v. 980; the translation is taken from Chrétien de Troyes, *Arthurian Romances*, trans. D. D. R. Owen (London: Dent, 1987), 106.
4. Raoul de Houdenc, *Le Roman des Eles*, ed. Keith Busby (Amsterdam: Benjamins, 1983).
5. Chrétien de Troyes, *Le Roman de Perceval, ou, Le Conte du Graal*, ed. Keith Busby (Tübingen: Niemeyer, 1993). On names in this romance, see Michelle Szkilnik, *Perceval ou le Roman du Graal de Chrétien de Troyes* (Paris: Gallimard, 1998), 51–66.
6. The nature topos becomes a personification here, as do *cuer* in the next line and *honor* in the quotation above: "La soe honor doit estre morte." As Armand Strubel has noted, personifications seem to abhor standing alone; see his "*Grant senefiance a": Allégorie et littérature au moyen âge* (Paris: Champion, 2002), 179.
7. As in vv. 7576–77: "de terres et d'onors / Desiretees" [disinherited of lands and fiefs].
8. Danièle James-Raoul, *Chrétien de Troyes, la griffe d'un style* (Paris: Champion, 2007), 282.
9. Guillaume de Lorris and Jean de Meun, *Le Roman de la Rose*, ed. Félix Lecoy, 3 vols. (Paris: Champion, 1965–70). By contrast, cf. Perceval's artless confusion about appropriate knightly attire (*Perceval*, vv. 1148–96).
10. On this sense of *richesse*, see Douglas Kelly, *Medieval Imagination: Rhetoric and the Poetry of Courtly Love* (Madison: University of Wisconsin Press, 1978), 68–69.
11. "The free and frank bearing that is visible testimony to the combination of good birth with virtue" (Maurice Keen, *Chivalry* [New Haven, CT: Yale University Press, 1984], 2).
12. Akin here to adolescent love play: "n'avoit pas encor passez. . . . XII. anz

d'assez" (*Rose*, vv. 1259–60) [she had not yet gone much beyond her twelfth year] and kisses her beloved as often and shamelessly as she likes.

13. On the erotic connotations of this word, see Kelly, *Medieval Imagination*, 77.

14. For Raoul de Houdenc the rose is superior to all other flowers and thus embellishes them when in their midst (*Eles*, vv. 581–614); just so, love illuminates all other human attributes ("teches," v. 617) it is conjoined with (vv. 616–19).

15. Doux Regard's arrows signify eyebeams. On sight extramission, see Douglas Kelly, *Internal Difference and Meanings in the "Roman de la Rose"* (Madison: University of Wisconsin Press, 1995), 125.

16. Alain Rey, ed., *Dictionnaire historique de la langue française* (Paris: Dictionnaires Le Robert, 1992), 2: 1948, s.v. *simple*.

17. *Courtoisie* signifies both the court and manners proper to it; see Nelly Andrieux-Reix, *Ancien français: Fiches de vocabulaire* (Paris: Presses Universitaires de France, 1989), 44–47.

18. Cf. Glasser, 47; Marjolein Hogenbirk, *Avontuur en Anti-avontuur: Een onderzoek naar "Walewein ende Keye," Arturroman uit de "Lancelotcompilatie,"* diss. Universiteit Utrecht (Amsterdam: Stichting Neerlandistiek VU, 2004), 116–21, 178.

19. Kelly, *Medieval Imagination*, 85–90; Andrieux-Reix, 160–62; Douglas Kelly, "*Fictio personae* and Subtle Rewriting in Later Medieval French Poetry," in *Essays in Later Medieval French Literature: The Legacy of Jane H. M. Taylor*, ed. Rebecca Dixon (Manchester: Manchester University Press, 2010), 94–96.

20. The transfer is from the villain that Amant represents to the villein who responds to him in the way a peasant might.

21. Kelly, *Medieval Imagination*, 90–92.

22. Keith Busby, "Plagiarism and Poetry in the *Tournoiement Antéchrist* of Huon de Méry," *Neuphilologische Mitteilungen* 84 (1983): 505–21.

23. Huon de Méry, *Le Tournoi de l'Antéchrist (Li Tournoiemenz Antecrit)*, text estab. by George Wimmer; ed. and trans. Stéphanie Orgeur; 2nd ed. rev. by Stéphanie Orgeur and Jean-Pierre Bordier (Orléans: Paradigme, 1995), v. 3271.

24. On this humorous encounter, see Ernstpeter Ruhe, "Die Turnierkunst des Huon de Méry," *Zeitschrift für romanische Philologie* 105 (1989): 73.

25. Douglas Kelly, *Machaut and the Medieval Apprenticeship Tradition: Truth, Fiction and Poetic Craft* (Cambridge: D. S. Brewer, 2014), 287–88.

26. Orgeur, ed., in Huon de Méry, *Tournoiement*, 24–25.

27. See Ruhe, "Turnierkunst," 68–69.

28. Ruhe, "Turnierkunst," 67. Matilda Tomaryn Bruckner uses the more precise term "middleness" in *Chrétien Continued: A Study of the "Conte du Graal" and Its Verse Continuations* (Oxford: Oxford University Press, 2009), 24–25.

29. Cf. Jung, *Études*, 66, 286–87.

30. On this personification, see Madelyn Timmel Mihm, ed., *The Songe d'enfer of Raoul de Houdenc* (Tübingen: Niemeyer, 1984), 91–93.

31. Richard Trachsler, *Disjointures-conjointures: Étude sur l'interférence des matières narratives dans la littérature française du Moyen Âge* (Tübingen: Francke, 2000), 318–23.

32. Cf. Ruhe, "Turnierkunst," 73; Michelle Szkilnik, ed., *Meraugis de Portlesguez*, by Raoul de Houdenc (Paris: Champion, 2004), 11–21.

33. Reminiscent of the *Songe d'enfer* in which Versez (Felled), son of Yvrece, wrestles with the narrator in Hell (vv. 216–302); see Mihm's notes, *Songe*, 105–6, 108–14.

34. This name is not otherwise identified in the *Tournoiement*. Ruhe, "Turnierkunst," 74, interprets it as the name of a demon. In the early fifteenth-century *Echecs amoureux* she is the goddess who represents a chaste love (cf. Jung, *Études*, 278; Kelly, *Machaut*, 266–71).

35. D. W. Robertson Jr., *A Preface to Chaucer: Studies in Medieval Perspectives* (Princeton, NJ: Princeton University Press, 1962), 231–33; Marc-René Jung, "*Poetria*: Zur Dichtungstheorie des ausgehenden Mittelalters in Frankreich," *Vox romanica* 30 (1978): 44–64. Cf. Glasser, 103; Pierre-Yves Badel, *Le Roman de la rose au XIV*^{e} *siècle: Étude de la réception de l'œuvre* (Geneva: Droz, 1980), 283–84; Strubel, 252–53.

36. I summarize here briefly the analysis of the two personifications in my "*Fictio*," 97–98. See also William W. Kibler, "*Le Joli Buisson de Jonece*: Froissart's Midlife Crisis," in *Froissart across the Genres*, ed. Donald Maddox and Sara Sturm-Maddox (Gainesville: University Press of Florida, 1998), 63–80.

37. Kelly, *Medieval Imagination*, 172–73.

38. Kelly, "La Spécialité dans l'invention des topiques," in *Archéologie du signe*, ed. Lucie Brind'Amour and Eugene Vance (Toronto: Institut Pontifical d'Études Médiévales, 1983), 101–25.

39. Kelly, *Medieval Imagination*, 137–39; Kelly, *Machaut*, chapter 1.

40. Douglas Kelly, *Christine de Pizan's Changing Opinion: A Quest for Certainty in the Midst of Chaos* (Cambridge: D. S. Brewer, 2007), 30, 47–48.

41. Kelly, *Medieval Imagination*, 161–66.

42. Glasser, 66–67.

43. *Aviser* connotes consideration and discretion, a thought process that culminates in description (*deviser*). Cf. *Eles*, vv. 267–69, and Kelly, *Medieval Imagination*, 39.

44. Ruhe, "Le Chevalier errant auf enzyklopädischer Fahrt," in *Artusrittertum im späten Mittelalter: Ethos und Ideologie*, ed. Friedrich Wolfzettel (Gießen: Schmitz, 1984), 159–76; Trachsler, 346; Kelly, *Machaut*, 244–63. Bruckner, 27,

finds the model already in Chrétien's *Conte du Graal* and its continuations; see as well Trachsler, 358–59.

45. Ruhe, "Chevalier errant," 167–73; Badel, 288–89. Cf. a similar, albeit more pessimistic, evolution of the Froissart narrator analyzed by Michael Schwarze, *Generische Wahrheit: Höfischer Polylog im Werk Jean Froissarts* (Stuttgart: F. Steiner, 2003).

46. Badel, 268–69, 286; Gianmario Raimondi, "Les Eschés amoureux: Studio preparatorio ed edizione (I: VV. 1–3662)," *Pluteus* 8–9 (1990–98): 72–73, 224; Kelly, *Machaut*, 263–72.

47. François Villon, *Le Testament Villon*, vol. 1, *Texte*, ed. Jean Rychner and Albert Henry (Geneva: Droz, 1974).

48. An obvious reference to how dull his formerly sharp feelings have become. On this word, see Rey, *Dictionnaire historique*, 2: 1466, s.v. *pelote*.

49. Charles d'Orléans, *Ballades et rondeaux*, ed. Jean-Claude Mühlethaler (Paris: Librairie Générale Française, 1992).

50. See Daniel Poirion, *Le Poète et le prince: L'évolution du lyrisme courtois de Guillaume de Machaut à Charles d'Orléans* (Paris: Presses Universitaires de France, 1965), chapter 16.

51. *Gradus amoris* and *cursus aetatum* are also blueprints for a mini-narrative plot.

52. Jung, "A propos de la poésie lyrique courtoise d'oc et d'oïl," *Studi francesi e provenzali* 84–85 (1986): 14; cf. Glasser, 80–81; Kelly, *Machaut*, 9–15 et passim.

53. Glasser, 63–67; Rohr, "Skala."

Chapter 2. "Je vueil ung livre commencier": The Othernesses of Othon de Grandson's "Je"

1. From the *envoi* devised by Chaucer to follow his translation of three of Othon de Grandson's ballades in his *Compleynt of Venus*; see Geoffrey Chaucer, *The Minor Poems*, ed. Walter W. Skeat (Oxford: Clarendon Press, 1883), 206.

2. See Arthur Piaget, *Oton de Grandson, sa vie et ses poésies*, Mémoires et documents publiés par la Société d'histoire de la Suisse romande, 3e série, 1 (Lausanne: Payot, 1941); Oton de Granson, *Poésies*, ed. Joan Grenier-Winther, Classiques français du Moyen Âge 162 (Paris: H. Champion, 2010). Note that the text, with a facing-page translation into English, is also now available online in *Oton de Granson: Poems*, edited and translated by Peter Nicholson and Joan Grenier-Winther (Kalamazoo, MI: Medieval Institute Publications, 2015); see https://d.lib.rochester.edu/teams/text/granson-nicholson-grenier-winther-le-livre-messire-ode. All three editions contain brief biographies of Othon; for a rather more romanticized account, see Esther Rowland Clifford, *A Knight of Great Renown: The Life and Times of Othon de Grandson* (Chicago: University of Chicago Press, 1961).

3. In Grenier-Winther's edition, 383–499; all citations are from this edition, by line number. Translations are my own.

4. Or "autography," as A. C. Spearing would have it: see his *Medieval Autographies: The "I" of the Text* (Notre Dame, IN: University of Notre Dame Press, 2012).

5. For a brief survey of the *mise à distance* associated with the literary dream, see Jean-Claude Schmitt, "Du 'moi' du rêve au 'je' du récit et de l'image," in *Le Rêve médiéval: Études littéraires*, ed. Alain Corbellari and Jean-Yves Tilliette (Geneva: Droz, 2007), 233–42.

6. Which is extant, complete, in only one manuscript: Paris, BnF fr. 1727; Brussels, Bibliothèque Royale, MSS 10961–10971 is incomplete; a sixteenth-century manuscript, Paris, BnF fr. 1952, contains a somewhat modernized version.

7. Laurence de Looze, *Pseudo-Autobiography in the Fourteenth Century: Juan Ruiz, Guillaume de Machaut, Jean Froissart, and Geoffrey Chaucer* (Gainesville: University Press of Florida, 1997).

8. On the late-medieval vogue for "anthologies" of this sort, see Jacqueline Cerquiglini, "Quand la voix s'est tue: La mise en recueil de la poésie lyrique aux XIVe et XVe siècles," in *La Présentation du livre: Actes du colloque de Paris X–Nanterre (4, 5, 6 décembre 1985)*, ed. E. Baumgartner and N. Boulestreau (Nanterre: Centre de recherches du Département de français de Paris X–Nanterre, 1987), 313–27; Nancy Freeman Regalado, "Gathering the Works: The 'Œuvres de Villon' and the Intergeneric Passage of the Medieval French Lyric into Single-Author Collections," *L'Esprit créateur* 33 (1993): 87–100.

9. For a more complete summary, see Sally Tartline Carden, "*Le Livre Messire Ode* d'Othon de Grandson: Un interrogatoire poétique," *Le Moyen français* 35–36 (1996): 79–90.

10. I say *seems to be*; Othon certainly seems to suggest so: "vouloie / En mon dormant ung songe faire, / Je m'endormy, et n'y mis guere. / Et en mon dormant je veoye, / Chevauchant par une saulsoye, / Dangier" (1878–83) [I wanted to have a dream in my sleep. I soon fell asleep. And in my sleep I saw Danger riding through a stand of willows]. But at this point the narrative voice virtually ceases, so it is unclear how this second dream is to be understood.

11. The form is unknown to either the *Dictionnaire du moyen français* (*DMF*) or to Godefroy's *Dictionnaire de l'ancienne langue française* (*DALF*). It must, of course, be related to *pasmee* and *pasmement*, both of which (see *DALF* 6: 19 and 10: 287) mean "pâmoison," but given that the *pasmerie* is conducive to dreams, is a particular sort of loss of consciousness implied? The text would suggest that *pasmerie* is to be distinguished from *resverie*, which, according to *DMF*, means simply "songe, état de songe." *Pasmer* has, of course, meanings to do with to swoon or faint, often from pain or distress: is Othon implying that this is a more

pathological condition? Certainly the context would suggest this: "Quant je l'oy, j'estoye en pasmerie, / Si prins adonc a ma teste lever / . . . / quant vint le matin, / De mes maulx fu allegré grandement" (1987–94) [When I heard this, I was still dreaming, but I immediately raised my head . . . when morning broke, I was much comforted in my ills].

12. As Catherine Attwood points out: see her "La dialectique amoureuse chez Othon de Grandson," in *Othon de Grandson, chevalier et poète*, ed. Jean-François Kosta-Théfaine (Orléans: Paradigme, 2007), 85–101. Piaget too wonders if the poem is unfinished; see his *Oton*, 150. For Kosta-Théfaine, on the other hand, what he calls Othon's "écriture fragmentaire" is deliberate, an objective correlative of his unsuccessful experience of love: see "Le *Livre Messire Ode* d'Othon de Grandson ou l'écriture fragmentaire d'un discours amoureux," *Germanisch-Romanische Monatsschrift* 53 (2003), 355–61.

13. There are some brief comments on Othon's dreams in Hélène Basso's article "L'envol et l'ancrage: La quête amoureuse dans *Le Dit de l'alérion* de Guillaume de Machaut et *Le Livre messire Ode*," in *Othon de Grandson*, ed. Kosta-Théfaine, 148–63, and in Carden, "*Le Livre Messire Ode*."

14. For the ubiquity in the late Middle Ages of literary pseudo-autobiographical dreams derived from the model of the *Rose*, see Armand Strubel, *"Grant senefiance a": Allégorie et littérature au Moyen Âge* (Paris: Honoré Champion, 2002), esp. 211–16; Virginie Minet-Mahy, *Esthétique et pouvoir de l'œuvre allégorique à l'époque de Charles VI: Imaginaires et discours* (Paris: Champion, 2005); see also, for a preliminary catalogue, B. A. Windeatt, *Chaucer's Dream Poetry: Sources and Analogues* (Cambridge: D. S. Brewer, 1982).

15. On these multiple perspectives, see Evelyn Birge Vitz, "The *I* of the *Roman de la Rose*," *Genre* 6 (1973): 49–73.

16. Othon's dream self insists heavily on *le livre*: on the act of writing as preservation, and on reading as communication: see lines 360–61, 505–11, 520–24, 580–82, 699–701, 834–35, 868–71, 942, 1078–80, 1086–89, 1120–24, 1412–13, 1727–28. For some similar strategies elsewhere in late-medieval French literature, see Jacqueline Cerquiglini, "L'échappée belle: Stratégies d'écriture et de lecture dans la littérature de la fin du Moyen Âge," *Littérature* 99 (1995): 33–52.

17. On the "I" of the *Rose* as a student, see Alan M. F. Gunn, "Teacher and Student in the *Roman de la Rose*: A Study in Archetypal Figures and Patterns," *L'Esprit créateur* 2 (1962): 126–34.

18. Kosta-Théfaine hints at a similar viewpoint: "[Othon] tente de brosser des portraits amoureux particuliers, s'apparentant au sien par une thématique identique, sans toutefois lui être propres" [Othon tries to sketch portraits of lovers as individuals, being thematically close to himself but still being sufficiently different]; see his "De la continuité à l'innovation: Le *Livre messire Ode*," *Cahiers*

de recherches médiévales 11 (2004): 241–53. I am aware, of course, of the specialized sense in which the word "projection" is used by psychoanalysts: for Freud, for instance, projection is a defense mechanism whereby unacceptable or unwanted thoughts are attributed to others. I shall, I am afraid, continue to use the term rather more loosely, to mean the creation of "other" or "alien" selves that correspond to, or contrast with, the particular narrating self.

19. The poem is found in *Le Lais Villon et les poèmes variés*, ed. Jean Rychner and Albert Henry, 2 vols. (Geneva: Droz, 1977); for the comment quoted, see 2: 123. Dialogue-poems are something of a commonplace in late-medieval verse: see Omer Jodogne, "La ballade dialoguée dans la littérature française médiévale," in *Fin du Moyen Âge et Renaissance: Mélanges de philologie française offerts à Robert Guiette* (Antwerp: Nederlandsche Boekhandel, 1961), 71–85, and more recently Emma Cayley, *Debate and Dialogue: Alain Chartier in His Cultural Context* (Oxford: Clarendon Press, 2006). I give the title as "so-called" because it seems not to have been Villon's but to have been first used in Pierre Levet's *editio princeps* of 1489.

20. Jacqueline Cerquiglini, "Le clerc et l'écriture: Le *Voir Dit* de Guillaume de Machaut et la définition du dit," in *Literatur in der Gesellschaft des Spätmittelalters*, ed. Hans Ulrich Gumbrecht, Grundriss der romanischen Literaturen des Mittelalters (Heidelberg: Winter, 1980), 1: 151–68, here 155.

21. Using birds as metaphors for lovers is, of course, conventional: I think of Machaut's *Dit de l'alerion* (on which see Basso, "L'envol et l'ancrage"), and indeed of Chaucer's *Parliament of Foules*. I am particularly reminded, in the present instance, of the scorn with which the *bouvier* (cowherd) in *Aucassin et Nicolette* treats Aucassin's absurdly hyperbolic grief for his *levrier* (greyhound), although I do not suggest any link; see the edition by Mario Roques (Paris: Honoré Champion, 1982), lines 25–26.

22. The *je* of the *dit* is, of course, frequently faintly comic: see Michel Zink, *La Subjectivité littéraire autour du siècle de saint Louis* (Paris: Presses Universitaires de France, 1985), 47–79; cf. Jacqueline Cerquiglini, "Le Clerc et le Louche: Sociology of an Esthetic," *Poetics Today* 5 (1984): 479–91, and Didier Lechat, *Dire par fiction: Métamorphoses du Je chez Guillaume de Machaut, Jean Froissart et Christine de Pizan* (Paris: Champion, 2005).

23. Pierre-Yves Badel, *Le Roman de la Rose au XIVe siècle* (Geneva: Droz, 1980).

24. See Badel, *Le Roman de la Rose*, 334–40; cf. Alain Corbellari, "Les limites du rêve-cadre: Prologues et épilogues dans les récits allégoriques du XIIIe au XVe siècle," in *Sommeil, songes et insomnies: Actes du colloque CELAM (Rennes 2) et Université de Bretagne Occidentale (Rennes 2), 28–29 septembre 2006*, ed. Christine Ferlampin-Acher, Elisabeth Gaucher, and Denis Hüe, special issue of *Perspectives médiévales,* juillet 2008, 127–41.

25. Badel, *Le Roman de la Rose*, 355.

26. And unusually lengthy: the prologues analyzed by Badel and Corbellari rarely exceed 60 or so lines, whereas Othon's has 190.

27. This cross-refers to Othon's *Complainte de saint Valentin*, where indeed the God of Love had presented him, Othon, to a *non pareille beauté* who was to be his *maistresse*; see *Poésies,* ed. Grenier-Winther, 183–97.

28. It is conventional, of course, for a "dream" to end with the speaker waking up, but Othon's *Livre* simply ends in a welter of lyrics, with no sign of a concluding episode or of an epilogue.

29. I am reminded of the state of *dorveille* in which, Guillaume de Machaut tells us, he has composed his *Fontaine amoureuse*; ed. Jacqueline Cerquiglini-Toulet (Paris: Stock, 1993).

30. Corbellari, "Les limites du rêve-cadre," 138–39.

31. See my *The Poetry of François Villon: Text and Context* (Cambridge: Cambridge University Press, 2001), 6–32.

32. Gay Clifford, *The Transformations of Allegory* (London: Routledge and Kegan Paul, 1975), 5.

33. David F. Hult, *Self-Fulfilling Prophecies: Readership and Authority in the First "Roman de la Rose"* (Cambridge: Cambridge University Press, 1986), 137.

34. Here *dangier* and *reffuz* are, studiously and rightly, lowercased.

35. Othon includes, for instance, a *lai*—the mode that, Froissart tells us in the *Espinette amoureuse*, is the most demanding of all lyric genres: "D'un lay faire c'est .I. grans fes, / Car qui l'ordonne et rieule et taille / Selonc ce que requiert la taille, / Il y faut, ce dient li mestre, / Demi an ou environ mettre" (2199–2203) [To compose a *lai* is very demanding, for anyone who embarks on the refining and reworking necessary will need, the authorities say, as much as six months' work] (ed. Anthime Fourrier [Paris: Klincksieck, 1963]).

36. On both of which see de Looze, *Pseudo-Autobiography in the Fourteenth Century*, and Daniel Poirion, *Le Poète et le Prince: L'évolution du lyrisme courtois de Guillaume de Machaut à Charles d'Orléans* (Paris: Presses Universitaires de France, 1965); for a study in particular of the technical complexity of Machaut's *Voir Dit*, see Jacqueline Cerquiglini, *Guillaume de Machaut et l'écriture au XIVe siècle: "Un engin si soutil"* (Geneva: Slatkine, 1985).

37. Othon remains much neglected; however, two recent articles appear in *Sens, rhétorique et musique: Études réunies en hommage à Jacqueline Cerquiglini-Toulet*, ed. Sylvie Lefèvre et al. (Paris: Champion, 2015). Hélène Basso's "L'audace et les doutes: Le lyrisme désaccordé d'Oton de Granson," 31–49, analyzes, with great subtlety, the unreliability of what she calls the "petrified" language of Middle French love-lyric: for her, the poet's voice, claimed as autobiographical and hence authentic, is in fact inflected by the traditional stances of the lover poet and

leads to a "décrochage" (40) between word and experience. Jean-Claude Mühlethaler's "*De Falcone Peregrino*: Subtilités de la communication au temps d'Othon de Grandson," 171–85, starts from what might seem a minor detail, the peregrine falcon, to show how it serves as a multifaceted metaphor: for the inconstant lover, for the perfect prince, and for that most hackneyed of late-medieval figures, the *amant martyr*.

Chapter 3. *Huon de Bordeaux*: The Cultural Dream as Palimpsest

1. Throughout the essay I will be referring to the edition by William W. Kibler and François Suard: *Huon de Bordeaux* (Paris: Champion, 2003). Although an earlier date had been proposed, Marguerite Rossi suggested 1268 as the year of composition in *Huon de Bordeaux et l'évolution du genre épique au XIIIe siècle* (Paris: Champion, 1975), esp. 157–67, and Kibler and Suard, in their edition, opt for "a few years after 1268" (xxii).

2. *Huon* is quite overt in its condemnation of Charlemagne and of his son. At both the beginning of the text and the end, Charlemagne is portrayed as indecisive, irrational, given to accesses of temper, and quick to flout traditional judicial practice.

3. It appears that contemporary listeners were most interested in the very same incidents. In the early fourteenth-century manuscript P, one of only three such extant manuscripts, the copyist has titled the work *Livre de Huelin de bourdialx et du roi abron*, and the 1,010-line continuation of the chanson included in the same manuscript is divided into three sections: *Huon, roi de féerie* (444 verses), *Combat de Huon contre les geants* (404 verses), and *Huon le desvey* (162 verses).

4. *Huon de Bordeaux*, vv. 2924–26.

5. *Huon de Bordeaux*, vv. 2928–35.

6. *Huon de Bordeaux*, vv. 2939–44.

7. Many of these descriptions are common to texts that discuss the lands surrounding Jerusalem and the major Middle Eastern cities after the First Crusade, and they are all indebted to passages from *Le Roman d'Alexandre* and the *Letter of Prester John*. See William Burgwinkle, "Utopia and Its Uses: Twelfth-Century Romance and Conquest," *Journal of Medieval and Early Modern Studies* 36.3 (Fall 2006): 539–60, and Anne Berthelot, "L'autre monde féerique comme distorsion de l'Orient dans *Maugis d'Aigremont, Huon de Bordeaux* et le *Roman d'Auberon*," in *L'Épopée romane: Actes du XVe Congrès international Rencesvals, Poitiers, 21–27 août 2000*, ed. G. Bianciotto and C. Galderisi (Poitiers: Université de Poitiers, Centre d'études supérieures de civilisation médiévale, 2002), 647–53, here 649.

8. *Huon de Bordeaux*, v. 3295.

9. *Huon de Bordeaux*, v. 3426.

10. Kibler and Suard, *Huon*, 187n2: "amitié passionnée pour Huon qui se tourne ici en haine."

11. *Huon de Bordeaux*, vv. 3506–11.

12. The following passage establishes Auberon's credentials:

> Je sai de l'omme le cuer et le pancez,
> Se li sai dire comment il ait ovrez,
> [Et] enaprés son peschief criminez.
> La thierce fee si volt muelx esprouver,
> Si moy donnait tel don com vous orez,
> Qu'il nen ait marche ne paiis ne rengnez
> Jusqu'a Sec Arbre, ne jusqu'a Rouge Mer,
> Se je m'y vuelz sohaidier en nom Dey
> Que je n'i soie tout a ma vollanteit
> Tout si errant com je l'ai devisez,
> A tant de gens come je vuelz demander.
> Et quant je vuelz .j. pallais massonneir
> a .xxx. chambre et a .xv. pilleir,
> je l'ai tantost, ja mar le mescroirez ;
> Et tel maingier com je vuelz deviser,
> Et sifait boivre com je vuelz demander. (vv. 3513–28)

[I know the hearts and thoughts of men; I know the things they have done and their mortal sins. The third fairy wanted to do one better so she gave me such a gift as you will soon hear. There is no marketplace, no land, no kingdom between here and the Dry Tree, or even the Red Sea that I couldn't get to on my willpower alone, in the name of God, just as quickly as I thought of it and with as many along for the ride as I desire. And if I want to build a palace with thirty sleeping chambers and fifteen pillars, I can have it that very day, and you had better believe me; and such food and drink as I can imagine is mine for the asking.]

13. *Huon de Bordeaux*, vv. 3626–27, 3654–62.

14. *Huon de Bordeaux*, vv. 3713–18.

15. Roger Kennedy, *Psychoanalysis, History, and Subjectivity: Now of the Past* (New York: Routledge, 2002).

16. "Les péripéties romanesques dont se nourrit la chanson procèdent du pèlerinage et tout le coeur de la chanson, qui se déroule entre le depart de Huon et son retour en France s'avère être un récit de pèlerinage" [The fanciful events that the song is based on are derived from pilgrimage and the chanson's core, which takes place between Huon's departure and his return to France, proves to be a pilgrimage story]: Valérie Galent-Fasseur, *L'Épopée des pèlerins: Motifs eschatologiques et mutations de la chanson de geste* (Paris: Presses Universitaires de France, 1997), 123.

17. Several of the locales alluded to in the text, however, do have Westerners present. Both Tormont (vv. 3950–4573), which is ruled over by Huon's uncle, and Dunostre, where Huon's cousin Sebille is held prisoner, are located in Outremer.

18. Berthelot, "L'autre monde féerique," 649.

19. For example, after the battles at Tormont (vv. 4555–60) and Dunostre (vv. 6955–60).

20. Such acts of heroism often take place through Huon's madness, a quality that marks him as a spontaneous child of instinct rather than a full-fledged military hero.

21. In Berthelot's words: "A côté de l'émir de Babylone ou d'Yvorin, il faut avouer que Charlemagne—sans même aborder le problème de la décadence morale subie par l'empereur Franc—fait bien piètre figure" [When looked at beside the emir of Babylon or Yvorin, one has to admit that Charlemagne—even without considering the moral decadence the Frankish emperor exhibits—cuts a decidedly poor figure] ("L'autre monde féerique," 649). It is on this basis that it is argued that *Huon de Bordeaux* can be seen as a rebel baron epic. Only the corruption of the court of Charlemagne and his sons can spur these local heroes to extraordinary actions.

22. As Berthelot points out, to associate Esclarmonde, Huon's Muslim lover, with a fairy is a natural step: "C'est qu'en tant que fille de l'émir de Babylone, elle appartient d'ores et déjà à ce monde quelque peu interlope qui rassemble l'Orient et la Féerie, sans qu'il soit possible d'en tracer les frontières" [Inasmuch as she is the daughter of the emir of Babylon, she belongs already to this somewhat interstitial world which collates the Orient and Fairydom while blurring decisively the borders between them] ("L'autre monde féerique," 653). Yet we must add that this realm, Esclarmonde included, is then reclaimed for Christianity.

23. This motif is further developed in the brief mention that Gériaume makes of a Saracen princess falling in love with him and securing his liberation. When he had been imprisoned by the Saracens and Eslavons ("Sairaisin et Escler," v. 3098), it was only through the efforts of the emir's daughter, who had fallen in love with him, that he was released (vv. 3101–3). The cry of the Eastern Christian calling out for Western liberation—here in the person of Auberon—of course recalls the fate of Outremer, the crusader settlements after the fall of Jerusalem in 1187.

Chapter 4. Ringing True: Shifting Identity in *Le Roman de la Violette*

1. Kara Doyle notes that a mere 1,500 or so lines detail Euriaut's plight; see "'Narratizing' Marie of Ponthieu," *Historical Reflections/Réflexions historiques* 30.1 (2004): 29–54, here 42.

2. Citations come from Gerbert de Montreuil, *Le Roman de la Violette ou de*

Gerart de Nevers, ed. Douglas Labaree Buffum (Paris: Champion, 1928). Translations into English are mine.

3. As Mireille Demaules observes, the ring and its stone symbolize union and fidelity; see "L'art de la ruse dans *Le Roman de la Violette* de Gerbert de Montreuil," *Revue des langues romanes* 104.1 (2000): 143–61, here 148.

4. Francine Mora, "Mémoire du narrateur et oublis du héros dans le *Roman de la Violette* de Gerbert de Montreuil," *Études de lettres* (2007): 119–37, here 134.

5. Mora, "Mémoire du narrateur," 134.

6. Gérard's revelation incites the soon-to-be abandoned Aiglente to try to strangle the sparrowhawk before she is restrained (vv. 4357–78). Her lack of success testifies to her inability to alter permanently the love that binds Euriaut and Gérard.

7. Demaules highlights the contrast in remarking upon the distinction between courtly love, which comes from the heart, and love born of a potion; see "L'art de la ruse," 149. In this case the lark evokes both false and true love: false because Gérard associates the bird's song with Aiglente, and true because it has come from Euriaut and will set in motion the chain of events reuniting the couple.

8. David S. King contends that Gérard himself unintentionally reveals his misjudgment of Euriaut. In the line immediately before he links Euriaut's infidelity to his shame, Gérard tells her: "Ves ci vostre martyre" (v. 1030) [See here your martyrdom]. King argues that with the term "martyre" Gérard acknowledges Euriaut's lack of sin; see "Learning from Loss: Amputation in Three Thirteenth-Century French Verse Romances," *Modern Philology* 110.1 (2012): 1–23, here 9. I see the line less as recognition—unconscious or not—by Gérard than as part of a pattern by which Gerbert consistently draws attention to Euriaut's innocence.

9. Kathy Krause, "The Material Erotic: The Clothed and Unclothed Female Body in the *Roman de la violette*," in *Material Culture and Cultural Materialisms in the Middle Ages and Renaissance*, ed. Curtis Perry (Turnhout: Brepols, 2001), 17–39, here 25–29.

10. Krause, "The Material Erotic," 31. Suzanne Kocher deems this approach a "repellent fiction" in "Accusations of Gay and Straight Sexual Transgression in the *Roman de la Violette*," in *Discourses on Love, Marriage, and Transgression in Medieval and Early Modern Literature*, ed. Albrecht Classen (Tempe: Arizona Center for Medieval and Renaissance Studies, 2004), 189–210, here 194.

11. Krause, "The Material Erotic," 32.

12. King, "Learning from Loss," 9.

13. Gérard thereby symbolically regains his own land, as Norris J. Lacy points out; see "Spatial Form in Medieval Romance," *Yale French Studies* 51 (1974): 160–69, here 162–63.

14. Doyle posits that Gerbert uses the episode as part of his "narratizing" of

Marie de Ponthieu, casting her in a passive role and representing Marie's exiled husband, Simon de Dammartin, in a positive and active light; see "'Narratizing' Marie of Ponthieu," 42.

15. Mora views Marote as "une image épurée, simplifiée, de l'amie" [a refined, simplified image of the *amie*] ("Mémoire du narrateur," 131). She thus subtly calls attention to Euriaut's worthiness and foregrounds the couple's reunion.

16. Because of the echoes created in these scenes, I do not entirely agree with Hans-Erich Keller's assertion that the romance is about how Gérard learns to be courtly. To be sure, there is the binary structure of error and redemption that Keller notes, and much of the tale details the exploits that prove Gérard worthy of Euriaut. Yet the similar tales that Gérard and Euriaut tell forge a bond between them, which suggests that Gerbert's goal is not solely to depict Gérard's progress toward courtliness. See "L'Esprit courtois et le *Roman de la Violette*," in *Courtly Literature: Culture and Context*, ed. Keith Busby and Erik Kooper (Amsterdam: John Benjamins, 1990): 323–35.

17. Kocher, "Accusations," 196.

18. For a reading of the judicial importance of the accusations against Euriaut, see Philippe Haugeard, "Preuve et Vérité dans le *Tristan* de Béroul et le *Roman de la violette* de Gerbert de Montreuil," *Cahiers de Recherches Médiévales et Humanistes* 34.2 (2017): 149–71.

19. John W. Baldwin, *Aristocratic Life in Medieval France: The Romances of Jean Renart and Gerbert de Montreuil, 1190–1230* (Baltimore: Johns Hopkins University Press, 2000), 156.

20. Krause, "The Material Erotic," 34.

21. King notes that Onestasse represents Euriaut and sees the episode's placement as significant: "With the examples of bodily imperfection before and after the rescue of the heroine, the poet highlights the one damaged body that enjoys restoration" ("Learning from Loss," 16).

22. For more on the ways in which Euriaut takes on an active role, see my "Re-Creating the Body: Euriaut's Tales in *Le Roman de la Violette*," *Symposium: A Quarterly Journal of Modern Literatures* 56.1 (Spring 2002): 3–16. Although I do not use the term "active passivity" there, the article demonstrates the ways in which Euriaut is less passive than she first seems, as she claims her right to interpret and modify the significance of her body.

23. Alberto Limentani and Laura Pegolo, "Marote ou de l'amour bourgeois," in *Epopée Animale, Fable, Fabliau: Actes du IVe Colloque de la Société Internationale Renardienne, Evreux, 7–11 septembre 1981*, ed. Gabriel Bianciotto and Michel Salvat (Paris: Presses Universitaires de France, 1984), 323–31, here 327.

24. Demaules, "L'art de la ruse," 148.

25. King notes that during their duels with Gérard, both Méliatir and Lisiart

receive facial injuries and then lose arms before being condemned to death for their treachery. He views Gérard's mutilation of the two men as evocative of the marks that Euriaut inscribes on herself after Gérard abandons her; see "Learning from Loss," 11. In this sense, too, Gérard takes on the active role of protecting and defending Euriaut, symbolically erasing the wounds she inflicts upon herself by transferring them to the villains.

Chapter 5. Inside Out and Outside In: (Re-)Reading the Other in the Guillaume Cycle

1. Léon Gautier, *Les Épopées françaises: Étude sur les origines et l'histoire de la littérature nationale*, 2nd ed., 5 vols. (1878–92; Osnabrück: Otto Zeller, 1966), 1: 13. The issue of nationhood was of great importance to critics such as Gautier, and the early nineteenth-century scholarly interest in folklore and oral literature as repositories of forgotten national ideals influenced those eager to find a provable historical basis for legendary tales and their heroes. Also belonging to this pioneering generation was Gaston Paris, much of whose work was devoted to investigating the "sources," historical, folkloric, or otherwise, of these poems supposed to illustrate the true "self" of the nation; see his 1865 *Histoire poétique de Charlemagne*, augmented, with new notes by Paris and Paul Meyer (Paris: Emile Bouillon, 1905). Such an approach is understandable following the Romanticism-influenced trend earlier in the nineteenth century for analyzing oral literature (ballads, fairy tales, pseudo-historical legends) as a source of information about a race or nation's origins and development; this approach was famously advanced by the Grimm brothers, among others. Later scholars would continue this search for the origins of epic, still emphasizing the desire for provable historical sources. See, for example, Joseph Bédier, *Les Légendes épiques: Recherches sur la formation des chansons de geste*, 3rd ed., 3 vols. (Paris: Champion, 1926–29), whose third volume examines the problems inherent in seeking to establish historical bases for epic; Ferdinand Lot, *Études sur les légendes épiques françaises* (Paris: Champion, 1958); Martín de Riquer, *Les Chansons de geste françaises*, trans. Irénée Cluzel, 2nd ed. (Paris: Nizet, 1957); Italo Siciliano, *Les Origines des chansons de geste*, trans. P. Antonetti (Paris: Picard, 1951). See also Emmanuèle Baumgartner et al., eds., *La Chanson de geste et le mythe carolingien: Mélanges René Louis, publiés par ses collègues, ses amis et ses élèves à l'occasion de son 75e anniversaire*, 2 vols. (Saint-Père-sous-Vézelay: Musée archéologique régional, 1982).

2. Michèle Gally, ed., *Comprendre et aimer la chanson de geste (à propos d'"Aliscans")* (Fontenay–St. Cloud: Feuillets de l'ENS, 1994), 6; Jean-Marcel Paquette, "Epopée ou roman: Continuité ou discontinuité?," *Études littéraires* 1 (1971): 9–38, here 12–13.

3. Huguette Legros, "Réalités et imaginaires du péril sarrasin," in *La Chrétienté*

au péril sarrasin, Senefiance 46 (Aix-en-Provence: CUER-MA, 2000), 125–45, analyzes Otherness in later chansons de geste, which she contends reveal complexities discovered by encountering "Saracens" in real life.

4. Bernard McGrane, *Beyond Anthropology: Society and the Other* (New York: Columbia University Press, 1989), ix. See also Michelle Houdeville, "Les Sarrasins, miroir des chrétiens?," in *La Chrétienté au péril sarrasin*, Senefiance 46 (Aix-en-Provence: CUER-MA, 2000), 77–83, on the reciprocal and mutually illuminating aspects of Christian/Saracen binarism.

5. See, for example, Henri Baudet's *Paradise on Earth: Some Thoughts on European Images of Non-European Man*, trans. Elizabeth Wentholt (New Haven, CT: Yale University Press, 1965).

6. Lynne Tarte Ramey's *Christian, Saracen and Genre in Medieval French Literature* (New York: Routledge, 2001) examines the topic of French identity and self as depicted by "interethnic" (French/Saracen) couples, whether lovers or friends, opposite or same sex, in a rather small corpus of works (eleven chansons de geste, *Aucassin et Nicolette*, and travel literature). There are many studies of the intersection of East and West in literature and history; see, for instance, *Images et signes de l'Orient dans l'Occident médiéval*, Senefiance 11 (Aix-en-Provence: CUER-MA, 1982), and John V. Tolan, *Saracens: Islam in the Medieval European Imagination* (New York: Columbia University Press, 2002). There are also numerous works on the theme of the Saracen Other in epic; these include Paul Bancourt's *Les Musulmans dans les chansons de geste du cycle du roi*, 2 vols. (Aix-en-Provence: CUER-MA, 1982); *Au Carrefour des routes de l'Europe: La chanson de geste*, 2 vols., Senefiance 21 (Aix-en-Provence: CUER-MA, 1987); and Marianne Ailes, "Chivalry and Conversion: The Chivalrous Saracen in Old French Epics *Fierabras* and *Otinel*," *Al-Masaq: Studia Arabo-Islamica Mediterranea, The Medieval Mediterranean Cultures in Contact* 9 (1996–97): 1–21.

7. David Richards, *Masks of Difference: Cultural Representations in Literature, Anthropology and Art* (Cambridge: Cambridge University Press, 1994), 1–2.

8. Raymond Corbey and Joep Leerssen, eds., *Alterity, Identity, Image: Selves and Others in Society and Scholarship* (Amsterdam: Rodopi, 1991), vii. Although "alterity theory" is a relatively recent term, the acknowledgment of alterity is not. We find an early theoretical discussion of the notion of Other by Hegel in *The Science of Logic*, where he also discusses the necessity of a third being to establish the existence of two somethings that are mutually other; see *Hegel's Science of Logic*, trans. A. V. Miller (London: George Allen & Unwin, 1969), 118. This is important in discussing the Other in French epic, for the narrator, the third being, is commenting on both the dominant discourse that he is excluded from, yet apparently endorsing, and those who are Other to that discourse. This necessarily imposes questions of subjectivity and objectivity, especially given the often questionable

social status of the performer, a medieval jongleur. Mark C. Taylor's chapters on Hegel's thought on alterity, and on Heidegger's development of Hegelian theory, provide interesting and useful summaries in *Altarity* (Chicago: University of Chicago Press, 1987). See also Michel de Certeau, *Heterologies: Discourse on the Other*, trans. Brian Massumi (Manchester: Manchester University Press, 1986); William Desmond, *Desire, Dialectic and Otherness: An Essay on Origins* (New Haven, CT: Yale University Press, 1987); Brian Massumi, *The Politics of Everyday Fear* (Minneapolis: University of Minnesota Press, 1993); and Michael Taussig, *Mimesis and Alterity: A Particular History of the Senses* (New York: Routledge, 1993).

9. Claude Régnier, ed., *La Prise d'Orange: Chanson de geste de la fin du XIIe siècle*, 3rd ed. (Paris: Klincksieck, 1970); Philip E. Bennett, ed. and trans., *"La Chanson de Guillaume" and "La Prise d'Orange"* (London: Grant and Cutler, 2000); François Suard, ed., *La Chanson de Guillaume* (Paris: Bordas, 1991); Claude Régnier, ed., *Aliscans*, 2 vols. (Paris: Champion, 1990); François Guessard and Antoine de Montaiglon, eds., *Aliscans: Chanson de geste, publiée d'après le manuscrit de la Bibliothèque de l'Arsenal et à l'aide de cinq autres manuscrits* (Paris: Vieweg, 1870). Orable/Guibourc appears in many other poems as well, including *Les Enfances Guillaume* and *La Bataille Loquifer*—see Patrice Henry, ed., *Les Enfances Guillaume* (Paris: SATF, 1935) and Monica Barnett, ed., *La Bataille Loquifer* (Oxford: Basil Blackwell, 1975)—but *La Prise d'Orange*, *La Chanson de Guillaume*, and *Aliscans* are the ones in which her character is most fully developed and her actions given the most scope. For Guillaume's defense of Louis's throne, and the king's weak character, see Ernest Langlois, ed., *Le Couronnement de Louis*, 2nd ed. (1925; Paris: Champion, 1984).

10. Régnier, *Aliscans*, vv. 3595–3603; see also vv. 3523–40.

11. Régnier, *La Prise d'Orange*, vv. 202–7.

12. See Peter S. Noble's discussion of class in epic in "Attitudes to Social Class as Revealed by Some of the Older Chansons de Geste," *Romania* 94 (1973): 359–85.

13. Guessard and de Montaiglon, *Aliscans*, vv. 4878–84.

14. Guessard and de Montaiglon, *Aliscans*, vv. 3847–55.

15. Joan B. Williamson, "Le personnage de Rainouart dans *la Chanson de Guillaume*," in *Guillaume d'Orange and the chanson de geste*, ed. Wolfgang van Emden and Philip E. Bennett (Reading: Société Rencesvals British Branch, 1984), 159–71, here 163, 167. See also Bennett's "Carnaval héroïque et écriture cyclique dans la geste de Guillaume," in *L'épopée romane*, ed. Gabriel Bianciotto and Claudio Galderisi, 2 vols. (Poitiers: Université de Poitiers, Centre d'études supérieures de civilisation médiévale), 253–63, which applies aspects of Bakhtinian theory to chansons de geste. According to Bennett, all major epic characters—not only one such as Rainouart—demonstrate how notions of carnival and dialogism illuminate the dynamic of both dominant groups and the Other.

16. Suard, *La Chanson de Guillaume*, v. 2818.

17. The distinction between "marginal" and "liminal" is one I developed more fully in relation to epic in my doctoral dissertation, "'Myriad with Difference': Alterity and Identity in Old French and Russian Epic" (University of Virginia, 1997). Briefly, I argue that the term "marginal," though traditionally used in literary, historical, and cultural studies, is insufficient to describe the variety of characters who are Other. A term used in ethnography, anthropology, and folklore, "liminality," seems to suit these needs. Jacqueline de Weever, in the final chapter of *Sheba's Daughters: Whitening and Demonizing the Saracen Woman in Medieval French Epic* (New York: Garland, 1998), contends that liminality involves temporary exclusion preceding return to one's place or point of origin (188, 191). This is merely one aspect of liminality, which can also involve temporary exclusion pending transfer from one group or status to another.

18. De Weever's *Sheba's Daughters* is valuable in analyzing the black Saracen woman in epic, a type previously relatively ignored. It also provides a history of rhetoric regarding skin color and aesthetic judgment from classical writers to the Renaissance. However, de Weever makes sweeping generalizations about race in epic, based on far too small a corpus (only eighteen chansons de geste listed in the bibliography).

19. John Boswell, *Christianity, Social Tolerance, and Homosexuality: Gay People in Western Europe from the Beginning of the Christian Era to the Fourteenth Century* (Chicago: University of Chicago Press, 1980), 6n7. This is a vital point when speaking of a genre in which the term "Saracen" denotes religious, but not necessarily racial, difference. While de Weever for one is right to point to the different representations of white and black Saracens in epic, we must remember that epic criteria of Otherness do not always include the race-gender-class triad assumed in the late twentieth and early twenty-first centuries. See also Sharon Kinoshita's "'Pagans are wrong and Christians are right': Alterity, Gender, and Nation in the *Chanson de Roland*," *JMEMS* 31.1 (2001): 79–111. In this special issue on race and ethnicity in the Middle Ages, Kinoshita emphasizes that epic alterity is primarily religious and cultural, not racial; anachronistic readings risk misreading this Otherness.

20. Michael Heintze, "La réception des plus anciens troubadours dans le 'Roman de Thèbes,'" *Romanistische Zeitschrift für Literaturgeschichte* 12 (1988): 226–41, here 228. See also Patricia Black, "The Gendered World of the *Chanson de Guillaume*," *Olifant* 21.3–4 (1997): 41–63, which sees Guibourc's actions as filling gaps created by Guillaume's absence. Daniel Rocher explores the character in "Guiborc, de *la Chanson de Guillaume* au *Willehalm* de Wolfram," in *Guillaume et Willehalm: Les épopées françaises et l'œuvre de Wolfram von Eschenbach*, ed. Danielle Buschinger (Göppingen: Kümmerle, 1985), 125–44.

21. Gautier, *Les Épopées françaises*, 1: 535. See also J. L. R. Bélanger, "Women's

Equal Rights in the Twelfth Century Church in France, as Seen in the Old French Epics, Especially *the Chanson de Roland*," in Bianciotto and Galderisi, *L'épopée romane*, 423–30; Sara I. James, "Making a Mark in a Man's World: Female Characters in the *Chanson de Bertrand Du Guesclin*," in *Epic Connections/Rencontres épiques: Proceedings of the Nineteenth International Conference of the Société Rencesvals, Oxford, 13–17 August 2012*, ed. Marianne J. Ailes, Philip E. Bennett, and Anne Elizabeth Cobby (Edinburgh: British Rencesvals Publications, 2014), 333–48.

22. Alain Labbé, "Les 'jeux d'Orange': Matériau onirique et illusion magique dans les *Enfances Guillaume*," in *Magie et illusion au Moyen Âge*, Senefiance 42 (Aix-en-Provence: CUER-MA, 1999), 269–91, analyzes Orable's association with the supernatural.

23. Philip E. Bennett and Leslie Zarker Morgan, "The Avatars of Orable-Guibourc from French 'chanson de geste' to Italian 'romanzo cavalleresco': A Persistent Multiple Alterity," *Francigena* 1 (2015): 165–214, here 166.

24. Bennett sees an interesting link between the two women: "The other female relative of Guillaume d'Orange who introduces a notable element of alterity into his family tree is his own mother, Hermenjart, wife of Aymeri de Narbonne" (Bennett and Morgan, "Avatars," 171).

25. Sarah Kay, *The Chansons de Geste in the Age of Romance: Political Fictions* (Oxford: Clarendon Press, 1995), 34. See also Kay, "La représentation de la féminité dans les chansons de geste," in *Charlemagne in the North: Proceedings of the Twelfth International Conference of the Société Rencesvals*, ed. Philip E. Bennett, Anne Elizabeth Cobby, and Graham Runnalls (Edinburgh: Société Rencesvals British Branch, 1993), 223–40.

26. Kay, *Chansons de Geste*, 35–36.

27. Peggy McCracken, *The Romance of Adultery: Queenship and Sexual Transgression in Old French Literature* (Philadelphia: University of Pennsylvania Press, 1998), in particular "Illegitimacy and Islam," 124–35. De Weever has also claimed that Guibourc's childlessness with Guillaume hints at the poet's ambivalence about the legitimacy of Guibourc's actions and status.

28. Suard, *Chanson de Guillaume*, vv. 683–86.

29. Bennett and Morgan, "Avatars," 172.

30. Bennett and Morgan, "Avatars," 166.

31. Edward W. Said, *Orientalism: Western Conceptions of the Orient* (1978; London: Penguin, 1995), 67.

32. Régnier, *Aliscans*, vv. 7536–54.

33. Suard, *La Chanson de Guillaume*, vv. 2530–31.

34. Suard, *La Chanson de Guillaume*, vv. 2590–94.

35. See James R. Simpson, *Fantasy, Identity and Misrecognition in Medieval French Narrative* (Oxford: Peter Lang, 2000).

36. Julia Kristeva, *Strangers to Ourselves*, trans. Leon S. Roudiez (New York: Columbia University Press, 1991), 1.

Chapter 6. *Ami et Amile* **and Jean-Luc Nancy: Friendship versus Community?**

1. Algirdas Julien Greimas and Joseph Courtès, *Sémiotique: Dictionnaire raisonné de la théorie du langage* (Paris: Hachette, 1979), 10.

2. François Suard, *La Chanson de geste* (Paris: Presses Universitaires de France, 1993), 19.

3. Cesare Segre, ed., *La Chanson de Roland*, rev. ed., French trans. Madeleine Tyssens, 2 vols. (Geneva: Droz, 1989), vol. 1.

4. The case is made eloquently by Simon Gaunt, *Gender and Genre in Medieval French Literature* (Cambridge: Cambridge University Press, 1995), chapter 1. Sarah Kay critiques readings of the genre as monolithically monologic in her introduction to *The* Chansons de Geste *in the Age of Romance: Political Fictions* (Oxford: Clarendon, 1995).

5. For example, John Benton, "'Nostre Franceis n'unt talent de fuïr': The *Song of Roland* and the Enculturation of the Warrior Class," *Olifant* 6 (1979): 237–58.

6. Christian readings include those by William Calin in *The Epic Quest: Studies in Four Old French* Chansons de Geste (Baltimore: Johns Hopkins University Press, 1966) and Gérard J. Brault, most influentially in his edition of the text with English translation, *The Song of Roland: An Analytical Edition*, 2 vols. (University Park: Pennsylvania State University Press, 1978). Christian geopolitics are stressed by Sharon Kinoshita in "'Pagans are wrong and Christians are right': Alterity, Gender, and Nation in the *Chanson de Roland*," *Journal of Medieval and Early Modern Studies* 31 (2001): 80–111; a slightly different version is found in her *Medieval Boundaries: Rethinking Difference in Old French Literature* (Philadelphia: University of Pennsylvania Press, 2006), chapter 1. Italian diffusion is discussed by Juliann M. Vitullo, *The Chivalric Epic in Medieval Italy* (Gainesville: University Press of Florida, 2000).

7. Capetian links are argued notably by Hans-Erich Keller, *Autour de Roland: Recherches sur la chanson de geste* (Paris: Champion, 1989); Keller's conclusions need revision in the light of more recent work on circulation and reception. On Norman expansion, see D. C. Douglas, "The *Song of Roland* and the Norman Conquest of England," *French Studies* 14 (1960): 99–116, and André de Mandach, *Naissance et développement de la chanson de geste en Europe*, 6 vols. (Geneva: Droz, 1961–93), especially "Le commonwealth normand et le mythe de Charlemagne et de Roland" (6: 123–37). Luke Sunderland emphasizes the varied and complicated medieval identifications with and investments in chansons de geste, and relates these to English and to French kingship, to places that those kings and others contested—Burgundy, Occitania, and the Low Countries—and to Italy, in *Rebel*

Barons: Resisting Royal Power in Medieval Culture (Oxford: Oxford University Press, 2017).

8. The reference, of course, is to Hegel, *Phenomenology of Spirit*, §475. I do not intend to invoke a Hegelian analytical framework in borrowing the phrase.

9. Martin Thom, *Republics, Nations and Tribes* (London: Verso, 1995); Patrick J. Geary, *The Myth of Nations: The Medieval Origins of Europe* (Princeton: Princeton University Press, 2002).

10. I refer primarily to the essay "La communauté désœuvrée" as printed in the collection of the same title: Jean-Luc Nancy, *La Communauté désœuvrée*, 3rd ed. (Paris: Bourgois, 1999), 11–102, hereafter *CD*. English translations are from "The Inoperative Community," trans. Peter Connor, in *The Inoperative Community*, ed. Peter Connor, trans. Peter Connor et al. (Minneapolis: University of Minnesota Press, 1991), 1–42, hereafter *IC*. First published in *Aléa* 4 (1983): 11–49, Nancy's essay elicited an indirect response from Maurice Blanchot, who disputed Nancy's interpretation of Georges Bataille in *La Communauté inavouable* (Paris: Minuit, 1984). Nancy continued the debate not only with *La Communauté désœuvrée*, first published in book form in 1986, but also in *La Communauté affrontée* (Paris: Galilée, 2001), hereafter *CA*, the body of which was written to preface an Italian translation of Blanchot's book, and in *La Communauté désavouée* (Paris: Galilée, 2014), which combines a critical reading of *La Communauté inavouable*, a detailed account of the whole exchange, and further development of Nancy's thought.

11. All references to *Ami et Amile* are to the edition by Peter F. Dembowski, CFMA 97 (Paris: Champion, 1969). Valuable introductions to critical issues raised by the text are the volume of essays *Ami et Amile: Une chanson de geste de l'amitié*, ed. Jean Dufournet (Paris: Champion, 1987), and "Sur *Ami et Amile*," special issue of *Bien Dire et Bien Aprandre* (Université de Lille 3, 1988). The themes of BnF fr. 360 are studied by Gaunt, *Gender and Genre*, 44–45.

12. On the different versions, see Alice Planche, "*Ami et Amile*, ou le Même et l'Autre," *Beiträge zum romanischen Mittelalter: Zeitschrift für romanische Philologie*, special centenary edition, ed. Kurt Baldinger (Tübingen: Niemeyer, 1977), 237–69, esp. 241–42, and MacEdward Leach's introduction to his edition of *Amis and Amiloun*, EETS o.s. 203 (London: Oxford University Press, 1937), ix–xiv.

13. Dominique Boutet, "Individu et société dans *Ami et Amile*," in *Actes du XIe Congrès international de la Société Rencesvals*, 2 vols. (Barcelona: Real Academia de Buenas Letras, 1990), 1: 75–86.

14. A redaction of the Latin vita is printed in *"Amis and Amiloun," Zugleich mit der altfranzösischen Quelle*, ed. Eugen Kölbing, Altenglische Bibliothek 2 (Heilbronn: Henninger, 1884). *Li Amitiéz de Ami et Amile*, in *Nouvelles françoises en prose du XIIIe siècle*, ed. L. Moland and C. d'Héricault (Paris: Jannet, 1856), 35–82, is a thirteenth-century French redaction.

15. The case has been argued recently by Huguette Legros, *L'Amitié dans les chansons de geste à l'époque romane* (Aix-en-Provence: Publications de l'Université de Provence, 2001), esp. 288–94, 369–89. Legros meticulously details the ethically questionable dimensions of the heroes' behavior and of the tensions within their friendship, elements that in her view are resolved by divine sponsorship. Although I do not challenge the text's drive toward divine ends, neither do I consider the problems to be exhausted by this teleology.

16. Different feminist critiques of the text's social modeling are given by Gaunt, *Gender and Genre*; Peggy McCracken, *The Curse of Eve, the Wound of the Hero: Blood, Gender, and Medieval Literature* (Philadelphia: University of Pennsylvania Press, 2003), 47–51; Yasmina Foehr-Janssens, "La Mort en fleurs: Violence et poésie dans *Ami et Amile*," *Cahiers de civilisation médiévale* 39 (1996): 263–74; Sarah Kay, "Seduction and Suppression in *Ami et Amile*," *French Studies* 44 (1990): 129–42.

17. René Zazzo, *Les Jumeaux: Le couple et la personne*, 2 vols. (Paris: Presses Universitaires de France, 1960).

18. The uncanny tendency of acts to adhere to both heroes is emphasized by Finn E. Sinclair, "The Imaginary Body: Framing Identity in *Ami et Amile*," *Neophilologus* 92 (2008): 193–204.

19. Nancy, *CD*, 30; *IC*, 9. "The French word 'immanence' means to be fully present with oneself, to be closed upon oneself" (Ignaas Devisch, "Jean-Luc Nancy," *Internet Encyclopedia of Philosophy*, www.iep.utm.edu/nancy, 4.a).

20. Nancy, *CD*, 74; *IC*, 29. All italics are original.

21. Nancy, *CD*, 81; *IC*, 33. Nancy is quoting Georges Bataille, *La souveraineté*, in *Œuvres complètes*, 8 vols. (Paris: Gallimard, 1970–76), 8: 243–56 (297). The published English translation of Bataille gives "my being is never *myself alone*; it is always myself and *my fellow beings*"; see Georges Bataille, Sovereignty, in *The Accursed Share: An Essay on General Economy*, trans. Robert Hurley, 3 vols. in 2 (New York: Zone, 1988–91), 3: 193–430 (253).

22. Nancy, *CD*, 83–84; *IC*, 33–34.

23. Nancy, *CD*, 74; *IC*, 29.

24. The quotation is taken from Micheline de Combarieu du Grès's magisterial *L'Idéal humain et l'expérience morale chez les héros des chansons de geste: Des origines à 1250*, 2 vols. (Aix-en-Provence: Université de Provence, 1979), 1: 248. The argument for sworn brotherhood as social institution throughout the Middle Ages and beyond is made notably by Alan Bray, *The Friend* (Chicago: University of Chicago Press, 2003).

25. Herman Braet, *Le Songe dans la chanson de geste au XIIe siècle* (Ghent: Romanica Gandensia, 1975): "Le rêve et la glose [du rêve] découvrent et voilent tout ensemble l'avenir: le héros appréhende les dangers qui le menacent, sans les

comprendre pleinement. Il ne possède pas l'information nécessaire pour conjurer une catastrophe que l'on sent imminente" (201) [The dream and its interpretation at once reveal and obscure the future: the hero apprehends the dangers that threaten him without fully understanding them. He does not have the information necessary to avert a disaster that we feel to be imminent].

26. Kay, "Seduction and Suppression," and William Calin's critique "Women and Their Sexuality in *Ami et Amile*: An Occasion to Deconstruct?," *Olifant* 16 (1991): 77–89.

27. *Amis and Amiloun*, vv. 2392–400.

28. Nancy, *CD*, 95; *IC*, 38.

29. Nancy, *CD*, 89–99; *IC*, 36–40. "Les amants" I translate as "loving couple" rather than as "lovers" because Nancy is keen to argue, against Bataille and Blanchot, that such couples are not necessarily heterosexual. I put aside for lack of space the thorny issue of the homoerotic both in Nancy's writing and in *Ami et Amile*.

30. Suard, *La Chanson de geste*, 48.

31. Nancy, *CD*, 42; *IC*, 15.

32. Nancy, *CA*, 11.

33. The various terms for friendship are analyzed by Huguette Legros in *L'Amitié dans les chansons de geste*. Combarieu du Grès argues that friendship and enmity similarly express a perpetual antagonism: "lorsque l'un et l'autre adversaire se seront (re)connus comme des égaux, quelle issue plus indiquée trouver à un affrontement qui ne peut, par lui-même, se résoudre, si ce n'est l'alliance des deux qui iront alors, de concert, mesurer à d'autres leurs forces additionnées?" (*L'Idéal humain*, 1: 247) [when the adversaries have recognized each other as equals, what better way to end their confrontation—which cannot be resolved through its own mechanisms—than an alliance between the two, who will then go, together, to measure their combined forces against others?]. Related to French philosophical work on community has been an exploration of friendship as the paradigmatic communal relation. The positions of some of Nancy's principal interlocutors are mapped by Patrick ffrench, "Friendship, Asymmetry, Sacrifice: Bataille and Blanchot," *Parrhesia* 3 (2007): 32–42. I am indebted also to Ian James, *The Fragmentary Demand: An Introduction to the Philosophy of Jean-Luc Nancy* (Stanford, CA: Stanford University Press, 2006).

34. Nancy, *CD*, 84; *IC*, 33.

35. Nancy, *CD*, 42; *IC*, 15.

36. Nancy, *CA*, 42; *IC*, 14.

37. Nancy, *CA*, 42–43.

38. Sunderland similarly stresses the socially constitutive nature of feud, and its concurrence with kinship and friendship, in *Rebel Barons*, 175–212, esp. 192–98.

39. Nancy, *CD*, 68; *IC*, 26–27.
40. Nancy, *CD*, 33–35; *IC*, 11–12.

Chapter 7. The Devil Inside: Merlin and the Dark Side of Romance

1. Francis Gingras, *Le Bâtard conquérant: Essor et expansion du genre romanesque au Moyen Âge* (Paris: Champion, 2011).

2. Edmond Faral, *La Légende arthurienne, études et documents*, pt. 1, *Les plus anciens textes*, 3 vols. (Paris: Champion, 1929); Paul Zumthor, *Merlin le Prophète: Un thème de la littérature polémique de l'historiographie et des romans* (1943; repr., Geneva: Slatkine, 2000), 33–35; Alexandre Micha, *Essais sur le cycle du Lancelot-Graal* (Geneva: Droz, 1987), 30–37, 174. On the parallel geneses of Merlin and Arthur, see Kate Cooper, "Merlin Romancier: Paternity, Prophecy, and Poetics in the Huth *Merlin*," *Romanic Review* 77 (1986): 1–24; Alexandre Leupin, *Le Graal et la Littérature: Étude sur la Vulgate arthurienne* (Lausanne: L'Âge d'Homme, 1982), 78–84; Anne Berthelot, "De Merlin à Mordret: Enfants sans père et fils du diable," in *Lignes et lignages dans la littérature arthurienne*, ed. Christine Ferlampin-Acher and Denis Hüe (Rennes: Presses Universitaires de Rennes, 2007), 35–45. On Arthur's conception, see Laurence Mathey-Maille, "Le roi Arthur chez Geoffroy de Monmouth et chez Wace: La naissance du héros," in *Arturus Rex: Acta conventus Lovaniensis 1987*, ed. W. Van Hoecke, G. Tournoy, and W. Verbeke (Louvain: Leuven University Press, 1991), 222–29; Denis Hüe, "Les variantes de la séduction: Autour de la naissance d'Arthur," in *Le "Roman de Brut": Entre mythe et histoire*, ed. Claude Letellier and Denis Hüe (Orléans: Paradigme, 2003), 67–88. On Merlin's conception, see Francis Dubost, *Aspects fantastiques de la littérature narrative médiévale (XIIe–XIIIe siècles): L'Autre, l'Ailleurs, l'Autrefois* (Paris: Champion, 1991), 710–51; Annie Combes, "Du *Brut* au *Merlin*: Le fils du diable et les incertitudes génériques," *Cahiers de recherches médiévales* 5 (1998): 15–32; Francis Gingras, "L'Autre Merlin," in *"Furent les merveilles pruvees et les aventures truvees": Hommage à Francis Dubost*, ed. Francis Gingras, Françoise Laurent, Frédérique Le Nan, and Jean-René Valette (Paris: Champion, 2005), 263–79.

3. Francis Gingras, *Érotisme et merveilles dans le récit français des XIIe et XIIIe siècles* (Paris: Champion, 2002), 406.

4. *Historia Regum Brittaniae of Geoffrey of Monmouth*, vol. 1, ed. Neil Wright (Cambridge: D. S. Brewer, 1985), 72. My translation.

5. Wace, *Roman de Brut: A History of the British*, ed. and trans. Judith Weiss (Exeter: University of Exeter Press, 1999).

6. Geoffrey of Monmouth, *Vita Merlini = Life of Merlin*, ed. and trans. Basil Clarke (Cardiff: University of Wales Press, 1973), vv. 779–84.

7. Godfrey of Viterbo, *Pantheon*, in *Patrologia Latina*, vol. 198, col. 1001c.

8. Ibid.

9. This definition germinates with Arnold of Villanova and is explicitly formulated by Bernard of Gordon in *Lilium medicinae* (ii.24), quoted by Maaike van der Lugt, *Le Ver, le démon et la vierge: Les théories médiévales de la génération extraordinaire; Une étude sur les rapports entre théologie, philosophie naturelle et médecine* (Paris: Belles Lettres, 2004), 329.

10. Caesarius von Heisterbach, *Dialogus miraculorum*, ed. Joseph Strange, 2 vols. in 1 (1851; repr., Ridgewood, NJ: Gregg Press, 1966), 1: 124 (III.xii).

11. "Crementum humanum, quod contra naturam funditur, daemones colligunt, et ex eo sibi corpora, in quibus tangi viderique ab hominibus possint, assumunt; de masculino vero masculina, et de feminino feminina" (ibid.).

12. Vincent of Beauvais, *Speculum Historiale*, bk. 20, chap. 30, *Bibliotheca Mundi Vincentii . . . Speculum quadruplex, naturale, doctrinale, morale, historiale* (1624; repr., Graz: Akademische Druck- und Verlagsanstalt, 1965), 791a.

13. "Post haec adamavit rex uxorem cuiusdam ducis, habuitque rem cum ea, de qua genuit celeberrimum illum Arthurum, et filiam nomine Amam [*sic*]" (ibid., chap. 49, 797b).

14. Raoul de Houdenc, *Meraugis de Portlesguez*, ed. Michelle Szkilnik, bilingual ed. (Paris: Champion, 2004), vv. 1303, 2019, 2665.

15. Girart d'Amiens, *Escanor*, ed. Richard Trachsler (Geneva: Droz, 1994), vv. 12972–13478.

16. Guillaume le Clerc, *Fergus*, ed. Wilson Frescoln (Philadelphia: W. H. Allen, 1983), vv. 775–76.

17. Apart from topographic and etiologic allusions—Merlin is responsible for the Round Table and the Perilous Seat in *La Queste del saint Graal*, ed. Albert Pauphilet (Paris: Champion, 1923), 77—Merlin appears fleetingly as a prophet in *La Queste del saint Graal*, 116, and in *La Mort le roi Artu*, ed. Jean Frappier (Geneva: Droz, 1936), 228–29.

18. Robert de Boron, *Merlin*, ed. Alexandre Micha (Geneva: Droz, 1979).

19. Robert de Boron, *Joseph d'Arimathie*, ed. Richard O'Gorman (Toronto: Pontifical Institute of Mediaeval Studies, 1995).

20. It is worth noting that one of this romance's modern publishers, William Nitze, also retained the title *Le Roman de l'estoire dou Graal* for his edition published at Champion in 1927, thus contributing to its popularization within the realm of French Arthurian criticism.

21. The shift to prose relies on a similar movement when it delivers the aforementioned verses as such: "Et de lors en ça fu clamee ceste estoire LE CONTE DEL GREAL" (lines 1081–82), designating the text less by its generic status and more through its narrative form and, mostly, by its detached position (second) in regard to history, thus excluded from the title. Even in the verse version of *Joseph d'Arimathie*, references to "la grant estoire dou graal" (vv. 3487, 3493) can also

relate to the original tale, that which the author "conte" (v. 3486) or "retrai[t]" (v. 3489).

22. Our referring edition is that of Alexandre Micha, who provides variations of the β version for § 11, lines 55–62. Bonn 256—which, with Paris BnF fr. 24324 among other manuscripts, kept the β version—was edited by Irene Freire-Nunes for the *Merlin* by Robert de Boron in *Le Livre du Graal* (Paris: Gallimard, 2001), here quoted at 1: 597–98, § 25.

23. That is, *Le Haut Livre du Graal: Perlesvaus*, ed. and trans. Armand Strubel (Paris: Livre de Poche, 2007), page 726, line 19. All further citations of this edition, hereafter *HLG*, give page and line numbers linked by a period.

24. "Il le fist muer en la samblance del roi Goloés" (*HLG* 728.16–729.1) [Merlin transformed Uther into the semblance of King Golés].

25. Notably through the "Beste Glatissant" episode in *La Suite du Roman de Merlin*, ed. Gilles Roussineau, 2 vols. (Geneva: Droz, 1996), § 5–7. All citations of this edition, hereafter *SRM*, give section and line numbers linked by a period.

26. "Sire, fait li preudom [Merlin], de chou ne vous devés vous pas mervillier, que il n'est nule si celee chose que elle ne soit descouverte. Et se la chose estoit faite desous terre, si en seroit la verité seue deseure terre" (*SRM* 14.27–29). [Sire, says Merlin, you should not be surprised by that since there is nothing so concealed that it could not be discovered. And even if such a thing was done under earth, the truth would be known upon earth.]

27. "Car par le descouvrir porra estre la terre garandie et par le celer perdue" (*SRM* 16.28–30). [Hence through discovery the land will be expanded, and through concealment it shall be lost.]

28. "Si moustra bien qu'il estoit estrais dou dyable et d'anemi" (*SRM* 30.25) [It showed clearly that he [Merlin] was descended from the devil and the enemy]; "Li fiex a l'anemi" (*SRM* 83.18–19) [the son of the enemy]; "fiex de dyable comme Merlins" (*SRM* 404.39) [son of the devil, as Merlin is].

29. "Car il le contrehaoient et despisoient por chou que il ne savoient nule chose de son parenté" (*SRM* 24.24–26) [For they [the barons] hated and despised him because they knew nothing about his family].

30. "Quant li rois ot oï toute sa naissance et son estre" (*SRM* 21.1) [Once the king had heard about his birth and his being].

31. On the specificity of Grail romances within the genre of Arthurian romance, see Mireille Séguy, *Les Romans du Graal ou Le signe imaginé* (Paris: Champion, 2001), and, by the same author, *Le Livre-monde: "L'Estoire del saint Graal" et le cycle du "Lancelot-Graal"* (Paris: Champion, 2017), as well as Jean-René Valette, *La Pensée du Graal: Fiction littéraire et théologie, XIIe–XIIIe siècle* (Paris: Champion, 2008).

32. Heldris de Cornuälle, *Silence: A Thirteenth-Century French Romance*, ed.

and trans. Sarah Roche-Mahdi (East Lansing, MI: Colleagues Press, 1992). The translations into English are my own.

33. The ridiculousness of the situation is also underlined by the narrator, who specifies: "Ki donc veïst ventre eslargir, / Estendre, et tezir, et bargir, / Ne lairoit qu'il n'en resist tost!" (*Silence*, vv. 6127–29) [Anyone who ever saw his belly swell up, / expand, inflate and dilate, / could not help but burst out laughing!]. The reader's laugh here precedes Merlin's laugh, associated with the conclusion of the tale and the revelation of the truth hidden behind appearances.

34. *Le Chevalier as deus espees*, ed. Paul Vincent Rockwell (Woodbridge: Brewer, 2006). All citations are from this edition. Translations into English are my own.

35. Giraldus Cambrensis [Gerald of Wales], *Descriptio Kambriae*, ed. James Francis Dimock, vol. 1, chap. 1 of *Giraldi Cambrensis Opera* (London: Longman, Green, Longman, and Roberts, 1868), 202.

36. In the *Première Continuation*, "Si com Bleheris nos dist," mss. *A S P U*, v. 6550 ("Si con Bliobliheri dist," ms. *L*, v. 6552). In the *Deuxième Continuation*, "Si con le conte Bleheris," variant of ms. *L*, v. 29351. *The Continuations of the Old French Perceval of Chrétien de Troyes*, ed. William Roach (Philadelphia: American Philosophical Society, respectively vol. III/1, 1952; vol. IV, 1971).

37. *Claris et Laris*, ed. Corinne Pierreville (Paris: Champion, 2008). All citations are from this edition.

38. Marthe Robert, *Roman des origines et origines du roman* (Paris: Grasset, 1972).

Chapter 8. Melly and Merlin: Locating Little Voices in Paris BnF fr. 24432

1. For edition, see B. Munk Olsen, ed., *Dits en quatrains d'alexandrins monorimes de Jehan de Saint-Quentin* (Paris: Société des Anciens Textes Français, 1978).

2. The thumbnail titles of the tales contained in the *Vie des Pères* were suggested by Gaston Paris in an initialed note added to Edouard Schwan's seminal study of the collection, "La Vie des Anciens Pères," *Romania* 13 (1884): 233–63, here 263. In most instances, as with *Merlin Mellot*, they reflect the rubrics in BnF fr. 24432.

3. For edition, see Félix Lecoy, ed., *La Vie des pères*, 3 vols., Société des Anciens Textes Français (Paris: Picard, 1987–99). For comment, see Adrian Tudor, *Tales of Vice and Virtue: The First Old French "Vie des Pères"* (Amsterdam: Rodopi, 2005); on *Merlin Mellot*, see particularly 288–300. On Gautier's verse, see particularly Tony Hunt, *Miraculous Rhymes: The Writing of Gautier de Coinci* (Cambridge: D. S. Brewer, 2007).

4. For description, see Olsen, *Dits en quatrains*, cxliii–cxlvii. Although superseded with regard to the material considered here, an earlier edition of Jehan's works can be found in Achille Jubinal, ed., *Nouveau Recueil de contes, dits, fabliaux*

et autres pièces inédites des XIIIe, XIVe et XVe siècles (1839; Geneva: Slatkine Reprints, 1975). Jubinal's compilation has the merit of assembling various texts from BnF fr. 24432 (formerly Notre Dame 198 as referenced in Jubinal) alongside those attributed to Jehan. A reproduction of the manuscript may be consulted via the Bibliothèque nationale's Gallica portal.

5. Contents include *Le Livre des songes Daniel et les songes Macrobe*; a treatise on the Mass; a translation of Innocent III's *On the Misery of the Human Condition*; philosophical and scientific material (*Lucidarius*) along with lyric (sirventes and "sottes chansons") and narrative lais (*Le Lai de l'oiselet* and *Yonec*); fabular material (a translation of Alexander Neckam); and five texts by Rutebeuf (*La Repentance Rutebeuf; Le Dit de l'herberie; La Disputaison de Charlot et du Barbier de Melun; La Complainte Rutebeuf; La Complainte de Sainte Eglise*). Other poems in the same form in BnF fr. 24432, such as "Le Dit des mais" (fols. 138v–142v), have been attributed to a certain Geoffrey. The complementarities between Jehan's and Geoffrey's works in this collection are arguably very interesting, although this would be a line of argument to be developed elsewhere.

6. *Le Dit qu'on clamme respon* (fols. 14–17); *Le Dit des trois chanoinnes* (fols. 36–42); *Le Dit des .iii. pommes* (fols. 53–57); *Le Dit de la bourjosse de Romme* (fols. 99–104); *Le Dit des .ii. chevaliers* (fols. 104–7); *Le Dit de l'enfant rosti* (fols. 107–9); *Le Dit du povre chevalier* (fols. 109–12); *Le Dit du chevalier et de l'escuier* (fols. 112–15); *Le Dit de la bourjoise de Narbonne* (fols. 115–18); *Le Dit du chevalier qui devint hermite* (fols. 118–20); *Le Dit du cordouanier* (fols. 120–23); *Le Dit du petit juitel* (fols. 123–25); *Le Dit de l'enfant qui sauva sa mere* (fols. 125–28); *Le Dit de l'eaue beneoite et du vergier* (fols. 128–30); *Le Dit du riche homme qui geta le pain a la teste du povre* (fols. 130–32); *Le Dit du chien et du mescreant* (fols. 132–35); *Le Dit de la pecheresse qui estrangla .iii. enfans* (fols. 135–37); *Le Dit de Merlin Mellot* (fols. 199–202); *Le Dit de Flourence de Romme* (fols. 215–26); *Le Dit des anelés* (fols. 231–41); *Le Dit du buef* (fols. 247–57); *Le Dit de la beguine qui mist le cors nostre seigneur avecques .i. crapaut en .i. escrin* (fols. 312–15).

7. In addition to these, two further texts found in other manuscripts have been attributed to Jehan: *La Vie saint sauveur l'hermite*, preserved in Paris, Arsenal 2115, and *D'une abesse que Nostre Dame delivra de confusion*, preserved in BnF fr. 12483.

8. Joseph Morawski, "Mélanges de littérature pieuse," *Romania* 65 (1939): 327–58.

9. The question of whether such a constellation should be regarded as polyphonically stabilized or tensely heteroglossic has considerable bearing on how this orchestration articulates the conflicts, negotiations, and appropriations of both discourses and practices through which individuals positioned themselves within faith communities. On the opposition between polyphony and heteroglossia, chiefly associated with the work of Mikhail Bakhtin, see "From the Prehistory of

Novelistic Discourse," in *The Dialogic Imagination: Four Essays by M. M. Bakhtin*, ed. Michael Holquist, trans. Caryl Emerson and Holquist (Austin: University of Texas Press, 1983), 41–83.

10. On medieval representations of peasants see notably Paul Freedman, *Images of the Medieval Peasant*, Figurae: Reading Medieval Culture (Stanford, CA: Stanford University Press, 1999).

11. On local sensibilities and cults vis-à-vis the broader church, see Dominique Iogna-Prat, *La Maison Dieu: Une histoire monumentale de l'Église au Moyen Âge (v. 800–v. 1200)* (Paris: Seuil, 2012), and his "Churches in the Landscape," in *The Cambridge History of Christianity*, vol. 3, *Early Medieval Christianities, AD 600–1100*, ed. Thomas F. X. Noble and Julia M. H. Smith (Cambridge: Cambridge University Press, 2008), 363–82. For case studies of marginal provincial cults, see notably Jean-Claude Schmitt, *The Holy Greyhound: Guinefort, Healer of Children since the Thirteenth Century*, trans. Martin Thom (Cambridge: Cambridge University Press, 1983); Patrick J. Geary, *Living with the Dead in the Middle Ages* (Ithaca: Cornell University Press, 1994); and Robert Bartlett, *The Hanged Man: A Story of Miracle, Memory, and Colonialism in the Middle Ages* (Princeton, NJ: Princeton University Press, 2004).

12. On the place of Mary in Jewish-Christian relations, see Miri Rubin's works *Gentile Tales: The Narrative Assault on Late Medieval Jews* (New Haven, CT: Yale University Press, 1999); "Mary," *History Workshop Journal* 58:1 (2004): 1–16; and, notably, *Mother of God: A History of the Virgin Mary* (London: Penguin, 2009).

13. Rubin, *Gentile Tales*, 8.

14. This is thus more reminiscent of the "narrative" use of the line in the chanson de geste, Jehan's verse certainly appearing much less ornate than the more "lyric" works in the same form attributed to Rutebeuf, whose intense use of sound play at and around the caesura provides a stronger secondary split. On which, see my "Turning Verse Conversions? *Mise en page* and Metre in Rutebeuf's *Le Miracle de Théophile*," *Pecia: Le livre et l'écrit* 16 (2014): 17–40. On epic resonances in moralizing works, see particularly Linda Marie Rouillard, "Warrior Relationships with God: From *Roland* to the *Chevalier au Barisel*," *Medieval Perspectives* 17 (2003): 129–50.

15. A moment perhaps reminiscent of Merlin's various cackles at the end of the *Roman de Silence* (vv. 6469–85). See Heldris de Cornuälle, *"Silence": A Thirteenth-Century French Romance*, trans. Sarah Roche-Mahdi (East Lansing, MI: Colleagues Press, 1992).

16. Miri Rubin, *Charity and Community in Medieval Cambridge*, Cambridge Studies in Medieval Life and Thought (Cambridge: Cambridge University Press, 2002), 6.

17. Rubin, *Charity and Community*, 8.

18. The idea of the struggle for daily bread as a recurring cycle appears in various discussions of urban poverty, notably Jacques de Vitry and Thomas Aquinas (see Rubin, *Charity and Community*, 8).

19. "Charity cannot satisfactorily be understood as a purely altruistic act since gift-giving is so rich in rewards towards the giver" (Rubin, *Charity and Community*, 1).

20. As Jubinal comments, there appears to be a missing strophe following v. 124. The further shift in address that it presumably contained can be inferred from Merlin's comments in v. 174.

21. *La Chanson de Roland*, ed. and trans. Ian Short, Lettres Gothiques (Paris: Livre de Poche, 1990); translation cited from Gerard J. Brault, ed. and trans., *The Song of Roland: An Analytical Edition*, 2 vols (University Park: Pennsylvania State University Press, 1978). In that respect, the peasant's reaction concatenates Ganelon's initial reaction to Roland's proposal ("Tut fel, pur quei t'esrages?" v. 286) and his later anger at Roland's laughter ("Dunc ad tel doel pur poi d'ire ne fent," v. 304).

22. Admittedly, this suggestion is somewhat problematic given that it would require Jehan to be echoing a version close to the Oxford text, whose casting of the line does not find a strong echo elsewhere in the tradition. Châteauroux–Venice 7—the only other French version sufficiently complete to contain a version of the counsel discussion—shows significant variation here: "en piez se drice, bien dit q'il ne l'otrie" (v. 241) [He stands up and says very clearly that he does not agree]; "lor ot tel doel por un petit ne fent" (v. 438) [He is so aggrieved that he nearly bursts]. For the texts of the other versions, see Joseph J. Duggan et al., eds., *La Chanson de Roland: The French Corpus*, 3 vols. (Turnhout: Brepols, 2005).

23. On the place of voice in inter-communal tensions, see notably Slavoj Žižek, *The Plague of Fantasies*, rev. ed. (London: Verso, 2008), 87–90.

24. The literature on voice in cultural studies is extensive. See notably Mladen Dolar, "The Object Voice," in *Gaze and Voice as Love Objects*, ed. Renata Salecl and Slavoj Žižek (Durham, NC: Duke University Press, 1996), 7–31, as well as her *A Voice and Nothing More* (Cambridge, MA: MIT Press, 2006). In the context of voice in medieval studies, see Bruce Wood Holsinger, "The Flesh of the Voice: Embodiment and the Homoerotics of Devotion in the Music of Hildegard of Bingen (1098–1179)," *Signs* 19.1 (1993): 92–125.

25. Anna Drzewicka, "Le Livre ou la voix? Le Moi poétique dans les *Miracles de Notre Dame* de Gautier de Coinci," *Le Moyen Âge* 96 (1990): 245–63, here 263. See also M.-C. Pouchelle, "Mots, fluides et vertiges: Les fêtes orales de la mystique chez Gautier de Coinci," *Annales: Economies, Sociétés, Civilisations* 42 (1987): 1210–20.

26. The fair was held between 11 and 24 June on the *plaine St Denis*, during

which period mercantile activity in Les Halles was transplanted outside the city walls, the area providing a key forum for students from the universities of Paris buying parchment, a significant moment of interaction between university and mercantile communities as well as with rural ones. See Anne Lombard-Jourdan, "Les Foires de l'abbaye de Saint-Denis: revue des données et révision des opinions admises," *Bibliothèque de l'École des Chartes* 145 (1987): 274–338; here, 328.

27. See Julia M. H. Smith, "Portable Christianity: Relics in the Medieval West (c. 700–c. 1200)," *Proceedings of the British Academy* 181 (2012): 143–67; and her "Rulers and Relics, c. 750–c. 950: 'Treasure on Earth, Treasure in Heaven,'" in *Relics and Remains*, ed. Alexandra Walsham, supplement 5 to *Past & Present* (Oxford: Oxford University Press, 2010), 73–96. In that sense, such accumulations appear as antecedents of the syncretistic practices centered on the piñata in late medieval–early modern Latin America. On the piñata, see *A Handbook of Hispanic Cultures in the United States* vol. 4, *Anthropology*, ed. Thomas Weaver (Houston, TX: Arte Público, 1994), 77. Such collections were not necessarily exclusively small or local in import, a case in point being a collection of objects that, according to Ekkehard, were rescued by monks of Stavelot-Malmédy from Viking raids on the imperial chapel and then placed by Charles the Fat in a gold capella reliquary. As Simon Maclean comments, the collection appears as "a miniature substitute Aachen, quite literally Carolingian legitimacy in a box" (*Kingship and Politics in the Late Ninth Century: Charles the Fat and the End of the Carolingian Empire* [Cambridge: Cambridge University Press, 2003], 157).

28. In this respect my work echoes Adrian Tudor's argument that the *Vie des Pères* draws on a thesaurus of names associated with other literary *matières*, notably from Arthurian tradition. See Adrian P. Tudor, "A Futile Quest? Seeking Arthurian Characters in Old French Short Narratives," *Studi Francesi* 56 (2012): 5–20.

29. Keith Busby, *Codex and Context: Reading Old French Verse Narrative in Manuscript*, 2 vols. (Amsterdam: Rodopi, 2002).

30. For a reproduction of Gaston Paris's 1884 critical edition, see *Nouvelles courtoises*, ed. and trans. Suzanne Méjean-Thiolier and Marie-Françoise Notz-Grob, Lettres Gothiques (Paris: Livre de Poche, 1997), 426–49. On the transmission of the poem, see 411–13.

Chapter 9. Sex, the Church, and the Medieval Reader: Shaping Salvation in the *Vie des Pères*

1. This study builds on ideas expressed in and background reading for two of my previous articles: "Concevoir et accoucher dans les fabliaux, les Miracles de la Vierge et les contes pieux," *Reinardus* 13 (2000): 195–213, and "Sexe et salut dans la première *Vie des Pères*," *Reinardus* 12 (1999): 188–203. I should like to recognize

the help of Wendy Bishop and Shu-Mei Li, without whose patience and support this work would not have been possible.

2. For the most profound explanation of this term, see Michel Zink, *Poésie et conversion au Moyen Âge* (Paris: Presses Universitaires de France, 2003). See also Zink's introduction to his Collège de France lectures at http://www.college-de-france.fr/media/michel-zink/UPL65512_zink.pdf. I use the words "reader" and "audience" almost interchangeably in the current context to mean "the medieval consumer of the text." See Joyce Coleman, "Audience," in *A Handbook of Middle English Studies*, ed. Marion Turner (Oxford: Wiley, 2013), 155–70.

3. In writing this essay there was one particular issue to resolve: does the present work address "sex" or "sexuality"? By opting for the first term, my intention is to examine in some detail the sex act itself within the broader landscape of how identities are shaped by an individual or a third party. April Harper and Caroline Proctor faced the same question when choosing a title for an edited volume a decade ago. On page 2 of their introduction to *Medieval Sexuality: A Casebook* (New York: Routledge, 2008), the difference between the words "sex" and "sexuality" is discussed. The first is understood to refer to the sex act only, whereas "sexuality" refers more to the perception of sex, "its role in law, literature, societies, religions and cultures." Sexuality is representative of "a culture's religion, attitudes, taboos and experience." I have preferred to use the word "sex" for the sake of focus, since this essay addresses shaping identity. My discussion of the nuts and bolts of cultural and legal issues is a conduit to considering the fluidity of identity—of which sex is just one element—in the *Vie des Pères*.

4. A great deal of ink has already been spilled on legal, canonical, and social attitudes toward the sex lives of the faithful in the Middle Ages. My aim is to draw on some of this scholarship as a means to studying a small number of instances drawn from a masterpiece of medieval French hagiography. I would encourage the reader to consider the work of some of the pillars of this area of study. James A. Brundage, John W. Baldwin, John Boswell, Vern L. Bullough, Joan Cadden, Ruth Mazo Karras, Kim M. Phillips, and others are all to be thanked for establishing and developing the conversation on sex, sexuality, and literature in the Middle Ages.

5. Marginal characters exist across the Christian world, whether excessively good or excessively bad. A Jew, a heretic, a Saracen, or an adulterer is clearly marginal. These do not represent what might be considered ideal examples for the Christian faithful. Recipients of miracles or figures who, as in the tale *Prévot d'Aquilée*, take what they consider to be their marital duty to something of an extreme are in their own way equally "different." Extreme, strange, different, marginal figures abound in religious literature. They represent what is very good, or very bad, or in a gray area of some sort. As with manuscript marginalia, they are for us (and presumably for the medieval audience) abnormal and very engaging.

6. According to Michel Zink, this text can stand shoulder to shoulder with Chrétien de Troyes's romances and the *Chanson de Roland*: "Voici une œuvre . . . dont la profondeur, la densité, l'audace parfois, l'habileté stylistique, la force poétique sont proprement stupéfiantes et devraient valoir à son auteur une place au voisinage de celle qu'occupent pour nous celui de la *Chanson de Roland* ou Chrétien de Troyes" [Here is a work . . . whose depth, density, occasional audacity, stylistic adroitness, and poetic potency are quite breathtaking and should bestow upon its author a place alongside the one we reserve for the *Chanson de Roland* or Chrétien de Troyes]. See preface to Adrian P. Tudor, *Tales of Vice and Virtue: The First Old French "Vie des Pères"* (Amsterdam: Rodopi, 2005), 11.

7. For an overview of scholarship regarding this text, see my brief note, "The One That Got Away: The Case of the Old French *Vie des Pères*," *French Studies Bulletin* 55 (1995): 11–15. See also Élisabeth Pinto-Mathieu, *La "Vie des Pères": Genèse de contes religieux du XIIIe siècle*, Nouvelle Bibliothèque du Moyen Âge 91 (Paris: Champion, 2008).

8. It was not until 1999 that a complete edition, *La Vie des Pères*, ed. Félix Lecoy, 3 vols. (Paris: Société des Anciens Textes Français, 1987–99), became available. All quotations are from this now standard edition.

9. See the introduction to Brian J. Levy, *The Comic Text: Patterns and Images in the Old French Fabliaux* (Amsterdam: Rodopi, 2000).

10. For *Barisel* the standard edition is Félix Lecoy, ed., *Le Chevalier au barisel*, Classiques Français du Moyen Âge 82 (Paris: Champion, 1955); English translation by Adrian P. Tudor, *The Knight and the Barrel* (Manchester: Manchester University Press, 2019). For text and translation of *Tumbeor* see Pierre Kunstmann, ed. and trans., *Vierge et merveille: Les miracles de Notre-Dame narratifs au Moyen Âge* (Paris: Union Générale d'Éditions, 1981). For *Jongleur* see Louis Karl, "La légende de L'Ermite et le jongleur," *Revue des Langues Romanes* 63 (1925): 110–41, and Louis Allen, ed., "*De l'Hermite et del Jougleour*," a Thirteenth Century "Conte Pieux": Text, with Introduction and Notes, Including a Study of the Poem's Relationship to "Del Tumbeor Nostre Dame" and "Del Chevalier au Barisel" (Paris: Solsona, 1925).

11. Essential reading for those interested in the exemplum includes Jean-Thiébaut Welter, *L'Exemplum dans la littérature religieuse et didactique du Moyen Âge* (Paris: Occitania, 1927; repr. New York: AMS, 1973); Claude Bremond, Jacques Le Goff, and Jean-Claude Schmitt, *L'"Exemplum,"* Typologie des Sources du Moyen Âge Occidental 40 (Turnhout: Brepols, 1982); Jacques Berlioz and Marie Anne Polo de Beaulieu, eds., *Les* Exempla *médiévaux* (Carcassonne: Garae/Hesiode, 1993); Jacques Monfrin, "L'exemplum médiéval: Du latin aux langues vulgaires," in *Les* Exempla *médiévaux: Nouvelles perspectives*, ed. Jacques Berlioz and Marie Anne Polo de Beaulieu, Nouvelle Bibliothèque du Moyen Âge 47 (Paris: Champion, 1998), 243–65; Jacques Berlioz, "L'Auditoire des prédicateurs

dans la littérature des *exempla* (XIIIe–XIVe siècles)," *Medioevo e Rinascimento* 3 (1989): 125–58. Oxford Bibliographies offer a useful and relatively up-to-date "Late Medieval Preaching" section at www.oxfordbibliographies.com.

12. Sarah Melhado White, "Sexual Language and Human Conflict in Old French Fabliaux," *Comparative Studies in Society and History* 24 (1982): 185–210.

13. Augustine, *Sancti Aurelii Augustini Confessionum libri tredecim*, ed. Pius Knöll, Corpus Scriptorum Ecclesiasticorum Latinorum 33 (Vienna: Tempsky, 1896), vol. 8, 10.30.41; *Confessions*, trans. R. S. Pine-Coffin (Harmondsworth: Penguin Classics, 1961).

14. Keith Busby, *Codex and Context: Reading Old French Verse Narrative in Manuscript*, 2 vols. (Amsterdam: Rodopi, 2002), 201.

15. James A. Brundage, *Law, Sex, and Christian Society in Medieval Europe* (Chicago: University of Chicago Press, 1987), 414–15. For a useful survey of both "normal" and "transgressive" sexual activity, see Ruth Mazo Karras, *Sexuality in the Middle Ages: Doing Unto Others* (Oxford: Routledge, 2005).

16. Michel Raby offers an excellent short introduction to this delicate topic in "Le Péché 'contre nature' dans la littérature médiévale: Deux cas," *Romance Quarterly* 44 (1997): 215–23, here 215.

17. Vern L. Bullough, *Sexual Variance in Society and History* (New York: Wiley, 1976), ix.

18. It is difficult to ascertain to what extent the treatment of sexual sins in the *Vie des Pères* reflects this codification. The seminal work on the subject is Brundage's *Law, Sex, and Christian Society*, which includes an impressive bibliography. For the development of papal authority in sexual matters, see also Bullough, *Sexual Variance*, chapters 13 and 14, and Jeffrey Richards, *Sex, Dissidence, and Damnation: Minority Groups in the Middle Ages* (London: Routledge, 1991). See also David d'Avray, *Medieval Marriage: Symbolism and Society* (Oxford: Oxford University Press, 2005). In legal and social practice, sexual intercourse as a symbol of Christ's union with the Church became increasingly important in the Middle Ages.

19. James A. Brundage, "Sex and Canon Law," in *A Handbook of Medieval Sexuality*, ed. Vern L. Bullough and James A. Brundage (New York: Garland, 1996), 33–51, here 40; Raby, "Le Péché 'contre nature,'" 215.

20. Raby, "Le Péché 'contre nature,'" 215.

21. See R. Foreville, *Latran I, II, III et Latran IV*, Histoire des Conciles Œcuméniques 6 (Paris: Editions de l'Orante, 1965); Pierre J. Payer, "Sex and Confession in the Thirteenth Century," in *Sex in the Middle Ages*, ed. Joyce E. Salisbury (New York: Garland, 1991), 126–44; and James A. Brundage, "Carnal Delight: Canonistic Theories of Sexuality," in *Proceedings of the Fifth International Congress of Medieval Canon Law*, ed. Stephan Kuttner and Kenneth Pennington, Series C, VI (Vatican City: Biblioteca Apostolica Vaticana, 1980), 361–85.

22. By far the most important recent accounts are William E. Burgwinkle, *Sodomy, Masculinity, and Law in Medieval Literature: France and England, 1050–1230* (Cambridge: Cambridge University Press, 2004), and Robert Mills, *Seeing Sodomy in the Middle Ages* (Chicago: University of Chicago Press, 2014). Other useful works are Albert Gauthier, "La sodomie dans le droit canonique médiéval," in *L'Érotisme au Moyen Âge*, ed. Bruno Roy (Québec: L'Aurore, 1977), 111–22; Joan Cadden, *Meanings of Sex Difference in the Middle Ages: Medicine, Science, and Culture* (Cambridge: Cambridge University Press, 1993), 214n161; and the groundbreaking work of John Boswell.

23. See, among others, Jessica Rosenfeld, *Ethics and Enjoyment in Late Medieval Poetry: Love after Aristotle* (Cambridge: Cambridge University Press, 2010); Françoise Laurent, *Plaire et édifier. Les récits hagiographiques composés en Angleterre aux XIIe et XIIIe siècles* (Paris: Champion, 1998); Jeannine Horowitz and Sophia Menache, *L'humour en chaire: Le rire dans l'Eglise médiévale* (Geneva: Labor et Fides, 1994); Damien Boquet and Piroska Nagy, *Sensible Moyen Âge: Une histoire des émotions dans l'Occident médiéval* (Paris: Editions du Seuil, 2015); and Peter Jones, "Preaching Laughter in the Thirteenth Century: The Exempla of Arnold of Liège (d. c. 1308) and his Dominican Milieu," *Journal of Medieval History* 41 (2015): 169–83.

24. Simon Gaunt, *Gender and Genre in Medieval French Literature* (Cambridge: Cambridge University Press, 1995), 180–233.

25. Evelyn Birge Vitz, review of Charles Muscatine, *The Old French Fabliaux* (New Haven, CT: Yale University Press, 1986), in *Speculum* 63 (1988): 199–202, here 201.

26. Alain-Julien Surdel, "Amour, mariage et . . . sainteté dans les légendes et les mystères hagiographiques," 73–91, in *Amour, mariage et transgressions au Moyen Âge*, ed. Danielle Buschinger and André Crépin (Göppingen: Kümmerle, 1984), 73.

27. Jean-Charles Payen, *Le Motif du repentir dans la littérature française médiévale* (Geneva: Droz, 1967), 532.

28. Payen, *Le Motif du repentir*, 534.

29. See Michel Zink, *La Prédication en langue romane avant 1300*, Nouvelle Bibliothèque du Moyen Âge 4 (Paris: Champion, 1976 [2nd ed., 1982]), 401. Whereas sermons require bare-bones exempla, perhaps just a line or two, which the preacher will expand on the spot to suit his purposes, and might be written down in full or partially, the tales of the *Vie des Pères* are literary works in their own right. An existing story, or a story of the authors' imagination, is the source of a self-standing tale that will not be expanded or embellished and will be unsuitable for use in a sermon. The tales are courtly literature which shares certain similarities with sermonizing material but operates quite differently; just to view

the *Vie des Pères* in its manuscript context shows how the work was considered by its medieval audience, whether occupying a codex of its own or copied alongside profane and religious courtly texts. Our tales exist within the framework of the collective text, with a general introduction and self-standing sermonizing sections. The stories can be read individually or in a series, with or without the introductions and *queues*, and are written in octosyllabic rhyming couplets. They are a world away from sermons and exempla as these latter texts have come down to us.

30. There are few details of the nun's debauchery, possibly because right from the outset it is clear that she will be saved, being described as "une nonne de sainte vie" (v. 6919), or perhaps because the story was so widely told that extra details might have appeared superfluous, or even in bad taste. Robert Guiette, *La Légende de la Sacristine* (Paris: Champion, 1927), remains the seminal study of this legend.

31. For a discussion of Gautier's miracle *De l'abeesse que Nostre Dame delivra de grant angoisse* (I Mir. 20) and *Abbesse grosse*, see my chapter "Telling the Same Tale? Gautier de Coinci's *Miracles de Nostre-Dame* and the First *Vie des Pères*" in *Gautier de Coinci, Les Miracles de Nostre Dame: Texts and Manuscripts*, ed. Kathy Krause and Alison Stones, Medieval Texts and Cultures of Northern Europe 13 (Turnhout: Brepols, 2007), 201–30.

32. Sex for pleasure rather than sex with the intention of procreating is *contra naturam*. For this distinction made in the twelfth century by Hugh of Saint-Victor, see Brian J. Levy, "Le dernier tabou? Les fabliaux et la perversion sexuelle," in *Sexuelle Perversionen im Mittelalter*, ed. Danielle Buschinger and Wolfgang Spiewok, (Greifswald: Reineke, 1994), 124.

33. For an interesting reading of this tale see Casey Casebier, "The Bestiary of Sin in *Ivresse* (*La Vie des pères*)," *Medieval Perspectives* 32 (2017): 7–26.

34. The same term is repeated in *Inceste* (vv. 17064–66). See Brian J. Levy, "Le dernier tabou?," 113.

35. Reminders of Original Sin—and specifically the role Eve played in this—are frequent (*Fornication imitée*, vv. 18–22; *Juitel*, vv. 381–82; *Prière à la Vierge*, vv. 19028–31; VdP II, *Coq*, vv. 19000–19004).

36. Elsewhere these words might be translated quite differently. "Guigniee" not only carries the idea of comeliness but, in a different context, could mean "tarted up." "Ace(s)mee" has a similar meaning, relating not just to her attractiveness but also to her preparedness. A soldier might be described in this way as he prepares for battle, whereas she is presumably preparing for sex. I would like to offer my utmost thanks to Alan Hindley for his generous help with this and other translations.

37. Duncan Robertson, *The Medieval Saints' Lives: Spiritual Renewal and Old French Literature* (Lexington, KY.: French Forum, 1995), 107.

38. Thaïs and the girl in *Nièce* among others certainly come across as noncompliant penitents.

Chapter 10. Roland's Confession and the Rhetorical Construction of the Other Within

1. Peter Brooks, *Troubling Confessions: Speaking Guilt in Law and Literature* (Chicago: University of Chicago Press, 2000), 101.
2. Paul Anciaux, *The Sacrament of Penance* (Tenbury Wells, Worcs.: Challoner, 1962), 54.
3. Ibid.
4. Brooks, *Troubling Confessions*, 96.
5. Jacques Chiffoleau, "Sur la pratique et la conjoncture de l'aveu judiciaire en France du XIIIe au XVe siècle," in *L'Aveu: Antiquité et Moyen Âge* (Rome: École Française de Rome, 1986), 341–80, here 341.
6. Brooks, *Troubling Confessions*, 95.
7. See William W. Kibler and Leslie Zarker Morgan, eds., *Approaches to Teaching the "Song of Roland"* (New York: MLA, 2006).
8. *La Chanson de Roland / The Song of Roland: The French Corpus*, gen. ed. Joseph J. Duggan, vol. 1, *The Oxford Version*, ed. Ian Short (Turnhout: Brepols, 2005). All references to the Old French Oxford version are to the edition by Short. Citations will include volume and line numbers.
9. *The Song of Roland*, trans. Glyn Burgess (London: Penguin, 1990). All English translations of the Oxford *Roland* will be from this edition.
10. Gerard J. Brault, *The Song of Roland: An Analytical Edition*, 2 vols. (University Park: Pennsylvania State University Press, 1978), 1: 252.
11. For a summary bibliography, see Kibler and Morgan, *Approaches to Teaching the "Song of Roland."*
12. Gaston Paris, "La Chanson de Roland et la nationalité française," in *La Poésie du moyen âge: Leçons et lectures* (Paris: Hachette, 1885) 1: 87–118; *La Chanson de Roland*, ed. T. Atkinson Jenkins (Boston: Heath, 1924); *The Song of Roland*, trans. Dorothy L. Sayers (Harmondsworth: Penguin, 1957); Mary Hackett, "Le Gant de Roland," *Romania* 89 (1968): 253–56; Faith Lyons, "More about Roland's Glove," in Société Rencesvals, *Proceedings of the Fifth International Conference, Oxford 1970* (Salford: University of Salford, 1977), 156–66. For a review of these positions, see Brault, *The Song of Roland*, 1:254–60. Peter Haidu considers it a sign of final and ultimate fealty; see *The Subject of Violence: The "Song of Roland" and the Birth of the State* (Bloomington: Indiana University Press, 1993), 123.
13. A good overview of opinions on Roland's guilt is found in Jean-Charles Payen, *Le Motif du repentir dans la littérature française médiévale des origines à 1230* (Geneva: Droz, 1967). On contritionism, see esp. 31–53.
14. Cited in Payen, *Le Motif du repentir*, 32.
15. Payen, *Le Motif du repentir*, 112.
16. Brault, *The Song of Roland*, 1: 254.

17. Payen, *Le Motif du repentir*, 49.

18. Payen, *Le Motif du repentir*, 113.

19. *La Chanson de Roland / The Song of Roland: The French Corpus*, vol. 3, *The Châteauroux–Venice 7 Version*, ed. Joseph J. Duggan (Turnhout: Brepols, 2005). As Duggan states (3: 33), this edition is an attempt to reproduce the text that was the basis of the manuscripts of C and V7. All references to the Châteauroux version are to Duggan's edition.

20. The translations of the Châteauroux version are from Joseph J. Duggan and Annalee C. Rejhon, *The Song of Roland: Translations of the Versions in Assonance and Rhyme of the "Chanson de Roland"* (Turnhout: Brepols, 2013).

21. An interesting detail, probably taken from the *Pseudo-Turpin*, and clearly visible in the death scene depicted in the narrative panels of the Charlemagne window at Chartres. See Mary Jane Schenck, "The Charlemagne Window at Chartres: Visual Chronicle of a Royal Life," *Word and Image* 28.2 (2012): 135–60.

22. *Historia Karoli Magni et Rotholandi ou Chronique du Pseudo-Turpin*, ed. Cyril Meredith-Jones (Paris: Droz, 1936). See 36–75 for a discussion of theories on origins; Meredith-Jones rejects Bédier's contention in *Les Légendes épiques: Recherches sur la formation des chansons de geste*, 3rd ed., vol. 3 (1928; Paris: Champion, 1966), 89–90, that the *Pseudo-Turpin* was part of the *Codex Calixtinus* generated at Cluny and part of the promotion of pilgrimage routes. He thinks it was an independent work written around 1120–30 in northern France, perhaps at Aix, to provide a model for the Spanish crusades, not pilgrimages to Compostella.

23. *The Old French Johannes Translation of the Pseudo-Turpin Chronicle*, ed. Ronald N. Walpole (Berkeley: University of California Press, 1976), xv. Walpole demonstrates that a translation of the *Descriptio* by Pierre de Beauvais was completed before 1206 and inserted near this time into the vernacular version by Johannes of the *Pseudo-Turpin*, which clearly predated it.

24. See note 22.

25. The Old French text is from the Walpole edition. English translations are mine.

CONTRIBUTORS

William Burgwinkle is professor of medieval French and Occitan literature at King's College, Cambridge. His books include *Sodomy, Masculinity, and Law in Medieval Literature: France and England, 1050–1230* and *Love for Sale: Materialist Readings of the Troubadour Razo Corpus*. He coauthored *Sanctity and Pornography in Medieval Culture: On the Verge* and coedited *The Cambridge History of French Literature*.

Kristin L. Burr is professor of French at Saint Joseph's University in Philadelphia. Her research focuses on thirteenth-century medieval French literature, and especially on questions surrounding gender roles. She coedited *The Old French Fabliaux: Essays on Comedy and Context* and has published widely on post-Chrétien Old French verse romance. She is currently working on a project that involves examining the representation of love tokens and relics.

Jane Gilbert is senior lecturer in French at University College London. She has published on medieval French and English literature both separately and comparatively, including a monograph, *Living Death in Medieval French and English Literature*. Her latest project is on literary form in translation.

Francis Gingras is professor in the Département des littératures de langue française at the Université de Montréal, where he is also the director of the Center of Medieval Studies. His books include *Érotisme et merveilles dans le récit français des XIIe et XIIIe siècles*; *Le Bâtard conquérant: Essor et expansion du genre romanesque au Moyen Âge*; and *Profession médiéviste*. After collaborating with Olivier Collet and Richard Trachsler on a project titled *Lire en contexte à l'époque prémoderne: Enquête sur les recueils manuscrits de* *fabliaux*, he is currently working on translations of the Bible and universal histories.

Sara I. James completed her PhD on alterity and identity in Old French and Russian epic literature at the University of Virginia. After several years of working in academia and publishing in the United States and the United Kingdom, she moved into IT and finance. Sara now runs a writing skills consultancy, Getting Words to Work (www.saraijames.com), delivering report-writing courses to clients across the globe. Sara continues her research on the chanson de geste and has focused recently on the *Chanson de Bertrand Du Guesclin*. Her most recent publications include "Bertrand Du Guesclin" in the *Literary Encyclopedia* (online) and "Chronique Qui Chante ou Chanson Qui Chronique? *La Vie du Vaillant Bertrand Du Guesclin*" in "*Il fist que proz*": *Essays in Honor of Robert Francis Cook*.

Douglas Kelly is professor emeritus of French and medieval studies at the University of Wisconsin–Madison. His scholarship has been devoted to the medieval art of poetry and prose and its application to and function in medieval works in French, Latin, and Occitan. His major publications include *The Art of Medieval French Romance*; *Internal Difference and Meanings in the "Roman de la Rose"*; *Christine de Pizan's Changing Opinion: A Quest for Certainty in the Midst of Chaos*; *The Subtle Shapes of Invention: Poetic Imagination in Medieval French Literature*; and *Machaut and the Medieval Apprenticeship Tradition: Truth, Fiction and Poetic Craft*.

Mary Jane Schenck is professor emerita of English at the University of Tampa. She has published extensively on the chanson de geste, the fabliaux, *Le Roman de Renart*, and more recently on the Charlemagne and Sylvester windows at Chartres. She coedited *Echoes of the Epic: Studies in Honor of Gerard J. Brault* and is the author of *The Fabliaux: Tales of Wit and Deception*.

James R. Simpson is reader in French at the University of Glasgow. He has published on French Arthurian romance, comic and satirical narratives, animal epic, and epic poetry. He is the author of three books: *Animal Body, Literary Corpus: The Old French "Roman de Renart"*; *Fantasy, Identity and Misrecognition in Medieval French Narrative*; and *Troubling Arthurian Histories: Court Culture, Performance and Scandal in Chrétien de Troyes's "Erec et Enide."* He also coedited *Heresy and the Making of European Culture: Medieval and Modern Perspectives.*

Jane H. M. Taylor is professor emerita of French at Durham University, following posts at Manchester and Oxford. She has published extensively on late-medieval, and more lately Renaissance, literature with books on François Villon, on manuscript anthologies, and on sixteenth-century rewritings of medieval Arthurian romances. She is now working on an in-depth study of the Stockholm manuscript (Vu 22) containing Villon's works. She has also, in collaboration with other scholars, translated *Jean de Saintré* and *The Chivalric Biography of Boucicaut* and is now translating Jean de Bueil's *Jouvencel.*

Adrian P. Tudor is senior lecturer in French at the University of Hull. He is the author of *Tales of Vice and Virtue: The First Old French "Vie des Pères,"* has translated Jehan Renart's *Lai de l'Ombre,* and has coedited several volumes, including *Performance, Drama and Spectacle in the Medieval City* and *Grant risee? The Medieval Comic Presence / La Présence comique médiévale.* He has also published numerous articles on the fabliaux and the *Vie des Pères.* His latest book is *The Knight and the Barrel,* an English translation of *Le Chevalier au barisel.*

INDEX

L'Abbesse grosse, 129–30, 136
Alien selves, 35, 38, 39, 40, 41
Aliscans, 69, 74, 75
Alterity, 68, 72, 74, 75, 78, 166n8; in Jean-Luc Nancy, 85, 88
Animal imagery, 111, 114; birds, 158n21; lark, 54, 55, 56, 57, 60, 64, 65; sparrowhawk, 32, 36, 56, 60, 64, 65, 163n7
Arthur, 92, 95, 96, 97, 99, 100–106
Assimilation, 75, 78
Auberon, 43, 44, 45, 47, 49, 50; Christianization of, 46, 48, 51, 52
Augustine, 124, 128, 136, 137

Bernard of Clairvaux, 124, 125
"Betweenness," 46, 47, 51
Bisclavret, 6

Caesar of Heisterbach, 95, 96
Canon law, 125, 127
Chanson de Guillaume, La, 69, 74, 79, 90
Chanson de Roland, La, 4, 79, 88, 90, 92, 116, 138
Charity, 108, 111, 112, 113, 114, 119
Charlemagne, 43, 67, 69, 81, 146, 148; Roland's memories of, 142, 143, 145, 150; success owing to Roland, 139, 140; weakness of, 44, 45, 46, 52, 75, 106n2
Châteauroux-Venice 7. *See* Roland (Châteauroux-Venice 7)
Chevalier aux Deux Épées, Le, 6, 103, 104

Chivalry, 16, 18
Chrétien de Troyes, 1, 4, 9, 21, 110; interiority in, 137, 150; personifications in, 15, 16, 18; as source for *Tournoiement Antéchrist*, 23, 25
Christine de Pizan, 27
Claris et Laris, 104–6
Cligés, 16
Communialty, 84, 86, 87, 89, 90, 91
Complainte, 30, 31, 32
Confession, 130, 135, 138; annual, 123, 126, 137, 150; through examples, 122, 124, 134; Roland's death and, 139–46, 148–49
Conquest, 42, 43, 47, 51
Conte du Graal, Le, 1, 9, 15, 16–18, 20, 21, 23
Contritionism, 143, 149, 150
Conversion, 111, 122, 124, 130, 132, 137; to Christianity, 45, 52, 69, 70, 71, 73, 133; literature of, 121, 123, 128, 134; Roland and, 143, 145
Corps, 33, 34, 41
Couronnement de Louis, Le, 90
Cueur, 33, 34, 40, 41
Cults, 109, 110

Dreams, 30, 38, 41, 51, 52, 85; conquest and, 43, 47; encounters in, 22, 32, 34, 40; garden in, 33; second in *Livre Messire Ode*, 31, 35, 156n11; visions in, 37
Durendal, 139, 140, 144–48

Escanor, 97
Estoire des Engleis, 8
Ethos, 138, 140, 144, 146, 149, 150

Fairy, 44–49, 52
Fantasy, 43, 45, 46, 51, 52, 95, 96
Fergus, 97
Fidelity, 22, 81, 125, 126, 146; in wager romances, 6, 53, 62, 65, 66
Fin'amor, 21, 56, 57, 125
Floris et Lyriopé, 4
Froissart, 26, 27, 30, 40

Garden, 31, 33, 37; of Deduit, 18–20, 26, 27
Gautier de Coinci, 7, 107, 124, 129
Gauvain, 6, 21
Gender, 11, 54, 62, 68; intersectionality and, 1, 7, 168n19; Guibourc/Orable and, 72–74
Geoffrey of Monmouth, 12, 92–94, 96, 97, 100
Gerald of Wales, 104
Gerbert de Montreuil, 53
Geste des Lorrains, La, 79
Girard de Vienne, 90–91
Godfrey of Viterbo, 95
Guillaume de Lorris, 18, 19, 21, 23, 32, 39, 41

Hagiography, 82, 121, 122, 127, 129, 132, 135
Haut Livre du Graal (Perlesvaus), Le, 99, 100, 101
Historia Regum Brittaniae, 93

Igraine, 94, 97, 101–3
Incubus, 93–96
Infidelity. *See* Fidelity
Interiority, 108, 137, 138, 150

Jean de Meun, 20, 21, 26, 41
Jerusalem, 3, 43, 44, 46, 47, 162n23

Jews/Judaism, 109, 123, 137, 182n5
Joseph d'Arimathie, 98

Kay, 4, 25

Lancelot-Grail cycle, 97
Lanval, 5, 47
Lateran IV, 122, 125, 126, 135, 137, 138, 150
Leprosy, 81, 83
Logos, 138, 144, 146, 148, 150
Love potion, 56, 58, 61, 64
Love token, 54, 58, 61, 62, 66
Lyric, 36, 38, 40, 56, 125, 127, 159n28

Machaut, 27, 30, 40, 41
Madness, 57, 61, 111, 162n20; holy fool, 91; mad with rage, 76, 115, 116
Marginalized characters, 53, 64, 71, 79, 182n5; Christianity and, 109–11, 122; in groups, 1, 9; as models, 123, 135, 136
Material culture, 108, 120
Meraugis de Portlesguez, 6, 25, 97
Merlin, 97, 98
Merlin Mellot, 107–10, 114, 117, 118, 120
Merveilleux, 43. *See also* Supernatural intervention
Middle East, 42, 46, 47, 49, 51, 52
Muslim, 45, 48, 49, 52

Olifant, 141, 142, 143, 144, 148

Passivity, 62, 63, 64, 65
Pathos, 138, 140, 141, 144, 146, 150; suffering and, 145; tears and, 142, 143, 148
Penance, 123, 129, 134, 137, 138
Perlesvaus, 99, 100, 101
Poverty, 61, 108, 112, 113, 180n18
Prise d'Orange, La, 69, 70
Pseudo-Turpin, 138, 146, 150
Psychomachia, 23, 24

Race, 1, 68, 72, 73, 165n1, 168n19
Raoul de Cambrai, 79, 87

Raoul de Houdenc, 15, 16, 23, 25, 153n14
Relics, 140, 144, 147
Ring, 54, 55, 56, 58, 61, 66; gender roles and, 62, 64, 65
Robert de Boron, 97, 98, 99
Roland, 110, 116, 138, 146, 148, 149, 150; Châteauroux-Venice 7 version of, 138, 144, 145, 180n22; death, 141, 142, 143; Durendal and, 139, 140, 144, 145, 147; Ganelon's betrayal of, 4, 116
Roman de la Rose, Le, 18–23, 25, 32, 33; intertextual echoes of, 30, 31, 37–41
Roman de la Rose ou de Guillaume de Dole, Le, 62
Roman des Eles, Le, 15, 20, 23
Roman de Silence, Le, 6, 102, 103
Round Table, 92, 100, 105

Salvation, 46, 116, 135, 140, 149, 150; forgiveness and, 128; of reader, 121; sex and, 122, 124, 136; stories and confession, 138, 142, 145, 146
Saracens, 4, 70, 72, 77, 146; attack in *Chanson de Roland*, 139, 144, 145; communialty and, 88; as Other, 68, 69, 75, 123; princess, 72, 73, 162n23; in *Pseudo-Turpin*, 147, 150; sexual temptation and, 133, 134
Self-projections, 33, 34, 36
Social class, 1, 68, 70, 73, 80, 127, 168n19

Songe d'enfer, Le, 15, 23
Suite du Roman de Merlin (Suite Huth), La, 101, 102
Supernatural intervention, 93–96

Tournoiement Antéchrist, Le, 15, 22–26, 27
Treasure (spiritual or worldly), 107, 109, 110, 113, 119

Uther Pendragon, 92, 93, 94, 96, 97, 104

Vie des Pères, La, 107, 122, 125, 126, 127–30, 136, 185–86n29; intertextuality, 110, 116, 118, 123, 124, 135
Villon, 16, 23, 28, 29, 30, 33
Vincent of Beauvais, 95, 96
Virgin Mary, 108, 109, 116, 119, 134, 145; as mother of Christ, 148, 149
Vita Merlini, 93, 94
Voice, 110, 113, 117, 118, 120, 131; attitudes toward, 118; Merlin's disembodied, 107, 109, 114, 116; mysterious, 104, 105, 106; narrative, 94, 96, 156n10; Roland's, 141, 149

Wace, 8, 92, 93, 94, 96, 100
William of Auvergne, 95

Yvain, 23

CPSIA information can be obtained
at www.ICGtesting.com
Printed in the USA
BVHW080840130719
553350BV00004B/8/P